The Status of Aliens in East Africa

Daniel D. C. Don Nanjira

The Praeger Special Studies program—utilizing the most modern and efficient book production techniques and a selective worldwide distribution network—makes available to the academic, government, and business communities significant, timely research in U.S. and international economic, social, and political development.

The Status of Aliens in East Africa

Asians and Europeans in Tanzania, Uganda, and Kenya

Praeger Publishers   New York   Washington   London

PRAEGER SPECIAL STUDIES IN INTERNATIONAL POLITICS AND GOVERNMENT

Library of Congress Cataloging in Publication Data

Don Nanjira, Daniel D.C.
    The status of aliens in East Africa.

    (Praeger special studies in international politics and government)
    Includes bibliographical references.
    1. Aliens—Africa, East.   2. Race discrimination—Law and
legislation—Africa, East.   I.   Title.
Law   341.48'4   75-19804
ISBN 0-275-55570-4

PRAEGER PUBLISHERS
111 Fourth Avenue, New York, N.Y. 10003, U.S.A.

Published in the United States of America in 1976
by Praeger Publishers, Inc.

Printed in the United States of America

To
My Mother
and
the Loving Memory of My Father

This study grew out of the thesis that I presented for my doctorate at the University of Nairobi in 1974, but my interest in the topic goes back to 1967-68, when the East African states began to implement in full force their declared postindependence policy of Africanization and noncitizen Asians were being expelled en masse. I asked myself, Was there any internationally recognized standard of substantive justice that the East African states were under a duty to observe? I was fully aware of the fact that there was no overall assessment of the international legal position of aliens, most particularly of Asians, in the East African context. I thought that the best way to tackle the problem was to try to place the question mainly in the context of the East African political, diplomatic, and socioeconomic situation, as well as in the light of international law on the topic of aliens. Such a procedure meant that I had to study the constitutions of Tanzania, Uganda, and Kenya, and the other East African laws concerning such issues as citizenship, immigration, work permits, nationalization, and business licensing.

To my great surprise, I found that there were no clear rules of international law on the question of aliens. I have consequently proposed in the book what I have felt such rules should be and have made recommendations for a better treatment of aliens in East Africa.

The starting point in Chapter 1 is the position of East Africa as terra nullius sine hominibus; then, there is a discussion of man's emplacement in the region, of native ethnic groups, of Arabs, Asians, and Europeans. The words "Indian" and "Asian" are used interchangeably. "European" has been used to mean a member of the white race, and not just a person or people from Europe. Chapter 2 reveals that, by legal definition, aliens in East Africa are found among Asians and Europeans. Chapter 3 establishes that Germany and Britain were the powers that eventually imposed their rule on East Africa. Chapter 4 examines the struggle for supremacy between Europeans and Asians in colonial East Africa. Chapter 5 discusses the African reactions to alien rule. Chapter 6 discusses the contributions of aliens in independent East Africa.

State responsibility for aliens in East Africa, the subject of Chapter 7, involves both the legal rights and the corresponding legal or moral duties of the East African states toward aliens, and of the latter toward the former. Chapter 8 analyzes Britain's duties toward her East African subjects of Asian origin. It should be noted here that a new liberal policy on immigration was introduced by the British Labour Government in February 1975; the slight relaxation in British immigration restrictions as announced on February 6, in the House of Commons by the home secretary, Roy Jenkins, directly affected the British Asians in East Africa. Entry of the Asians into the United Kingdom was facilitated through quota increases, which rose from 3,500 to 5,000 per year. The increase mostly went to Kenya, where U.K. passport-holders were estimated to be 23,000 at that time. Five categories were covered by new concessions, over and above the quota allocation, applying only to U.K. passport-holders. First, unskilled workers will be admitted on one-year permits provided they have a job to go to. Employers' guarantees will be required. Second, businesses and traders with funds in the United Kingdom to reestablish themselves will be admitted on one-year permits in the first instance. Third, parents providing proof of retirement and who are under 65 (the present qualifying age for admission to Britain) will now be allowed to join their families as dependents. Fourth, young people over 21 who at present must queue for a voucher for themselves will now be allowed in with their parents. Finally, students will be freely admitted on producing evidence of admission to colleges and payment of fees.

In Chapter 9, the heart of the book, I have tackled the question of human rights and the legal prevention of discrimination in the East African context, and have made practical proposals for a better treatment of aliens in the region. In Chapter 10, I have pointed out the conditions that must be fulfilled if the general position of aliens—and most particularly of resident Asian aliens—is to be improved in East Africa.

In writing the thesis from which this study evolved, I regularly sought and received advice from Professor Preston King. I owe him a debt of gratitude for his encouragement and for assistance at various stages of the work. I should also like to thank the Kenya Directorate of Personnel, especially its director, Joseph A. Gethenji, for the arrangement made for me to go to the University of Nairobi and embark upon a six-month, full-time research program. I am also greatly indebted to Professor John Joseph Okumu of the University of Dar-es-Salaam, and to Dr. T. A. Mugomba of the University of Nairobi, for their comments on the manuscript.

In the Kenya Ministry of Foreign Affairs, I am particularly grateful to I. S. Bhoi, former senior deputy secretary, and his successor, C. N. Kebuchi, for the opportunity I had of listening to their views on the legal and political implications of the subject. I further thank the library staffs of the University of Nairobi, the Kenya Attorney General's Office, and the Kenya Ministry of Foreign Affairs, for their kind cooperation and help. Finally, I express my gratitude to Nancy

Kilonzi, who typed the work in its final form. My principal debt of gratitude, however, is to my wife Jane, without whose patience, affectionate forbearance, and invaluable assistance, it is doubtful whether I could have found time or the peace necessary to write this book.

This work was written in a purely academic environment, and the arguments, ideas, conclusions, and recommendations are entirely my own, as are the general interpretations and views expressed in the book.

CONTENTS

LIST OF TABLES

LIST OF ABBREVIATIONS

ANC	African National Council
BEAA	British East Africa Association
CMS	Church Missionary Society
CRC	Community Relations Committee
EAP	East Africa Protectorate
ECHR	European Commission on Human Rights
ICB	Immigration Control Board (Uganda)
ICJ	International Commission of Jurists
KADU	Kenya African Democratic Union
KASU	Kenya African Study Union
KAU	Kenya African Union
KCA	Kikuyu Central Association
KPU	Kenya People's Union
NCCK	National Christian Council of Kenya
TAA	Tanganyika African Association
TANU	Tanganyika African National Union
TNS	Tanganyika National Society
UNC	Uganda National Council
UNHCR	United Nations High Commission for Refugees
UPC	Uganda People's Congress

The Status of Aliens
in East Africa

THE AFRICAN BACKGROUND

East Africa—Kenya, Uganda, and Tanzania—has been inhabited by man from the remotest antiquity. The remains of one of the earliest Homo sapiens have been found near Lake Victoria, while bones and tools of the Stone Age are plentiful in the Rift Valley and other areas of East Africa. And long before the coming of early alien traders and explorers, and the first written histories of East Africa, the peoples of present-day Uganda, especially those of the three largest kingdoms—Buganda, Bunyoro, and Toro—had committed to memory oral traditions celebrating their lineages, great events, and great men.

The expressions "tribe" and "race" have conflicting meanings, which will not be examined closely here. Rather, it will suffice to indicate briefly the sense in which each expression will be used in this book. "Tribe" will indicate some form of subordinate, social, and cultural group. "Race" will refer to large divisions of humans into physical types determined solely by some combination of skin, color, facial characteristics, and other imponderables.

It is believed that the earliest inhabitants of East Africa, normally referred to as the Bushmen, were short in stature, and that the Pygmies are the closest descendants of those inhabitants.[1] Intermarriages among the aboriginals produced mixed stocks such as the Bantu ethnic groups, which were the products of intermarriages between Negroid and Hamitic clusters. The latter can be divided into tribes, clans, lineages, classes, families, and so on. Hamites are (supposedly) descendants of Ham. They originally came from Asia and include the Boran, the Galla, and the Rendille.

A different mixing of Negroes and Hamites produced the Nilotic tribes of which an influx came from the north—mainly Egypt and the Sudan—and occupied the Upper Nile in Uganda; one branch of these tribes, the Luo, penetrated to the eastern shores of Lake Victoria, inhabiting what are now Kenya and Tanganyika.

Similarly, the Cushitic peoples from the Horn of Africa entered Kenya and northern Tanganyika from Ethiopia around 2000 B.C. The invasions by Hamites became very strong between the 14th and 15th centuries A.D. From the 15th to the 19th centuries, various Galla and Nilotic tribes arrived in East Africa via Ethiopia and points down the East African coast; the presence of the Galla peoples in Africa can in fact be traced as far back as 1000 B.C., when they arrived in northern Somalia from southern Arabia. While Cushites, Hamites, Nilotes, and their resulting mixed stocks were entering East Africa from the north and northeast, Bantu groups in southern Africa advanced northward, crossing Rhodesia and entering Tanganyika.

In the coastal regions, as we shall see, more than 3,000 years of contact introduced considerable Arab and Asian elements into the native people themselves, and also into their culture. Many of the tribes are loosely grouped together as Swahilis, and speak the Bantu language of that name. "Swahili" means "coast." The Swahilis are the descendants of the Bantu, Persians, and Arabs, although the strongest influences on Swahilis have come from Arabs. Swahilis are in fact a mixed race of varied hue and status, of Muslim and hybrid speech, and of Afro-Indian and Afro-Persian origin, among other ancestries.

THE ARAB BACKGROUND

Of the other ethnic races in East Africa, it is generally understood that both Arabs and Asians were the first invaders of East Africa, and that they were merchant adventurers who had learned to use the monsoons, or trade winds, between the Persian Gulf or the Arabian coast and the East African coast long before the Europeans had discovered the use of the monsoons. It has been argued, however, that Assyrians, Hindus, Jews, and Phoenicians were the first visitors to East Africa, and that they came to that part of Africa long before the birth of Christ. They were followed first by Greeks—between 247 B.C. and A.D. 45—and then by Arabs in the fifth century A.D. It has been argued further that Arabs and Persians were the first adventurers in East Africa whose contacts with the East African coast could be traced as far back as the sixth century B.C. and even earlier, and that Indians joined them later. By the time the Greek merchant seaman of Berenike wrote his "Periplus of the Erythrean Sea,"

probably in Alexandria around A.D. 100, Arabs had already been
well established on the east coast of Africa. They began to mix freely
with natives, intermarried with them, and learned the native languages.
By A.D. 600, Arabs and Persians had mastered the Indian Ocean region commercially—commerce having been the main cause of their
migration to that part of the world—and their settlements on the East
African coast had been completed.

Thus out of these foreign settlements in East Africa resulted
not only mixtures of culture but also of architecture and pottery.
Settlement of the East African coast by Arabs and Persians was followed by their colonization of the coast, which, like the settlements,
was a very long and gradual process started in remote antiquity and
continued more or less steadily for centuries; on occasion the colonization was carried out by bands of fugitives, whether from local feuds
along the Arabian and Persian littoral, or from the waves of war and
conquest "that swept from time to time through the backlands in the
north, and sometimes also by zealots of some persecuted sect who,
like the Puritan founders of New England, sought in the colonial field
the religious freedom denied to them at home."[2]

THE ASIAN BACKGROUND

Early Asian Contacts with East Africa

If we consider all early invaders of East Africa to have been
foreign visitors or traders, then Indians (Hindus) were definitely
among the invaders whose connections with the East African coast go
back many centuries before Christ. For by the time the Arabs had
colonized the eastern coast of Africa and become an aristocracy there,
Indians were already residents.

It seems almost certain that Indian connections with the East
African coast were from the very start most welcome to the Arabs,
who were not as good businessmen as the Indians. Indians thus became from the very early days the masters of finance, the bankers,
the money-lenders and money changers, and the main suppliers to
East Africa of goods such as cotton cloth, metal ware, grain beads,
and sundry manufactured articles.

India also supplied skill to East Africa, for Indian sailors,
pilots, and administrators constantly visited East Africa. The latter
in turn supplied to India goods such as ivory, gold, iron, gum, gum
copal, hides, horns, copra, ambergris, and incense. Thus over the
centuries, Indians became very closely associated with the Arabs in
East Africa, and this was because of the similar interests developed
by the minority races in the region.

Trading, visiting, or establishing contacts with East Africa did not mean permanent settlement, however. We can talk of real Indian immigration and/or settlement in East Africa only as from the 19th century, for it was only then that the Asian immigrant became less of a temporary visitor and gained an increasing stake in and commitment to the region.

During the 19th century, the traditional Indian trader connections with the East African coast were revived after the prolonged vicissitudes of Portuguese rule and recurrent hostilities in the Indian Ocean among seamen of rival powers. The revival of Indian commercial enterprise along the East African coast was encouraged by the recovery of the former Indian influence in Zanzibar by the imams of Muscat, by the establishment of British rule in India, and by the emergence of British naval supremacy in the Indian Ocean after the Napoleonic Wars. Also during the 19th century, the growth of British influence and the activities of the Indian traders were quite closely interrelated.

Indian Labor System in East Africa

The Indian immigration was a direct result of the European colonization of East Africa,[3] with the indentured, or hired, Indian labor system in British and other colonial possessions having been started in 1834. Because of increasing demands for labor in East Africa, the application of this system was sanctioned by the Indian government and extended to East Africa following the decision in 1895 to construct the Uganda Railway.

The Indian Emigration Act of 1883, for instance, had permitted Indians to travel, without any restrictions, to East Africa and elsewhere. Thus skilled Asian workers could be recruited even in what later became known as German East Africa, particularly for work on the construction of the German East African Railway.

In 1896 the Indian government amended the 1883 Emigration Act, thereby specially legalizing and encouraging Indian emigration to East Africa, particularly for the construction of the Uganda Railway, under three-year contract terms.[4] Thus from 1896 onward, agents were established in several Indian cities, such as Karachi and Calcutta, to deal with coolie (laborer) emigration and shipment to East Africa for the railway.

The reasons, then, for the immigration of Asians to East Africa, followed by their settlement there, were mainly commercial. They included aspirations for trade prosperity for both the immigrants and their kith and kin in East Africa and at home; the search for better living standards than those in their poor native regions at home,

such as the dry and arid Kutch; enhanced pay for recruited Asian
soldiers; and the lack of sufficient local manpower on the Uganda Railway, which forced the British government to import Indian coolies in
large numbers and encourage voluntary Indian immigration to eastern
and even southern Africa. Furthermore, encouragement of Indian
immigration to East Africa occurred in 1893 after the signing of the
so-called Heligoland Treaty. (The conditions that led to the signing
of the treaty will be examined in Chapter 3.)

Without the coolie labor (the term "coolie" comes from the
Hindu word "quli" which means "laborer") there would certainly not
have been any Kenya-Uganda Railway for many years.

Most of the Asian immigrants to East Africa came from Punjab
and Gujerat and were Muslims. The other sources of Indian immigration to East Africa included Bombay and Surat—Muslims; Kutch,
Jamnaggar, and Porpundar—both Muslims and Hindus; and Goa—Catholics.

The emplacement of British Indian troops in East Africa during
the 1890s helped to strengthen the growing Asian presence in the East
African interior, and contributed to future immigration from the Punjab, where most of the soldiers originated from. Moreover, the
short-lived influx of a large number of Indian troops and their array
of camp followers boosted the enterprises of some Asian traders who
either established dukas (small shops) in the vicinity of their camps
or became official agents for the supply of provisions, transport services, and so on.

The stimulation of Asian immigration into East Africa in the
19th century occurred therefore in two ways: as a result of the need
for coolie and other labor (sought, or promoted, immigration) and as
a result of private initiative to exploit the opportunities opened up by
colonization (private immigration). Most of the Asians who emigrated
to East Africa belonged to that second category. And the typical form
of their early activities was the small shop, or duka.

The growth of the Asian population in East Africa became rapid
at the end of the 19th century, as Table 1 clearly shows.

Between 1896, when the first group of Indian coolies arrived in
Mombasa, and 1901, the year the Uganda Railway was completed,
about 32,000 Indian workers were recruited for service on the railways, at an average overall cost of 30 rupees (Rs) per month per
coolie. A total of 16,312 indentured Indians returned to India at the
end of their contracts; 6,724 stayed on in East Africa; 6,454 were
invalidated and sent home; and 2,493 died as a result of the many
tropical diseases that obviously slowed down work as the railway
pushed through forests, swamps, and plains. In 1898 the "Man-Eaters of Tsavo" (lions) began to terrorize the coolies' camps and thus
added to the already existing hazards: malaria, dysentery, scurvy,

TABLE 1

Indian Immigration to East Africa, 1896-1902

Year	Number of Coolies Imported	Number Repatriated	Number Invalidated	Deaths
1896-97	4,269	—	200	121
1897-98	7,131	—	705	340
1898-99	15,593	773	1,206	611
1899-1900	23,379	2,761	3,424	1,164
1900-01	31,646	4,109	5,811	1,984
1901-02	31,983	9,616	6,354	2,367
1902-03	31,983	16,312	6,454	2,493

Source: Compiled by the author.

ulcers, and chiggers. In fact, 28 coolies and an unspecified number of Africans were killed and eaten by lions. Nearly all of the Indian coolies who decided to remain lived in Mombasa.

The years from 1886 to 1945 were crucial for the process of transforming the scattered Asian commercial population along the coast into a major settlement in the interior of East Africa. The shift of emphasis from the coast to the interior formed the background to the unprecedented and increasing influx of Asian immigrants into East Africa during the colonial period that lasted until the enforcement of identical immigration restrictions in the colonial territories. Among the pioneer Indian traders who penetrated into the East African hinterland following the changed economic emphasis from the coast to the interior, one deserves mention here. Alibhoy Mulla Jeevanjee (1856-1939) came from Karachi and launched the East African Standard at Mombasa in 1901. The paper was sold in 1903 to Maia Anderson, who renamed it the Mombasa Times and subsequently the East African Standard.[5] Within a short time, shops, trading centers, and Indian bazaars were established throughout the region. The barter economy was replaced by a money economy after the introduction of the Indian rupee currency. The latter and the pice in turn replaced the Maria Theresa dollars (thalers), which were the principal currency in circulation in the 19th century in East Africa. The Indian rupee thus laid the foundations of a modern, money-based economy in East Africa. The rupee helped solve some of the problems facing the establishment of colonial administration in the East African territories, particularly those regarding the collection of taxes, or the payment of employees.

In German East Africa, the population of Asian traders had grown to about 3,000 by the end of the 19th century. Most of them were also concentrated at the coastal settlements. A growing number of them had, however, opened stores and agencies along the caravan routes and the advancing railways, with Ujiji and Tabora representing major concentrations of their population in the interior.

The caravan route from Mombasa through Mumias and Kisumu was also used by the Asian traders who penetrated into Uganda before the completion of the Uganda Railway. Donkeys and carts were used as means of transporting goods. In 1899, for instance, some Mill Hill Fathers used the transport facilities provided by the Indians in order to carry their goods from Nairobi to Uganda.[6]

THE EUROPEAN BACKGROUND

The last of the four ethnic-racial groups in East Africa that deserves discussion are the Europeans.* However, the European background in East Africa does not need any elaboration here, since European immigration to, and impact on, East Africa will be discussed in Chapter 3.

European arrivals and settlements in East Africa are, for all practical purposes, very recent phenomena. Although they took place both before and after the colonization of East Africa, they occurred mainly in the 19th century, when European influences and interests were making themselves felt in the East African interior; rivalries in the interior among European powers—particularly French-British rivalry—had already taken shape. European emigration to East Africa was caused by such forces as commerce, national strategy, imperial expansion, humanitarianism, and Christianity.

Soon after Vasco da Gama's arrival at the east coast of Africa in 1498, the Portuguese seized control of the Sofala gold trade. Their unwillingness to penetrate into the East African interior, as well as their ruthlessness, brutality, and perfidiousness toward the native coastal inhabitants, clearly showed that the Portuguese were not interested in a long (political) colonization of East Africa, and that even if they had wanted this, they would not have been successful in it.

---

*The word "European" or "Europeans" is used to mean the white race, and not just a person or people from Europe. Thus although the Portuguese staged the first European "invasion" of East Africa, and were later followed by the English, French, and Germans, there were other members of the white race who also came and established themselves in that part of Africa. Americans were among the latter group.

France developed, with the years, strategic, labor, and even
political interests along the Indian Ocean region, both before and after the Revolutionary and Napoleonic Wars, and in the 1840s. Thus
the French, unlike, as we shall see below, the Germans and Americans at that time, were interested not only in trade, but also in politics in East Africa and in the Indian Ocean area as a whole.

The initiative to end slavery and slave trade in East Africa was
taken by Britain. Termination of the slave trade was supposed to be
achieved in 1845 when, on October 2, an agreement was signed by
Zanzibar's Sultan Said and Captain Atkins Hamerton, the British consular and political agent in Zanzibar, for the termination of the trade
in the Sultan's dominions. Unfortunately, the trade did, in practice,
continue.

Other European visitors to East Africa included the Greeks,
Poles, Jews, Americans, and Germans. These foreigners also had
mainly commercial aims.

The Americans likewise opened up great commerce in the Indian
Ocean region, in and after the 18th century. In fact, from 1820 onward, American whalers and other ships in East African waters were
frequently recorded. Americans later negotiated with Sultan Seyyid
of Muscat a settlement on the East African coast; a treaty of amity and
commerce was signed between the Sultan and the United States on September 21, 1833.

THE MISSIONARY INVOLVEMENT
IN EAST AFRICA

European Protestant and Roman Catholic missionaries arrived
at and established themselves on the coast of East Africa in the early
19th century. Their aims, under the cover of "preaching the word of
God and converting the heathen to God," were many and varied, and
included scientific, economic, political, colonial, and humanitarian
aims, and the elimination of poverty, ignorance, and disease. The
same aims were nurtured by explorers, who were also interested in
the conversion, education, and general development of Africa. Thus
missionaries, explorers, traders, and later settlers, besides administrators who came to Africa, often had coinciding adventures, and
sometimes the same people played different roles simultaneously.
Similarly, empire builders in Africa and elsewhere such as Lord Lugard and Cecil Rhodes, philanthropic societies, and chartered companies performed many different functions at the same time.

Alien commerce, then, and exploration, science, and religion
all invaded Africa. German missionaries were foremost; Hornemann,
Rupell, Barth, and Vogel crossed the Sahara, Libyan, and Nubian
deserts from North Africa.

A remarkable alien missionary invasion of East Africa occurred between 1844 and 1850; German missionaries Johann Ludwig Krapf and Johann Rebmann became the first Europeans to explore equatorial East Africa at any distance from the coast. They were, like many other German missionaries, such as Barth—sent by the British government—and Hornemann—sent by the African Association in London—agents of a British institution called the Church Missionary Society (CMS). The King of Buganda, Mutesa, very warmly welcomed the Protestant and Catholic missionaries, because he saw in Christianity the possibility of a new political power that might prove a useful weapon against both Egyptian advances southward and the Arab influx from the east. Christianity was not the only alien religion in East Africa at that time. By 1879, Islam had already gained converts in the East African interior. The consequence of the three religious invasions of East Africa was the division of African natives into traditional believers and "foreign," international believers. Thanks to the missionary impact, closer relations between natives and Europeans were established.

The European missionaries impressed the inland kings (paramount chiefs like Mumia) and their subjects, and the missionary settlements paved the way for further European settlements in the East African region.

CONCLUSIONS

Arguments regarding man's first emplacement in East Africa are inconclusive. According to some historians, most of what are termed aboriginal peoples (Africans or Negroes as the European slave overlords labeled them) entered the African continent through Arabia and Persia about 10,000 years ago. Other historians have argued that there are no Negro skulls of such antiquity, since the oldest known was dated only about 6000 B.C. But according to some anthropologists, man lived in East Africa as far back as 12 million years ago.[7] Some even claim that man had his origins in East Africa. But most information on the subject comes from linguistic studies and traditional oral legends that provide little sound material for historical reconstruction.

What is certain, however, is that East Africa has been the meeting place of many diverse ethnic groups, most of them immigrants from the west and north. On a linguistic basis, the indigenous peoples of East Africa can be classified mainly into four groups: Nilotes, Nilo-Hamites, Bantu-speakers, and Cushites, that is, Somalis. But on a genetic basis, the same native groups have come from three main stocks: the aboriginal, the Negroid, and the Hamitic.

At present, there are more than 192 native tribes in East Africa, of which more than 35 and 37 and 120 inhabit Kenya, Uganda, and Tanzania, respectively.

In the days of alien immigration to East Africa, the term "Asians" referred to all the Asiatic races mentioned above. Nowadays, the word "Asians" refers only to those people who come from, or whose ancestors were the native inhabitants of, the Indian subcontinent. The present strong commercial position of Asians in East Africa had its origins in the very early days of Asian settlement in East Africa.

The criticism and opposition voiced by the Europeans against the prosperous Asian immigrants were not justifiable, for until 1903, East Africa was actually a "native protectorate" with Asian settlement. It was therefore quite irrational for the Europeans to blame the Asians for having, under such circumstances, made a position for themselves in the region. In fact, the Asians materially assisted the colonial administration in the early days of the development of the protectorates by "working on the railway, building houses, and taking contracts at a time when there was practically no one else to do so."[8]

The main consequence of the building of the Uganda Railway was thus a further development of European and Asian colonization of East Africa. From the beginning, Asian settlers in East Africa were always far more numerous than Europeans. It is notable when local forces comprising Indian, Swahili, and loyal Sudanese troops failed to control various rebellions against the colonists, launched by the Mazrui Arabs at the coast and by Africans in the East African interior, reinforcements were sought from India, and in March 1896, 700 troops were dispatched from Bombay to Mombasa. In 1897 additional reinforcements were also sought from India following the mutiny of Sudanese troops in Uganda. Troops totaling 360 finally arrived in East Africa in the following year but returned to India after performing their "required functions." The position of Asians in East Africa was further internationalized by the growing nationalism in India, coupled with the deplorable treatment of the Indians in some overseas territories that were British colonial possessions.[10]

The real importance of the role in East Africa of the Asians who were indentured to work on the Kenya-Uganda Railway lay in the stimulation their officially sponsored immigration, and the Asian presence in the interior initiated by it, provided for the future Asian immigration to East Africa. For in addition to the indentured workers and British Indian troops mentioned above, there was a continued rise in the number of other voluntary immigrants to East Africa whose main attraction was also the prospect of enhanced pay. Table 2 illustrates the growth of the Asian population in East Africa between 1917 and 1961.

TABLE 2

Growth of Asian Population in East Africa, 1917-61

Year	Kenya	Uganda	Tanganyika
1917	11,787	—	—
1921	25,253	5,604	—
1931	43,623	14,150	—
1945	—	—	—
1948	97,687	35,215	46,254
1956	149,000	62,900	74,300
1961	176,613	77,400	88,700

Source: Compiled by the author.

The problem of Indians in the East African region was closely connected not only with the European colonization of East Africa but also with slavery, legal definition, and racial awareness in that region. The colonial power—the United Kingdom—introduced the Asian population in East Africa but did not nationalize it, as was the case with the Arabs. Given a different kind of legal definition, Indians might not have been regarded as aliens in East Africa. Thus the difference between Arabs and Indians was brought about by legal definition and by the colonial power of the time.

The first contacts between Africans and Europeans occurred in the 19th century. Rebmann was the first European to see Mount Kilimanjaro, on May 11, 1847, while Krapf was the first European to see Mount Kenya, on December 3, 1849.

When the Kenya-Uganda Railway reached Lake Victoria, Europeans started to settle in Kenya; for example, Lord Delamare came to Kenya from Somaliland in 1897 and settled in what became known as the "White Highlands." Similarly, Colonel E. S. Grogan came to Kenya from the Cape of Good Hope and settled near Kilimanjaro.

The United States in 1830 became the first Western nation to have consular representation in East Africa by setting up a consulate in Zanzibar. However, European settlers in East Africa resented American moves as an endeavor to usurp their own declining position. Thus some of the leaders of the U.S. liberal organizations, such as Marcus Moziah Garvey and his associates, were banned from entering what later became known as Kenya, by the Kenya (colonial) government.

NOTES

1. See generally A. J. Hughes, East Africa, Kenya, Tanzania, Uganda (Harmondsworth, Eng.: Penguin Books, 1969).

2. R. Coupland, East Africa and Its Invaders (London: Oxford University Press, 1961), p. 24.

3. See generally D. P. Ghai and Y. P. Ghai, eds., Portrait of a Minority: Asians in East Africa (Nairobi: Oxford University Press, 1970); and J. S. Mangat, History of the Asians in East Africa: 1886-1945 (London: Oxford at the Clarendon Press, 1968). See also R. Coupland, The Exploitation of East Africa: 1856-1890 (London: Oxford University Press, 1939).

4. London, Foreign Office, Coolie Emigration from India to African Protectorates, 1895-1902; "India Office," October 23, 1895; India Office to Government of India, October 31, 1895; and Hardinge to Salisbury, August 24, 1900.

5. See East African Standard (Nairobi), November 16, 1962, December 31, 1965, and January 1, 1966.

6. For a fuller account of this subject see Harry Hamilton Johnston, The Uganda Protectorate, vol. 1 (London: Hutchinson Publishers, 1902), p. 294.

7. See New York Times, May 16, 1968.

8. London, Colonial Office, Confidential Paper no. 879/2/844, p. 169.

9. R. S. Hollingsworth, The Asians of East Africa (New York: Macmillan, 1960), pp. 39-41 and 47-59.

10. See Anirudha Gupta, "Indians Abroad—in Asia and Africa," Africa Quarterly (New Delhi), 1968.

2

LEGAL DETERMINATION
AND CLASSIFICATION
OF ALIENS IN THE EAST
AFRICAN TERRITORIES

THE VIEWPOINT OF INTERNATIONAL LAW

The question "Who is an alien in East Africa?" is, from the standpoint of international law, principally one for the laws of Kenya, Uganda, and Tanzania to determine. At a glance, the answer seems obvious. When we examine it more closely, however, we find that it is a tricky question. Attempts continue to be made both at the national and international levels to reach a legal, uniform definition of nationality and citizenship. Lack of uniformity still reigns, but, despite it, some progress has been made since World War I. It is notable that in common-law nations, the distinction between "subject," "national," and "citizen" is important only for purposes of franchise, immigration, and the like. In these cases, stress should not be placed upon nationality but on allegiance.

The right to determine the nationality and citizenship of a person rests solely with the state in whose territory the person resides. This right results from the famous principle of state territorial sovereignty. A state determines nationality and citizenship by its domestic jurisdiction. Municipal laws such as constitutions and immigration and deportation rules also determine other similar issues such as the acquisition or loss of nationality or citizenship; the length of the "alien period" between the time of immigration and the time of naturalization; expatriation, extradition, admission, and expulsion of aliens; and treatment of aliens.

These issues, however, though regulated by municipal law, are governed by principles of international law. For treaty obligations may restrict the competence of a state as to the determination of nationality or citizenship. No state may, for instance, arbitrarily impose its nationality or citizenship on persons outside its territory who have no connection with it, or on persons residing in its territory without any intention of permanently living there.

A number of existing international instruments support in full the foregoing observations.[1] The Universal Declaration of Human Rights, approved by the UN General Assembly at its Third Session in Paris on December 10, 1948, provided: (1) "Everyone has a right to nationality"; and (2) "No one shall be arbitrarily deprived of his nationality nor the right to change his nationality."

Since the declaration is not a treaty, it does not impose any legal obligation. It provides a moral entitlement, as opposed to a legal entitlement, to nationality. The essence of nationality is, then, that a foreigner or alien remains a guest in the host state until his naturalization.

Today, states are, as we have seen, grouped into different types of nationality as a result of the lack of uniformity in state nationality laws. Four doctrines have been expounded on the acquisition of nationality.

First, a person's nationality should be determined by the nationality of his parents at birth, or the jus sanguinis (law-of-blood) doctrine. Second, nationality should be determined by blood and by territory of birth, or the jus soli (law-of-the-soil) doctrine. Third, nationality should be determined principally by blood and only partly by territory of birth. And fourth, nationality should be determined principally by territory of birth and only partly by blood. If the nationality of a person raises doubt, then the final decision rests with the municipal law of the state to which the person claims to belong, or to which it is alleged that the person belongs. There are other, less practiced methods of acquiring these qualifications: by naturalization (admission to citizenship by marriage, by legislation, or by official grant of nationality on application to the state authorities); by option; by entry into the public service of the state concerned; and by assumption by the inhabitants of a subjugated or conquered or ceded territory of the nationality of the victorious state, or of the state to which a territory is ceded.

The law-of-the-soil doctrine is practiced mainly by the United Kingdom, the United States, and the Latin American states. The law-of-blood method is applied mainly by such Western European states as France and West Germany, and by the Eastern European states, including the Soviet Union.

The term "nationality" does not connote only the quality of a person physically or naturally belonging to a population of a certain state. Nationality also implies a tie between a person and a comparable entity, for example, a trust corporation, a mandated territory, or a free state. "Personality" must likewise include legal persons. This is important, especially when dealing with aliens.

A corporation is a legal civil person. It can also be an alien. However, the nationality and legal status of a corporation are matters of private international law, and as such, most, though not all, of the effects of being either a "citizen" of a state or an "alien" are not applicable to corporations.

Some legal persons that are not sovereign staters—the primary subjects of international law—have international legal capacity, which enables them to possess specific treaty-making powers; these are international institutions that can also conclude treaties among themselves or with states and are thus endowed with international privileges and immunities. This privileged situation makes certain international organizations subjects of international law and capable of possessing rights and duties. It also gives them the capacity to bring international claims before international tribunals. However, not every international person has the capacity to conclude treaties.[2]

In the same way that the expressions "national" and "citizen" have been used interchangeably, the terms "alien," "foreigner," "foreign national," and "foreign citizen" have likewise been used interchangeably to mean the same thing—to avoid their abstractness and ambiguity. However, "alien" and "foreigner" cannot be used interchangeably in all cases. Clear-cut distinctions occur. To this writer, the term "foreigner" indicates a native or citizen of a nation other than the one he is now living in or visiting and who has no intention of becoming the host country's citizen, or of remaining in it permanently. An immigrant is a foreigner who resides or intends to remain permanently in his new country, but who may or may not intend to become a citizen of his country of residence.

An alien is, on the contrary, an immigrant who resides in another country permanently and intends to become a citizen of that country. An alien who becomes a citizen might nevertheless still be regarded as an "immigrant" by others, so long as his speech, clothes, or living habits reflect his country of origin and remain in contrast to the national norm in the country of domicile. Thus, those unduly fearful of what is foreign, and especially of people of foreign origin (the xenophobic), could in fact call such a naturalized citizen a "foreigner" to express their own intolerance for any departure from the norm.

EAST AFRICAN CITIZENSHIP LAWS

The citizenship and nationality laws of the East African states were modeled entirely on the British Nationality Act of July 30, 1948.[3] An alien in East Africa, according to the Tanzanian law, "is a person who is not a Commonwealth citizen, a British protected person or a citizen of the Republic of Ireland."[4]

The Uganda Aliens (registration and control) Act currently in force provides in Section 2: "In this Act, 'Alien' means a person who is not a citizen of Uganda or a Commonwealth citizen within the meaning of Section 13 of the Constitution, or a protected person within the meaning of Section 2 of the Uganda Citizenship Act, or a citizen of the Republic of Ireland."

The Kenya Citizenship Laws in force until the end of 1972 did not expressly define an alien in Kenya but contained provisions on aliens similar to those in the above-mentioned Citizenship Acts of Tanzania and Uganda. But the so-called Aliens Restriction Act (in Kenya) of 1973 does contain an express definition of an alien in Kenya: "In this Act, unless the context otherwise requires, 'alien' means any person who is not a citizen of Kenya."[5]

In the East African practice, an African national of any of the three East African states living in one of them that is not his home country is not and should not, therefore, be called an alien (in the strict sense) in the host country. He can live in it as long as he wants and even permanently—provided that is the wish of the host state and the person in question fulfills the conditions of his "survival" in that state—but he will be neither an alien nor a citizen of that state. He is, then, a foreigner there. It is nevertheless undeniable that from the legal standpoint, such a person should not be described as a "foreigner" but as an "immigrant." This simple position is complicated by the abovementioned legal definition of an alien in the region as "a person who is not a Commonwealth citizen, a British protected person or citizen of the Republic of Ireland."[6]

Whereas the constitutions of Uganda and Kenya contain provisions on citizenship, human rights, and fundamental freedoms of the individual, the Interim Constitution of Tanzania (1965) currently in force does not contain any chapter on citizenship or a "Bill of Rights." The only mention about human rights appears in the Preamble to the constitution, while the question of citizenship and nationality has been regulated by a series of acts enacted at various times—both before and after the union of Tanganyika and Zanzibar. We are mainly concerned with those laws ("acts of union") that deal with matters of citizenship, nationality, and alienage in the Republic of Tanzania.

Chapter 500 of the Tanganyika Revised Laws (1964) provided that the existing citizenship laws would continue to be the law after the commencement of the Republic of Tanganyika.

Thus the Tanganyika Citizenship Act and Citizenship Ordinance, both adopted in 1961, were the two laws relating to citizenship enacted to give effect to the citizenship provisions of Chapter 500. A presidential decree known as the Extension and Amendment of Laws Decree[7] was signed on November 3, 1964. By this decree, the existing citizenship laws of Tanganyika were amended and extended, except Sections 1 and 2 of the Tanganyika Citizenship Act of 1961, to Zanzibar as part of the law thereof.

For the purposes of determining any person as a citizen of the United Republic of Tanzania, the extension of the laws of Tanganyika then in force concerning citizenship would be deemed to have come into force on April 26, 1964. In this way, the 1964 decree also repealed the existing citizenship law of Zanzibar.

However, it was clearly stated in the 1964 decree that nothing in any such amendment as provided for in subsections (1) and (2) of Section 2 of the same decree "shall be construed as depriving any person entitled or eligible, in accordance with the Citizenship Act, 1961, or the Tanganyika Citizenship Ordinance, 1961, as in force prior to the commencement of this Decree, to be registered as a citizen of Tanganyika, of such entitlement or eligibility to be registered as a citizen of the United Republic of Tanznia in accordance with such laws." This provision refers specifically to categories of people referred to in Sections 1 and 2 of the revised (Tanganyika) Citizenship Act of 1961, which, as mentioned above, were not extended to Zanzibar. Sections 1 and 2 are as follows:

> Section (1) Every person who, having been born in Tanganyika is on the 8th day of December, 1961, a citizen of the United Kingdom and Colonies or a British protected person, shall become a citizen of Tanganyika on the 9th day of December, 1961 [Independence Day]:
>
> Provided that a person shall not become a citizen of Tanganyika by virtue of this subsection if neither of his parents was born in Tanganyika.
>
> (2) Every person who, having been born outside Tanganyika, is on the 8th day of December, 1961, a citizen of the United Kingdom and Colonies, or a British protected person shall, if his father becomes, or would but for his death have become, a citizen of Tanganyika in accordance with the provisions of subsection (1) of this section, become a citizen of Tanganyika on the 9th day of December, 1961.
>
> Section 2(1) Any person who, but for the provision to subsection (1) of section 1 of this Act, would be a citizen of Tanganyika by virtue of that subsection, shall be entitled, upon making application before the specified date in such manner as may be prescribed by Parliament, to be registered as a citizen of Tanganyika:

Provided that a person who has not attained the age of 21 years (other than a married woman) may not himself make an application under this subsection, but an application may be made on his behalf by his parent or guardian.

(2) Any woman who, on the 8th day of December, 1961, is, or has been married to a person—

(a) who becomes a Tanganyika citizen by virtue of section 1 of this Act; or

(b) who, having died before the 9th day of December, 1961, would, but for his death, have become a citizen of Tanganyika by virtue of that section shall be entitled upon making application in such manner as may be described by Parliament, to be registered as a citizen of Tanganyika.

(3) Any woman who, on the 8th day of December, 1961 is married to a person who subsequently becomes a citizen of Tanganyika by registration under subsection (1) of this section shall be entitled, upon making application before the specified date in such manner as may be prescribed by Parliament, to be registered as a citizen of Tanganyika.

(4) Any woman who, on the 8th day of December, 1961, has been married to a person who becomes, or would, but for his death, have become entitled to be registered as a citizen of Tanganyika under subsection (1) of this section, but whose marriage has been terminated by death or dissolution, shall be entitled, upon making application before the specified date in such manner as may be prescribed by Parliament, to be registered as a citizen of Tanganyika.

(5) Any person who, on the 8th day of December, 1961, is a citizen of the United Kingdom and Colonies, having become such a citizen by virtue of his having been naturalized or registered in Tanganyika under the British Nationality Act, 1948, shall be entitled, upon making application before the specified date in such manner as may be prescribed by Parliament, to be registered as a citizen of Tanganyika.

Provided that a person who has not attained the age of 21 years (other than a married woman) may not himself make an application, but this may be made on his behalf by his parent or guardian.

(6) In this section, "the specified date" means—

(a) in relation to a person to whom subsection (1) of this section refers, the 9th day of December, 1963 [two years after independence];

(b) in relation to a woman to whom subsection (3) of this section refers, the expiration of such period after her husband is registered as a citizen of Tanganyika as may be prescribed by or under an Act of Parliament;

(c) in relation to a woman to whom subsection (4) of this section refers, the 9th day of December, 1961;

(d) in relation to a person to whom subsection (5) of this section refers, the 9th day of December, 1963, or such later date as may in any particular case be prescribed by or under an Act of Parliament.

Provisions very similar to the above citizenship law of Tanganyika exist in the nationality/citizenship laws of Uganda (as at October 9, 1962) and of Kenya (as at December 12, 1963). Furthermore, these laws contain other identical legislative provisions on such questions as loss of nationality, dual citizenship, and acquisition of nationality/citizenship by registration or naturalization.

Thus a "citizen-by-birth" of any of the East African countries is a person whose parents and/or grandparents and he, himself, were born in the country in question, and were citizens of that country or of the United Kingdom and colonies at the time of that country's independence. A "citizen-by-descent" in any of the countries of East Africa is a person who is a citizen of that country—"(a) if his father is a citizen of the same country otherwise than by descent; or (b) the person was both born outside the country before independence and his father was a citizen of that country otherwise than by descent, and at the same time the person was, at the independence of the same country, a citizen of the United Kingdom and Colonies, or a British protected person—but only if his father became, or would but for his death have become, a citizen of the said country by birth."

In the case of Tanzania alone, a citizen-by-descent also means a person who is a citizen of Tanzania by virtue of the combined effect of his being a Zanzibar subject-by-descent in accordance with the former law of Zanzibar, had that law remained in force until immediately before Union Day, and of paragraph 2 of the Fourth Schedule to the Presidential Decree of 1964. Also, Zanzibar subject-by-birth and Zanzibar subject-by-descent were to be construed in accordance with the former law of Zanzibar. A protected person is any person who, under any enactment for the time being in force in any country that is part of the Commonwealth, is a protected person of that country.

Commonwealth countries are the United Kingdom and its colonies, Canada, Australia, New Zealand, India, Pakistan, Ceylon (now Sri Lanka), Ghana, Malaysia, Cyprus, Malta, Nigeria, Sierra Leone, Singapore, Jamaica, Trinidad and Tobago, Uganda, Kenya, Tanzania, Malawi, Zambia, Gambia, Guyana, Botswana, Lesotho, Barbados, Swaziland, Mauritius, and Rhodesia. Moreover, an East African parliament has power to determine which other country can be given the status of a Commonwealth country. A birth of a person on a registered ship or aircraft shall, by East African law, be deemed to have occurred in the place or country in which the ship or aircraft was registered. Finally, a consulate of an East African state means an office of a consular officer of the government of that state where a register of births or residents is kept, or such (other) office as may be prescribed.

The parliaments of Kenya, Uganda, and Tanzania have a very large say in the determination, acquisition, or loss of East African citizenship. Parliamentary determination of the legal status of individuals in East Africa is a sine qua non exercise in any effective acquisition of citizenship in the region. The minister responsible (for citizenship cases), however, has also power to approve, for instance, citizenship by registration through a statutory order, if he is satisfied that such citizenship will not be detrimental to established state government policy. The decision of the minister in such matters is considered final. East African citizenship is determined by the previously mentioned law-of-soil and law-of-blood doctrines and their combinations. However, the East African countries mainly use the law-of-soil method, which applies normally to people who acquire what is referred to as East African "automatic" citizenship.

The other methods of acquiring East African citizenship are by registration, naturalization, or a special grant of citizenship. Acquisition of citizenship by a special grant takes place under special circumstances—for instance, when a president or minister grants citizenship as an honor.

At independence, those categories of people in East Africa considered as aliens thereof had to apply for citizenship in the newly independent East African country. If granted citizenship, they became citizens by registration or naturalization. Certificates of registration or naturalization were effective on the day they were issued. If refused citizenship, the people remained aliens.

The conditions for registration and naturalization are quite similar in each of the East African nations. The only discernible difference between naturalization and registration is that, whereas naturalization is normally the method of acquiring East African citizenship that is used by aliens only, registration is the method of acquiring such citizenship for people who may or may not be aliens: minor children (under 21 years old) of East African citizens; people who ac-

quire East African citizenship as a special offer; alien wives of East
African citizens; people of African descent; and African citizens of
non-Commonwealth African countries.

Africans and Arabs born in East Africa are considered by law
to be "the indigenous inhabitants of East Africa," and consequently acquire East African citizenship by the automatic method.

According to the nationality laws of the East African states, an
alien acquires East African citizenship if he possesses certain qualifications, that is, if he fulfills certain conditions. For the sake of
convenience and ease of reference, the writer has divided these conditions into two groups: "common" conditions, that is, those that are
exactly the same in the citizenship laws mentioned above; and "non-
identical" conditions, that is, those that are characteristic only of
each of the countries of East Africa. The division of the conditions
into two groups should not, however, impair the validity of our previous assertion that the legislative provisions in the aforementioned
citizenship laws are identical.

NATURALIZATION IN EAST AFRICA:
IDENTICAL PROVISIONS

An alien can acquire an East African citizenship by fulfilling the
following requirements: attaining full age and capacity; making application to the minister responsible, in the prescribed manner; making
a declaration, in writing in the prescribed form, of his willingness to
renounce any other nationality or citizenship he may possess; taking
an oath of allegiance in the form specified in the First Schedule attached to each East African Citizenship Act (no dual nationality);
possessing a good character; satisfying the minister that he (the alien)
would be a suitable citizen; making his ordinary and lawful residence
in the East African country concerned throughout the period of 12
months immediately preceding the date of application to the minister,
but during the seven years immediately preceding the said period of
12 months, making his residence in that country for a period of, or
periods amounting in the aggregate to, more than four years; having
the intention, if registered or naturalized, to remain in the East African country permanently; and not being an enemy alien. Registration
is effective on the same day the alien is registered. Similarly, naturalization is effective on the date of grant of a certificate of naturalization. A man (or his wife) who, at the age of 21 is a citizen of an
East African country by registration, and is also a citizen of some
other country, must, if his East African citizenship is to be valid,
renounce his/her other citizenship and take an oath of allegiance,
within three months (12 months in Tanzania) after his acquisition of

an East African citizenship, or within such further period as an act
of parliament may prescribe, or as the minister or his appointed officer may permit. A naturalized or registered citizen of any of the countries of East Africa must produce, within the period specified above,
enough evidence of his renunciation of any other citizenship he may
have possessed before becoming a citizen of an East African nation.

On the question of citizenship by registration alone, the minister
has power to decide on, and allow the registration of, a minor child
as a citizen of an East African country where obviously that minister
exercises that power.

NATURALIZATION IN EAST AFRICA:
NONIDENTICAL PROVISIONS

Naturalization requirements characteristic of Tanzania alone
are birth outside Tanzania but of a father who was a citizen of Tanzania by descent at the time of the person's birth; ordinary residence
in the country for five years; and adequate knowledge in the minister's
judgment of Swahili or English.

Characteristic of Kenya alone are the following conditions: adequate knowledge of Swahili (in the minister's judgment); and ordinary
and lawful residence in Kenya for a period of, or for periods amounting in the aggregate to, not less than four years in the seven years
immediately preceding the aforesaid period of 12 months.

Characteristic of Uganda alone are the following conditions:
adequate knowledge of a prescribed vernacular language or of the English language; and being a wife of a Uganda citizen, who acquired on
October 8, 1962 Uganda citizenship by registration, on application in
the prescribed manner. Uganda citizenship by registration may be
granted to a national of an African non-Commonwealth country, if the
minister is convinced that reciprocal provisions are or may be made
in respect of Uganda citizens under the law of that country.

RENUNCIATION AND DEPRIVATION OF
EAST AFRICAN CITIZENSHIP

Other similar stipulations provided for in the East African nationality laws concern matters of renunciation and deprivation of East
African citizenship. Renunciation by a person himself, or deprivation
of his citizenship, does not affect that person's liability for any offense
committed by him before the renunciation or deprivation. Further,
the renunciation of such citizenship can be effective only if it is done
under certain conditions: It can be done only by an East African citi-

zen of full age and capacity, who is also (1) a citizen of any country to
which sections 7, 13, and 96 of the constitutions of Tanzania, Uganda,
and Kenya respectively apply or a citizen of the Republic of Ireland;
and (2) a national of a foreign country who makes a declaration, in the
prescribed manner, of renunciation of the citizenship of an East African country.

The minister may, however, refuse registration of such renunciation, if the renunciation is declared during a war in which that
country may be engaged, or if the declaration is contrary to that country's public policy.

The reasons for deprivation of citizenship in East Africa are
many and varied. A registered or naturalized citizen of an East African country shall be deprived of his citizenship if the minister is convinced that that fully grown and capable citizen has acquired such citizenship by means of false representation, fraud, or the concealment
of any material fact; has shown by act or speech to be disaffected or
disloyal toward an East African nation of which he is a citizen; has,
at any time while a citizen of an East African country, voluntarily
claimed and exercised, in a foreign country or in any other country
under the law of which provision is in force for conferring on its own
citizens, rights not available to Commonwealth citizens generally, or
any right available to him under the law of that country (being a right
accorded exclusively to its own citizens), and that as a result, it is
not conducive to the public good that he should continue to be a citizen
of the East African country in question; has, during any war in which
his East African country was engaged, unlawfully traded or communicated with any enemy, or been engaged in or associated with any business that was to his knowledge carried on in such a manner as to assist an enemy in that war; has, within seven years of his being naturalized (in Tanzania and Uganda) or five years commencing with the date
of the registration or naturalization (in Kenya), been sentenced in any
country to imprisonment for a term of not less than 12 months (in
Tanzania and Uganda), or a term of or exceeding 12 months that has
been imposed on that citizen by a court in any country, or that has
been substituted by a competent authority for some other sentence imposed on the citizen by such a court (in Kenya); has been ordinarily
resident in foreign countries for a continous period of seven years and,
during that period, has not registered annually, in the prescribed manner, with a consulate of Tanzania/Uganda, or by notice written to the
minister, his intention to retain his Tanzanian/Ugandan citizenship;
has, for a continuous period of seven years and during that period,
neither been at any time in the service of Kenya or of an international
organization of which Kenya was a member, nor registered annually—
with a Kenya consulate—his intention of retaining his Kenya citizenship.

The decision of the responsible minister (in these cases) in any
of the three countries of East Africa is considered final. Furthermore,
the minister may, as regards naturalization, allow a continuous period
of 12 months, ending not more than 6 months before the date of application, to be reckoned for the purposes of, and in accordance with, the
provisions set out in subparagraph 1(a) of the Second Schedule to each
of the Citizenship Acts (of Tanzania and Uganda), as though it had immediately preceded that date. That subparagraph (a) enumerates, as
one of the qualifications for naturalization of an alien who applies thereof, residence in any of the countries of East Africa, throughout the
period of 12 months immediately preceding the date of application to
the minister.

The minister may also allow periods of residence earlier than
eight years before the date of application, to be reckoned in computing
the aggregate cited in the abovementioned Second Schedule, namely,
that during or in the seven years immediately preceding the said period of 12 months, the alien in question has ordinarily and lawfully resided in an East African country for a period of, or periods amounting
in the aggregate to, not less than four years (in Kenya) or five years
(in Tanzania and Uganda). The Kenya Citizenship Act of 1967 does
not contain a schedule on qualifications for naturalization, but provisions on these qualifications are scattered throughout the Kenya Constitution.

FOUR SCHEDULES OF THE CITIZENSHIP ACTS
OF EAST AFRICAN COUNTRIES

The four schedules of the Citizenship Acts of Kenya, Uganda,
and Tanzania are as follows: the First Schedule concerns the "Oath
of Allegiance," and it is the same for the three nations; the Second
Schedule of the Ugandan and Tanzanian Citizenship Acts is entitled
"Qualifications for Naturalization," and the Second Schedule in the
Kenya Citizenship Act is entitled "Declaration Concerning Citizenship";
the Third Schedule in the Kenya Citizenship Act is entitled "Declaration
Concerning Residence," and the Third Schedule for Uganda and Tan-
zania is entitled "Declaration Concerning Citizenship"; the Fourth
Schedule for Uganda and Tanzania is entitled "Declaration Concerning
Residence." Thus although the headings vary in the different schedules,
the contents arc in fact the same in corresponding schedules.

WHO IS AN ALIEN IN EAST AFRICA ?

The backgrounds of each of the various racial groups in East Africa reveal that all the groups have inhabited East Africa for centuries.

One must therefore be very careful when stating that Asians—and for that matter Europeans and Arabs—are aliens in East Africa. If such a statement is made, then the criteria determining the alienage of these three racial minority groups in the region must be clearly given. Otherwise the statement would be sweeping and false. Countless statements of this sort have been made, unfortunately. Arabs, Asians, and Europeans in East Africa cannot be called aliens just because they happen to be brown or white and not black people. Arab emplacement in East Africa is, in many cases, older than that of many of the so-called indigenous peoples of East Africa. Similarly, the connections of Asians with East Africa are, really, just as old as those of the Arabs.

The question before us then is significant, but it is a difficult one. The definition of who is, and who is not, an alien in East Africa is a matter of legal definition. The real question that arises, then, is why and how some aliens became citizens in East Africa, while others did not.

The East African laws localized Arabs who inhabited East Africa permanently and bestowed upon them East African citizenship by the previously mentioned automatic method. Those Arabs who fell outside this category were described as aliens in the region. As for the Asians, they were defined as aliens in East Africa, despite their permanent residence in East Africa and long connections with the region, as archaeological evidence shows.

CONCLUSIONS

Legal determination and classification of aliens in East Africa conforms to the general rules of international law. Thus aliens can be classified into three broad groups.

One group consists of aliens in transit, that is, those who cross one East African state's territory to reach another state. A second group comprises aliens in route: These stay on in one East African country's territory for a limited period of time, for business and other purposes. Such people are usually known as the "temporary subjects" of the state. And under a third group fall aliens who stay and reside in an East African country temporarily or permanently. This class of aliens can, in turn, be divided into two groups that comprise people who are allowed to take up permanent residence in the East African state concerned: One group consists of resident aliens and domiciled aliens, and another group consists of immigrants.

It would, however, be a sweeping statement to say that the East African experience does not go against some of the rules of international law regulating questions of nationality and alienage. Such deviation in the East African law and practice from international law may be

justified, or unjustified, depending on whether or not the issues in ques-
question fall exclusively under domestic jurisdiction or international
law, and whether the East African state concerned adopts a "self-
styled" government policy that is implemented in complete defiance or
disregard of the rules of international law. Although the question of
who is or who is not an alien in East Africa is principally a matter of
legal determination and definition, the role of other forces in the determination of the situation of aliens in the region should not be overlooked
or underestimated. No doubt, the problem has also political, economic,
diplomatic, and sociological implications.

Four factors assist in determining generally the situation of
aliens in East Africa: the recentness of arrival of the alien; ethnic
or racial identity; enjoyment of an alternative citizenship status—a
matter to be decided by the government (where there is no option,
there is no alienage); and the functional position of the individual—
what he can do and under what conditions he can do it. In other words,
to qualify a person as an alien, racial identity alone is not enough.

Asians and Europeans were, and are still, the ethnic minority
groups in East Africa. They are distinguished from Africans physically and culturally. Arabs should also be grouped under the category
of the minority alien group, but, because Arabs have resided in East
Africa the longest of any minority group, they can safely be considered
nonaliens. Before independence, the ethnic minorities in East Africa
were classified under one general group—"British subjects." However,
distinctions were made between British citizens who then lived in the
colony of Kenya and British-protected persons—those who inhabited
the then Uganda protectorate and the then Tanganyika trust territory.

The position of all these alien ethnic minorities in the colonized
territories of East Africa will be the subject of the following chapter.

NOTES

1. For example, Hague Convention on the Conflict of Nationality
Laws (Geneva: League of Nations, April 12, 1930).

2. A fuller discussion on the question of legal personality appears in Don Nanjira, "The Legal Position of the United Nations Personnel and of Other International Organizations" (master's thesis,
Warsaw University, 1969), pp. 10-16.

3. See Laws, Reports, Statutes, 1948, vol. 2 (London: His
Majesty's Stationery Office, 1948), pp. 1241-65. See also "The
United Republic of Tanzania Citizenship Act, 1961," sec. 10(1) and
"The Uganda Citizenship Act," October 9, 1962, in Laws of Uganda,
vol. 2, rev. ed., 1964.

4. See Laws of Uganda, op. cit., chap. 63. See also Uganda, Ordinance 23 (1949), Ordinance 4 (1952), Ordinance 56 (1962), and Legal Notice, nos. 1 and 61 (1962), and S. 1. and 134 (1964).

5. See Republic of Kenya Acts, 1973, sec. 2. See also Kenya, Constitution, rev. ed., 1969, secs. 87, 93, and 95; and sec. 11(1), Kenya Citizenship Act, 1967.

6. Tanganyika Citizenship Act, 1961, sec. 6, subsec. (3), par. b, and subsec. (6), pars. a, c, and d.

7. Tanganyika, Government Notice No. 652, November 13, 1964. See also Tanganyika Subsidiary Legislation, 1964, p. 1061 et seq., and Tanganyika Revised Laws, vol. 13, chap. 557.

3

THE IMPOSITION OF ALIEN RULE IN EAST AFRICA

The imposition by foreign governments of their control on East Africa was piecemeal. And in this process, four elements were crucial: the migration of alien peoples to East Africa; the establishment by these peoples of colonies in East Africa; the subjection and exploitation by the newcomers of the newly colonized peoples in the region; and the ultimate duty of the colonizers to develop the colonized peoples and their territories.

After the creation of the United Nations, the expression "non-self-governing territory" was substituted for "colony" in official discussion. In more recent times, the expression "alien rule" has been used to mean "European colonial rule."[1] In the case of East Africa, however, colonization was shared by Europeans and Asians.

THE FIRST ALIEN ADMINISTRATION OF EAST AFRICA: THE CHARTERED COMPANY SYSTEM

The first alien attempt to administer and develop an East African territory—economically and even politically—actually occurred in 1876. In that year, Sir William Mackinnon's group of "influential (British) gentlemen" approached the Sultan of Zanzibar and expressed their intention to occupy his territory between the coast and Lake Victoria in his name, to protect it from any invasion and to develop it without costing his government anything. The Sultan granted the group a 50-year lease to administer his ten-mile coastal belt. The group henceforth exercised all the powers of a colonial government: It appointed officials and officers of justice; passed laws for the government of the various districts; raised an armed force for the protection of those districts; concluded treaties/agreements with the neighboring

governments or with subordinate or other chiefs; and acquired and
regulated the disposal of land not yet occupied, and appointed commissioners to rule, in the name or on behalf of the Sultan of Zanzibar,
any districts in the Sultan's territorial possessions. The group also
levied and collected taxes as might be necessary for the maintenance
and support of such local governments, forces, and administration of
justice, as well as for improvement of roads, water communication,
or other public works, defensive or otherwise, and for the liquidation
of debts and payment of interest on the capital expended.

On September 3, 1888, Queen Victoria granted the Mackinnon
group, which became known as the Imperial British East Africa Company, a royal charter—giving charter rights—to exploit the vast hinterland of British East Africa. Also in 1888, the company undertook
the government of the vast region between the Mombasa Coast and
what was then the Victoria Nyanza. In 1890, the company assumed
the direct administration of Uganda.

The administration of German East Africa was handled by the
Imperial German East Africa Company, founded by Karl Peters on
February 12, 1885. On February 27, 1885, the German Kaiser Wil-
helm issued an official notice of the extension of his protection to the
territories acquired, or which might be acquired, in East Africa. On
the same day, the Kaiser, at Bismarck's request, signed a "Charter
of Protection" taking the territories (acquired by Peters) under the
Kaiser's and Bismarck's imperial legal, commercial, political, and
administrative protection. Peters' Colonization Society was thus
granted complete jurisdiction over the natives as well as German and
other nationals in the German sphere of influence.

Owing, however, to lack of funds, both the British and German
companies failed in their duties. They consequently withdrew their
colonization of their respective areas of control. And the Sultan retained his suzerainty over the coastal zone.

ESTABLISHMENT OF DIRECT ANGLO-GERMAN CONTROL OVER EAST AFRICA: THE PROTECTORATE SYSTEM

According to some authors, the origins of the German government's direct administration of the German colony can be traced to
May 25, 1887, when Hauptmann Leue, a German administrator, arrived in Dar-es-Salaam. According to others, the German government
assumed direct responsibility for its East African colonial territory
in the same year that the British government did, that is, 1895.

The establishment of colonial rule in German East Africa was
done in two phases: at the coast between 1890 and 1891, and in the

interior between 1891 and 1895. There were three stages in the latter process. First, the German colonial administrators entered into
treaty agreements with local chiefs; they then set up military posts on
caravan routes and at maritime trade centers; and finally, the colonial
military government was replaced by a government of civilian district
officers who exercised both executive and judicial powers. Second,
the management of the German and British colonies in East Africa
was placed at first under the Foreign Offices of the governments of
the two countries. Third, new departments were created later in
Britain and Germany specifically for the direct management of all
colonial affairs. In Britain the new department was called the Colonial
Office. The Colonial Office assumed direct responsibility for the
British territory between the coast and Lake Victoria on April 1, 1905.
In the same year also, the administration of the Uganda protectorate
was passed from the Foreign to the Colonial Office. This transfer of
responsibility followed the absolute administrative confusion caused
by increased white settlements in East African highlands. The British territory, Uganda, and Somaliland were put under one East African Department of the Colonial Office.

In Germany a new Colonial Office was created in May 1907, and
the administration of the German protectorate in East Africa was dele-
gated to a secretary of state. Before the creation of the Colonial Office, all the German colonial affairs affecting German East Africa
had, for 106 years (1801-1907), been placed under the direction of
the German chancellor through a controller (a director after 1894) of
the Colonial Department in the German Foreign Office. Finally, the
assumption by the colonizing governments of direct responsibility for
their colonies in East Africa was immediately followed by proclamations
of protectorates over the colonial territories.

On April 1, 1894, a British protectorate was declared over Buganda; the proclamation of provisional British protection over Buganda
on April 1, 1893 had been the first British colonial administration on
the East African mainland. Then on June 18, 1894, the British government officially accepted and endorsed the British protectorate previously declared over Buganda, with a maintenance of British garri-
sons in the kingdoms of Bunyoro and Toro; the kingdom of Ankole
would also be protected, but there was to be no British responsibility
in these three kingdoms. Finally, in August 1894, the British Parliament (Gladstone was prime minister) confirmed the official British
protectorate over Buganda. That confirmation gave Buganda the new
name of the "Kingdom of Uganda."[2]

Actually, the British protectorate over the whole of Uganda was
effected on April 13, 1894. Then on June 30, 1896, the British protectorate was extended to the whole of Bunyoro, and the British special
commissioner, later governor, was given overall authority in the five

Ugandan kingdoms: Ankole, Bunyoro, Busoga, Toro, and Buganda.
By 1919, the political reconstitution of Uganda into one territory had
been completed.

As for the area between Uganda and the coast of East Africa,
the British government asked the bankrupt British East Africa Company in 1894 to surrender its charter and concession in the area in return for a £250,000 compensation. In March 1895, the company accepted the British government's proposal, and a British protectorate
over that area was proclaimed at Mombasa on July 1, 1895. In 1896,
the area was joined with the coast protectorate, and the resulting mer-
ger was referred to as the East Africa Protectorate (EAP).

The EAP therefore comprised a protectorate area and a colony
area. The former portion was held by the British on lease from the
Sultan of Zanzibar; it was variously known as a coast protectorate, a
coastal strip, a coastal belt, and a coastal zone. From 1920, it became
Kenya Protectorate, following a British order-in-council issued in the
same year. That arrangement between the British and the Sultan
meant that the coast protectorate would in the future be administered
as an integral part of the colony area.

Zanzibar was usually referred to as a protectorate because the
control exercised over it by Britain did not differ greatly from that
normally characterizing a protectorate. The only distinguishing element of the status of a protected state retained by Zanzibar was that
British authority in Zanzibar was represented not by a governor but
by a resident.

However, Zanzibar seemed to fall officially under the category
of a protected state, because of the treaty arrangement between Britain and the Sultan. Thus the treaty arrangement brought about an element of division of sovereignty. The actual original agreement by
which the Sultan formally accepted the protection of Britain was
reached on June 14, 1890.[3]

However, the British signed in December 1895 a "practical"
agreement with the Sultan for the administration of the Sultan's 10-
mile coastal belt. And in 1924-25, a British order-in-council was issued under the British Foreign Jurisdiction Act of 1890. The order
laid down the jurisdiction to be exercised in the coastal belt and the
classes of people who were to be subject to that jurisdiction.

The colony area of the EAP was constituted a Crown Colony in
1920. From 1921 onward, the name "Kenya" was applied to the EAP
as a whole; the expression "Colony and Protectorate of Kenya" began
to be used.

The first serious British thought of developing the EAP was nurtured between 1901 and 1903. The colony was at first (during this
period) administered from Zanzibar. Arthur Hardinge, the British
consul-general in Zanzibar and the first high commissioner of the

EAP, now had power over both the protectorate and colony of Kenya;
Hardinge combined the two posts in order to avoid additional expenses.
In 1905, the government was officially moved from Mombasa to Nairo-
bi.

BRITISH COLONIAL POLICIES AND
PRACTICES IN EAST AFRICA

The aim of British colonial policies consisted of two significant
elements: the divide-and-rule policy, which was basically a method
of imposing alien rule by force; and the determination to suppress and
abolish slavery and the slave trade, and to protect British interests in
East Africa. The British colonial administrator Frederick Lugard believed it was the duty of the white man to assist the African. His belief that the white man had a moral obligation to "civilize"—that is,
to develop—the African had been expressed by David Livingstone, who
had declared his aim as being to introduce the black family into the
"corporate" body of nations.

At the same time, in Kenya, the "white man's country," the system of "native reserves" introduced by the British colonial administrators encouraged corruption and tribalism, particularly after World
War I. The policy of "native reserves" called for the protection of
Africans in their own area and gave them the same security there as
the Europeans were given in the White Highlands. The divide-and-rule
policy impoverished the African, divided Africans, and made them
not only hate but also envy and compete with one another. It was a
system of local government that promoted the evil policy of racial
segregation. It was applied throughout the region.

This practice was definitely against the historic and long-de-
clared purpose of British colonial policy favoring fair representation
of all the major communities in the local legislatures, which have always been the organs of self-government.

The main British interest, then, in East Africa was political.
The British officials therefore rightly believed their ultimate task
was to promote and spread British rule in the region. But the British
also aimed at safeguarding native interests and training Africans in
such a way that they should eventually stand on their own feet. Hence
the eventual achievement of self-rule by the colonial peoples and territories was the main long-term objective of British colonial policy in
general. Self-rule in East Africa had to include a proper provision
for all the main communities that had made their home in that region.

Because of the great challenge to that objective from the white
settlers, it was absolutely essential that Britain should maintain her
control until the assistance given to the indigenous peoples in develop-

ing their own resources and institutions had set them so far on the road
to progress that they could take their full part, together with the political and economic life of the region.

Up to 1898, British policy in East Africa consisted of communications and strategy. The first British colonial administrative involve-
ments in the region were caused, inter alia, by Britain's wish to control Egypt, the headwaters of the Nile (the Nile Valley and the White
Nile), and Uganda; the need to secure the sea route (Suez Route) to India; and Britain's determination to control the territory between Lake
Victoria and the East African coast.

In the EAP, one of the purposes of British policy was to work for
the rapid financial welfare of the protectorate through encouragement
of immigration, especially of the European settlers, and of capital investment.

As for British policy in Uganda, successive governors stressed
the need to develop Africans and their land as an African country.
The Africans had to be consulted before any alienation of their land
could be effected. Developments in Uganda were hence the reverse of
those in Kenya and Tanganyika. Explaining, for instance, the British
policy toward local government authorities, the 1951 Uganda Protectorate Report declared:

> They [local government authorities] are designed to
> ensure the closest co-operation between chiefs and
> people, to provide the people as a whole with some
> experience of local government on democratic lines,
> to promote the growth of executive responsibility and,
> in the case of the Agreement Districts [the Ankole,
> Busoga, Bunyoro and Toro Kingdoms], to supplement
> the traditional personal relations between ruler and
> ruled with more democratic institutions.[4]

The obstacle to British policy was Buganda's strong separatist
attitudes. In 1953, the Lukiko (Parliament) in Buganda and the Bugandan people demanded an increased isolation and a strengthening of the
special position of Buganda, which would eventually emerge as a separate entity. The British, however, rejected Buganda's demands for
autonomy and separate statehood. In short, the essence of the "Pax
Britannica" policy lay in bringing peace, prosperity, and justice to the
less fortunate peoples of East Africa. After the creation of the British
Commonwealth, the British colonial policy was dominated by the hope
of persuading Britain's restive non-European colonial peoples to remain affiliated with Britain through the Commonwealth. Britain's
long-range purposes of colonial policy included the following:

1. Education was calculated to train a class of native leaders capable of manning the institutions of self-government and a modern economy.

2. Economic development and foreign investment were designed to raise the living standards of the colonial peoples and to develop agricultural, mining, and simple industrial facilities sufficient to assure the colony an income from the world market when the colony achieved independence.

3. Self-government was gradually introduced, advancing from self-rule at the village and district level to the establishment of colonial legislatures with elected majorities and increasing autonomous powers and ending with the choice of a native cabinet from among the freely elected parliamentarians. At that stage, independence would be achieved, and the former colony was free to decide whether to remain in the British Commonwealth. Thus, while Burma and Ireland eventually refused to remain in the Commonwealth, other former British colonies accepted Commonwealth membership; Kenya, Uganda, Tanganyika, and Zanzibar were among the latter group.

Britain sought to export her institutions and values but permitted native groups to adapt these to their own requirements as they saw fit. Colonial reforms were sometimes accelerated by unrest in the colonies and, as we shall see, by pressure from the United Nations.

GERMAN COLONIAL POLICIES AND PRACTICES IN EAST AFRICA

German colonial policy in East Africa was quite different from British policy. The Germans ruled Tanganyika with a very tough hand. They were ruthless and inflexible in character, and austere colonial administrators. The Germans had to be tough because African resistance was strong and persistent. The Swahilis described the German administrator Zelewski as "Nyundo"—"the hammer." Edward von Liebert, for example, who became governor of German East Africa in 1896, summed up the attitude of the German administrators by saying that it was impossible in Africa to get on without cruelty. The brutalities of the Germans, their use of the kiboko—"the whip of hippopotamus hide"—and the frequency with which the death sentence was lightly awarded were characteristic of the methods of German colonial rule in East Africa.

The German administrator Von Weissmann, for instance, could "neither bribe a single tribe in German East Africa to side with him, nor play off missionary against missionary," and thus "a seed had been sown which was to bear fruit in the years of tribulation lasting until 1907."[5]

Of all the German colonial administrators in German East Africa, Peters is the most remembered. And this is because he was an exceptionally cruel and ruthless administrator; his methods of rule were unacceptable not only to the Africans, Arabs, and Asians but also to the German settlers in German East Africa. At home, German's Social Democrats in the Reichstag also bitterly opposed Peters' inhuman methods of colonial rule. Peters kept a harem of African women and mercilessly killed those who escaped from him and were recaptured later. Peters even castrated those who followed after wives or fiancees he had accumulated for himself. The Africans remembered Peters as "Mkono-wa-damu," that is, "the man with the bloodstained hands." Peters was eventually indicted by a German judge "for excessive cruelty to Africans and for misuse of official power."

Peters died in 1918, and he was referred to by Hitler in 1934 as a "model, though stern, colonial administrator." Hitler then issued a series of propaganda stamps in honor of Peters.

German colonial policies and practices in East Africa were hence characterized, among other things, by:

1. Extreme cruelty exercised by the German colonists toward the Africans;

2. Extreme cruelty by German agents, called akidas (who were usually Swahilis and Arabs) in the administering of groups of villages;

3. Expropriation of the African lands and the granting of them to the German emperor;

4. Forced labor imposed on the Africans on the alien settler plantations, and on the government public workers; and

5. The introduction of a hut tax of three Indian rupees per year despite the fact that the Africans had no money.

The system of harsh, direct rule was started in German East Africa by the aforementioned Imperial German East Africa Company. That harsh system, together with the land alienation and forced labor policies applied by the German colonial administrators, prompted African rebellions, and a take-over in 1891 of direct colonial administration first by the German government's Foreign Office and later by its Colonial Office.

THE DOCTRINE OF INDIRECT RULE IN
COLONIAL EAST AFRICA

The central German colonial policy in East Africa, and indeed elsewhere in German colonial possessions, was that of direct rule; however, the British basic colonial policy was, for a long time, that of indirect rule. In fact, the indirect rule system was started by the British, and only later applied by the Germans in their colonies. The direct rule system was first applied by the chartered companies, and later by the colonial administrators, when direct management of the colony concerned was transferred to the colonizing government. The people advancing the indirect rule doctrine were traditional and other (appointed) local rulers. The system continued to function even after the transfer of direct control and administration to the government of the colonial power concerned.

By "indirect rule" was generally meant the heavy reliance by the early colonial administrators upon the work of local "officials" who functioned under "instruction." Indirect rule was therefore a system of mixed administration. It was considered a practical solution to the problems of administering colonial territories where communications were poor, money was short, and the number of European functionaries was low. The colonial powers used the already established traditional African authorities (chiefs, emirs, sultans) where possible as the basis of local government, while European officials occupied higher posts in the administration and retained ultimate responsibility for government. As a kind of "native administration," the indirect rule system was formulated when a colonial country or territory became a protectorate or protected state.

In East Africa, the early colonial administrators, especially in the case of the Germans, relied on the Sultan of Zanzibar's former system of officials. However, in areas such as Buganda, only a few of the African authorities were seemingly important. Therefore some of the local rulers were used only as a means of governing.

The indirect rule system was effectively developed in the British Protectorate of Northern Nigeria by the system's pioneer—Lugard— and by Donald Cameron, who was under Lugard. Lugard also applied the policy in Zanzibar and in the Bugandan protectorate. The system was later applied by Harry Hamilton Johnston in Buganda. Incidentally, Lugard, Cameron, and Johnston were the leading exponents of the British-initiated policy of indirect rule.

The so-called referents were the heads of the departments into which the central government was divided in German East Africa. At the decentralized level, the German colonial territory was administered by the provincial commissioners, district commissioners, liwalis ("headmen"), and the abovementioned akidas. The district commissioner headed the district and was the lowest European colonial official. The liwalis were actually governors in charge of the coastal towns. Under the liwalis were the akidas, or political agents, actually subheads of subdistricts; they were concerned with the direct administration of the Africans of the interior.

The liwalis and akidas were (as mentioned above) usually of Swahili or Arab origin. They were empowered to exercise limited

judicial duties, administer corporal punishment, and collect taxes.
The akida was usually an alien to the people he controlled: under him
were village elders or chiefs.

In what became Tanganyika, the Germans introduced the indirect
rule system and divided the territory into 21 districts administered by
21 German administrative officers as outlined above.

All these administrative officials aimed at the elimination of
tribalism in the colony. And in fact the present lack of open tribal
clashes in Tanganyika owes its origins to the German colonial rulers;
they were harsh administrators but established a principle—lack of
open tribalism—from which Tanganyika (Tanzania) has benefited ever
since.

Moreover, while these administrators functioned in the colonies,
German East Africa was actually ruled from Berlin through a governor
assisted by an official advisory council.

The origins of British administration over German East Africa
can be traced to the end of 1916, when Horace Byatt was appointed administrator over the northern half of Tanganyika, which Britain controlled. Byatt introduced an ad hoc administration. In January 1919,
Byatt's rule was extended to the whole of Tanganyika.

CAMERON: THE ARCHITECT OF INDIRECT
RULE IN TANGANYIKA

Cameron is the greatest figure in the history of British rule in
Tanganyika. He ruled the territory from 1925 to 1931. Cameron had
been greatly influenced by Lugard's system of indirect rule. Disagree-
ing, therefore, with Byatt's method of direct rule, Cameron introduced
a system of indirect rule in Tanganyika, which he called "local native
administration." Cameron asserted that his system was based on ex-
pediency. Hence traditional institutions had to be preserved and improved. Cameron first selected as chiefs the most able natives acceptable to the African people, and then endowed the chiefs with administrative duties and powers.

Cameron advanced the belief that Africa was to be left entirely
for the Africans, who should be given every opportunity to participate
in public affairs affecting them, whether directly or indirectly. He
strongly believed that one day Africans would, or should, rule not
only Tanganyika but the whole of East Africa; all foreigners, that is,
Europeans, Asians, and even Arabs, had to remember that always.

On December 7, 1926, Cameron inaugurated in Tanganyika a
legislative council of 26 members. Of these, 13 were senior officials
of the government and seven were nominated members—five Europeans
and two Asians.

After 1929, unfortunately, Cameron decided to exclude Africans from the legislative council, and they would thenceforth be represented on the council by the governor, the chief secretary, and the secretary for native affairs. The reason for the exclusion of the Africans was their lack of sufficient knowledge of the English language. Education, therefore, conditioned indirect rule and the preparation for self-rule and eventual independence. And thus Cameron placed great emphasis on education in his efforts to elevate Africans.

Cameron left Tanganyika in 1931, after having strongly opposed the idea of "closer union" in East Africa that was penetrating slowly into Tanganyika. Cameron had further abolished in 1928 the whipping and flogging of Africans by administrative colonial officers. He had banned head porterage and had also sponsored and supported the foundation of the Tanganyika African Association (TAA). The TAA was an African political organization created to operate in those urban areas that the Germans had destroyed beyond the point of revival. The TAA's main aim was to provide Africans with a further means of developing self-reliance and responsibility.

In the 1950s, every tribe in Tanganyika had its own tribal council, court, and other tribal institutions, schools, dispensaries, and so on, based on the elective principle. All decisions were to be taken by the tribal chief together with the council, and not just by the chief alone.

The system of indirect rule had its own good and bad features.

On the positive side, indirect rule was valuable economically, since the lack of funds and of trained (European) personnel did not allow for a system of direct rule. In addition, the indigenous institutions of indirect rule were undoubtedly democratic, for all the members of a tribe understood their purposes and participated in their institutions. British practices could be grafted on these institutions in due course and would eventually bring modern democracy to East Africa as a practical and workable form of government.

The negative aspects of the indirect rule method were many and varied. Many mistakes were made, especially when newly arrived European functionaries picked apparently influential tribal figures to act as links in the chain of command. Despite the endeavors of the colonial administrators to promote native rule, impediments developed when new provincial administrations were introduced. And the provincial and district commissioners suppressed the native authorities. Other disadvantages of the indirect rule method included the following:

1. The system encouraged tribalism, which has always been one of the greatest diseases in the developing and former colonial societies. The strict demarcation of tribal boundaries (regionalism, or "majimbo") in Kenya was a good case in point.

2. The system was an enforcement of the divide-and-rule policy, by which tribal groups were made to fight against one another.

3. The system made people turn inward toward their tribe, and hence back to the past, instead of forward and outward to the ideas of nationhood and Pan-Africanism.

4. The system deterred progress toward East African unity.

5. Cameron's exclusion of Africans from the legislative council in Tanganyika and his inclusion in it of more foreigners—after 1829—on the grounds that Africans could not speak English was the lamest of excuses.

6. The system failed to train Africans for "Western" posts, especially in the civil service.

In spite of these disadvantages, the colonists soon realized that they had challenging responsibilities: to raise the living standards of the East African inhabitants and introduce better farming methods, better medical, transport, and educational facilities, and so on.

ADMINISTRATIVE AND STRUCTURAL ORGANIZATION OF THE EAST AFRICAN COLONIES

As the years passed, a colonial administration in East Africa was, as indicated above, developed both at the centralized and decentralized levels. In German East Africa, each one of the districts was placed under a German district administrator called bekirksamtmann; and under him, there were other administrative officers, both at the vertical and horizontal levels.

The British adopted a similar administrative and governmental policy in the region.[6] The body that advised and assisted the high commissioner in the government of the EAP was called the East African Protectorate Council. And the high commissioner was eventually replaced by a governor who was the colony's commander-in-chief of the armed forces and had immense statutory and discretionary powers. He was answerable only to the colonial secretary in London.

At the decentralized level, there were organs of provincial, district, and local administration. Under these were the police and armed forces.

In Kenya, for example, a village headmen ordinance was enacted in 1902 that provided for the appointment of "official headmen," whose responsibility would be to keep public roads in repair. The headmen were simultaneously the principal agents for tax collection in what were called the native land units. The area under a headman became known as a "location," and the institution of the local native council was brought into existence. The district commissioner became chairman and chief executive authority, and an African his deputy, of the council. At first, each tribe had a separate local native council. Later, one council only existed in each district.

The main job of the councils was to levy rates and pass resolutions on issues affecting purely local native administration. The resolutions had the legal effect of by-laws once they were approved by the governor. From 1948 onward, local councils assumed responsibility for the construction and maintenance of dispensaries, cattle dips, markets, all primary education, and small roads. In 1950, the African District Councils Ordinance 12 was enacted, and by it, African district councils were created. Henceforth, the local native councils became known as the African district councils. These ranked with the municipalities and district councils in the European areas as organs of the Kenya Local Government Board. The district commissioner still remained the chairman of the new council, and African members on the council were appointed by the provincial commissioner. The procedure for the application of the local native councils was the most characteristic feature of the British policy in the administration of African affairs in colonial East Africa. The system of local administration—or, for that matter, local government—as introduced by the British in East Africa has been withheld up to today.

At the decentralized level also, native tribunals were set up by the British Native Courts Regulations of 1897. Administrative officers were authorized to try all cases arising within a radius of 15 miles from a government post. Outside this radius, certain tribal authorities were given contemporaneous jurisdiction. Native tribunals had, as their main duty, to administer native law and custom, but subject to reasonable supervision. In 1907 and in 1911, a courts ordinance and tribal rules respectively were enacted. Their central purpose was to empower the councils of elders, constituted under native law and custom, to exercise judicial powers in the native tribunals.

Administrative procedures at the decentralized level in Uganda, Tanganyika, and Zanzibar were similar to that in Kenya. In Zanzibar the last in the hierarchy of officials were Africans appointed as headmen, but the Africans were responsible only for the control of other Africans. The native courts set up in Zanzibar administered Muslim law.

In Uganda, especially Buganda, a strong system of local administration and political organization already existed before the advent of the Europeans. When the Europeans arrived, they used the strong traditional system in Buganda Kingdom as a kind of local rule. When the British signed an agreement with the kingdom's ruler in 1900 and with the rulers of the other Ugandan kingdoms (states) in the following years, the British created, in the whole Ugandan protectorate, a system of local administration of three different types: that existing in

Buganda State; that of the three states of Ankole, Toro, and Bunyoro in the western province; and that existing in the remaining eight districts of the Ugandan protectorate, in the eastern and northern provinces (native courts were also established in Uganda).

THE LEGISLATIVE AND EXECUTIVE COUNCIL SYSTEM

At the centralized level of colonial administration in East Africa after 1919, there were four essential organs: the governor, the legislative council, the executive council, and the judiciary.

The judiciary was appointed by the British colonial secretary on behalf of the British Crown, but on the advice and consent of the colony's governor and chief justice. Although the governor had no power over the high court, the Crown's prerogative of mercy was vested in him.

Constitutionally, the main task of the legislative council was to advise the governor—its chairman—but the council also made laws. Actually, the governor had the duty to make laws with the advice and consent of the legislative council. [7] Such laws were to be styled "ordinances," and the enacting words were to be "enacted by the Governor of" (for example, Tanganyika). The legislative council comprised two classes of members: ex officio and "unofficial" members.

The ex officio members were actually officials, that is, British civil servants from the British Colonial Office. The "unofficial" members were noncivil servants appointed by the governor of the colony in question. In practice, all the council members were nominated by the governor of the colony concerned.

As for the executive councils in the colonies, each one usually consisted of three classes of members. Ex officio members were those on the government side. They were in charge of the various governmental departments; Whitehall in London "knew" of them. They all worked under the direction and responsibility of the government. The so-called official members were those whom the governor appointed, in (their) personal capacity, to the executive council. And the unofficial members were ex officio members of the legislative council on the government side, but unofficial members of the executive council (after 1957). The officials (ex officio members) were initially the only persons with the right to belong to the executive council. The unofficials enjoyed that right only from 1918. At the beginning of colonial rule, these unofficials were Europeans only.

There were five indispensable officials (ex officio members) of the executive council: the governor, who was the council's chairman; the chief secretary, who was the head of the civil service (his was a

role of supervising permanent secretaries in all the governmental departments, answerable to the governor); the treasurer, who was in
charge of government finances; the attorney general, or the governor's
legal adviser; and the director of medical and sanitary services, who
was responsible for health matters. The development over the years
of the institution of the executive council turned these officials into
ministers. In Tanganyika, ex officio members became known as ministers from 1957, whereas the unofficials became assistant ministers,
although they did not sit in the executive council.

THE QUESTION OF LAND IN COLONIAL
EAST AFRICA

A significant and most sensitive issue that occupied a special
place in the European colonial policies and practices in East Africa
was the question of land. Broadly speaking, land problems were similar in all four East African territories. In all of them, Africans owned
land from time immemorial by custom and tradition. They therefore
had, for many years, what one may call traditional rights to occupy
the land.

In Zanzibar, for example, the African traditional land-tenure
system did not recognize any type of land alienation. This was still
the situation even as late as the 1950s. The Arabs, however, were
allowed to possess—and did possess—lands for more than one-and-a-
half centuries before independence—either by purchase, by grants
from the Sultan, or by simple occupation. In these cases, land rights
were not legally defined, but they were equivalent to freehold.

The African traditional and customary land tenure systems un-
derwent great changes during the Anglo-German colonization of East
Africa.

For example, in Zanzibar, it became compulsory to register
all land transactions, although no system of record titles nor a cadas-
tral survey existed. However, Zanzibar was, by constitution, an
Arab state under the protection of the British government; there was
therefore no claim by the British Crown to the disposal of any land in
Zanzibar. But nevertheless legal arrangements were made between
the British and the Sultan of Zanzibar concerning the occupation of
Zanzibari land. In 1921 a public land decree was enacted. The decree
contained three key provisions: the Sultan was given full powers and
rights over all waste besides unoccupied land and all land occupied according to tribal or local customs; subject to compensation, the British resident in Zanzibar could occupy any such land on behalf of the
Sultan; and, to be valid, any document authorizing the disposition of
such land required the "ratification" of a (British) district commis-

sioner in Zanzibar. Another decree—Land Alienation Decree No. 9, of 1939—prohibited attachment of debt on African or Arab lands, or their produce, and subjected all land alienation to the control of a board appointed by the British resident in Zanzibar.

In what is now Tanganyika, traditional land tenure systems were also retained, although with some modifications. Customary land tenure methods differed from one tribe to another.

The European colonizers enacted rules to regulate succession and rents. Provisions were made for the registration of land, and for the collection of registration fees. Land rules to protect peasants were also introduced.

As far back as November 26, 1895, a German imperial decree proclaimed that all land in the German protectorate was Crown Land. However, the right of the Crown was subject to the rights of private individuals and corporate bodies (juristische person) or of chiefs and native communities. The imperial decree further provided for the establishment of native reserves—for the cultivation of the natives. It also provided for the appointment of land commissions that would demarcate the native reserves. As a result of this German land policy, the local African tribes lost vast areas of land, which became Crown land.

When the British took over the administration of Tanganyika from the Germans, they also introduced their own land policy as they thought fit. That was all the more necessary, since the mandatory agreement under which the British government assumed direct responsibility for German East Africa (Tanganyika) in 1920 vaguely outlined the policy to be adopted concerning rights in the native lands. The agreement merely declared that no rights were to be enacted in favor of nonnatives without the prior consent of the public authorities.

The administering authority adopted a careful policy with regard to the extension of European settlement in Tanganyikan territory. Priority was given to native rights from the beginning, and even in the ordinances that were enacted over the years, emphasis was all the time placed upon the need to develop the native tribes, using, inter alia, the lands the Africans had occupied and utilized from time immemorial.

In 1923, a land ordinance was enacted in which three major stipulations were laid down: All lands in Tanganyika were proclaimed to be public lands to be administered for the common benefit of the territory's inhabitants with the exception of acquired lands; to be valid, however, the title to the occupation and utilization of any such lands required the consent of the governor; and thenceforth, the title would take the form of a certificate granting a right of occupancy for not more than 99 years, and such title could be granted both to Africans and non-Africans.

In 1926, Cameron made it clear at the East African Governors'
Conference that he was not ready to adopt the policy of "native reserves" as practiced in neighboring Kenya.

A particularly important land law enacted in colonized Tanganyika was the Land Ordinance of 1950. The main aim of the ordinance
was to acquire control (over land), which, while recognizing African
customary rights over land, would enable the colonizing government
to intervene in order to prevent undue alienation of land to non-Africans. That meant that, after 1950, an individual title over land
could be secured only by the grant of a right of occupancy. An omni-
racial Land Utilization Board was established in 1950 whose stated
aim was to recommend "on the measures to be adopted to encourage
and develop a suitable system of agricultural land tenure for Africans
giving the stability and continuity required by modern conditions."

In Uganda, the Bugandan Kabaka signed an agreement with the
British East Africa Company in 1892. By that agreement, the Kabaka
was bound not to alienate African land rights to Europeans without the
company's consent. In 1894, the British still affirmed that the pro-
mulgation of a protectorate over Buganda did not give the British
Crown any legal powers over the control of land. The turning point
occurred in 1899, when the British government decided to claim control over waste or unoccupied land in those Uganda protectorates
where no "settled" form of government existed and land had not been
appropriated either by the sovereign or by individuals.

The above stipulation mainly affected Ankole, Busoga, Bunyoro,
and Toro. In 1900, the British signed another agreement with Buganda, by which Buganda came under the class of a "settled" government,
and all of Buganda's land that was not occupied became a gift of the
Kabaka. A few months later, the British reached agreements with
the Mukama and chiefs of Toro, and in 1901 with the Mugabe of Ankole.

The Buganda agreement (1900) reserved 9,000 square miles of
land for the benefit of the Kabaka and his chiefs, totaling about 3,700
persons. The reserved land was not regarded to be a grant, but
merely as property to which the British Crown had no claim. It was
this land that became known, over the years, as the Buganda mailo
lands. In 1908, an ordinance called the Buganda Mailo Law was enacted
that granted to chiefs and private landowners a right approximating
freehold. However, transfers to non-Africans required the previous
consent of the governor of Uganda and the government of Buganda. All
the remaining lands and forests of Buganda were vested, by the agreement, in the Uganda colonial administration.

As for Ankole and Toro, the (British) agreements with these
kingdoms merely stated that all "waste and uncultivated lands" would
belong to the British government. In their case only, small areas
were granted to the rulers and to a few prominent chiefs.

British land policy in Uganda was also outlined in other legal instruments, of which the following are noteworthy: the Uganda Lands Order-in-Council of 1902; the Crown Lands Ordinance of 1903; the Uganda Land Ordinance of 1910; and the so-called Announcement of 1950.

The 1950 land "announcement" had the intention of developing Uganda primarily as an African country. After 1950, Crown land was described as "African trust land." In 1956, the colonial administration enacted a law declaring all lands hitherto held as Crown lands (barring those gazetted in townships) to be "African lands."

The British East Africa Company obtained rights over land from the Sultan of Zanzibar in 1887. Right from the beginning of the colonization of the EAP, the European and other alien settlers were able to acquire lands either by purchase from chiefs or from the British East Africa Company. Land regulations in the EAP were basically similar to those in neighboring Uganda. In 1899, the British government started to implement the view that the declaration of a protectorate enabled the British Crown to claim sovereign rights then in existence. This meant that the Crown was given the right to dispose of unoccupied lands.

In 1901, the British colonial administration in the EAP enacted an East Africa (Lands) Order-in-Council, which controlled land for the purpose of colonization. The land required for disposal had first to be brought into the class of Crown property—that is, "all public lands" that for the time being were subject to the control of the Crown. As in Uganda, the expression "public lands" in the EAP simply meant all those unoccupied lands over which the protectorate would henceforth have powers of control.

In 1902, another East Africa (Lands) Order-in-Council was enacted, establishing the terms under which Crown lands could be granted and permitting the lease or sale of Crown lands. Up to 640 acres could be granted. In 1902 also, a Crown lands ordinance was enacted providing that, in all dealings with Crown land, regard should be given to the rights and requirements of the natives, and in particular, the EAP high commissioner should not sell or lease any land in the actual occupation of the natives. This significant provision led to the appointment, by the Kenya administration in 1904, of a local committee that recommended the establishment of reserves for Africans, to enable Europeans to settle in the best lands.

A short comparative analysis of colonial land policies in East Africa reveals that Zanzibar's "special" (constitutional) status as an Arab state under the British government's protection hindered not only the British Crown from claiming lands in Zanzibar, but also the British government from formulating any land policy in Zanzibar, in the same manner as it did in Kenya, Uganda, and Tanganyika.

As in Tanganyika, the question of land rights in Uganda was not influenced to the same extent as it was in Kenya by a policy of colonization. Similarly, no serious alien-native clashes over land, as in Kenya, existed in Uganda or Tanganyika. The main reason for this situation was the fact that the areas best suited for colonization had been withdrawn from Uganda and transferred to Kenya in 1902. Similarly, the problem of alienation of land (to aliens) in Tanganyika was not as serious as in neighboring Kenya. There were three major reasons for this situation:

1. The administration in Tanganyika favored African priorities. In Kenya, the administration favored European priorities.
2. In Tanganyika, compensation and good conditions were given to the Africans who lost or leased their traditionally possessed lands to aliens. In Kenya, nothing of that sort existed.
3. In Tanganyika, land could not—especially from 1953 onward —be allocated for non-African settlement unless it was not likely to be required for non-African occupation in the foreseeable future. Land was to be used for the development of Africans. In Kenya, the idea was to demarcate as native reserves the worst land and allocate it to Africans, while the best land was to be delimited exclusively for the development and utilization of the Europeans.

TREATIES REGARDING EAST AFRICAN TERRITORIES

Of all the possible ways of settling the territorial disputes between Britain and Germany regarding East Africa, the best way available to them was obviously the "treaty" method.[8]

The colonial treaties on East Africa were concluded either between the Sultan of Zanzibar and the alien European powers or among the alien powers themselves. The treaties signed with the Sultan were either "protective" (as was the case between Sultan Barghash and the British), "of eternal life" (as was the case between Sultan Barghash or the local chiefs and Germany's Karl Peters), "commercial" (Barghash and Britain on April 30, 1886), or "political" (Germany and Britain in 1886 and 1890).

The first and most significant political treaty of the period was the Anglo-German Partition Treaty (agreement) of 1886. Previous to the conclusion of the treaty, an Anglo-German-French agreement had established a Joint International Delimitation Commission at Zanzibar, whose duty was to demarcate the Zanzibari Sultan's possessions in East Africa. The Commission delimited on December 14, 1885, and recognized as the Sultan's dominions, the islands of Zanzibar and Pem-

ba, and any islets within 12 miles of them; the work of the commission
was considered unacceptable.

On June 9, 1886, a proces-verbal was recorded among Britain,
France, and Germany in which the European powers unanimously recognized, at Zanzibar, the sovereign rights of the Sultan of Zanzibar
over certain maritime, littoral, and continental possessions. These
possessions included Zanzibar, Pemba, Lamu, Mafia, Malindi, Dar-
es-Salaam, Mogadisho, Mombasa, Pangani, Kilwa, Wanga, and other
smaller islands, plus certain territories on the East African mainland—a 10-mile coastal strip, measured from the coast directly into
the interior from the high-water mark.

In short, then, the significance of the Anglo-German Treaty of
1886 lay both in the restriction of the Sultan's power to a 10-mile
coastal belt and in the delimitation of a German "sphere of influence"
from the Ruvuma River to the Umba River—the present border with
Kenya—and inland thence to Lake Jipe and thence again to Lake Victoria; lying ill at the time, Sultan Barghash (of Zanzibar) could do
nothing but concur.

The scramble for East Africa between Germany and Britain
was completed in 1890, with the signing in Berlin (on July 1) of the
so-called Heligoland Treaty. Heligoland is a useful naval base off
the coast of Germany. Whereas the 1886 treaty had favored Germany,
which had wanted British friendship, the 1890 Treaty certainly favored
Britain, which then wanted German cooperation against any possible
French or Russian war or threat of war. Inter alia, therefore, the
1890 treaty accomplished the following:

1. Germany agreed to withdraw in favor of Britain her protection over Witu and all her claims to the coast up to Kismayu, or inland
to all the other territories to the north of the Tana River, including
Patta and Manda Islands (Article 2).

2. Germany accepted the extension of the border dividing the
two spheres of influence westward to Lake Victoria and across it to
the frontier of the Congo Free (Independent) State.

3. Germany recognized a British protectorate over the dominions of the Sultan, including Zanzibar, Pemba, and Witu (Article 11).

4. Britain agreed to cede to Germany the portion of the mainland already leased to the German East Africa Company in return for
an "equitable indemnity" (Article 11). Britain also agreed to cede to
Germany the tiny island of Heligoland. Finally, both Britain and Germany agreed to recognize the Sultan's sovereignty over his coastal
and hinterland dominions.

The mapping of Anglo-German East Africa was completed when
the two alien powers subsequently signed three protocols and two

agreements, which fixed the final borders of the colonial territories
acquired by Britain and Germany in East Africa.

The first of the agreements was a protocol signed at Taveta on
October 27, 1892, by Peters and Charles Stewart Smith, the British
consul at Zanzibar, and the second was also a protocol, signed at
Zanzibar on December 24, 1892, again by Peters and Smith. The
third was an agreement in respect to boundaries in East Africa from
the mouth of the Umba River to Lake Jipe and Kilimanjaro; the agreement was signed at Berlin on July 25, 1893. The fourth was a protocol
containing the decisions of the commissioners appointed to delimit the
Nyasa-Tanganyika border; the protocol was signed at Ikawa on November 11, 1898. And the fifth was an agreement signed at Berlin on
July 18, 1906, by delegates from Britain and Germany. It was signed
in accordance with the Heligoland Treaty, and determined the frontier
between the respective German and British territories in East Africa
that were east and west of Lake Victoria.

The two powers undertook to implement Section 2 of Article 5
of the Berlin General Act of February 26, 1885. In that section, it
had been provided that persons and the property of foreigners had to
be assured of security. Those provisions had to be applicable to
British subjects in German protectorates, and no differential treatment of British subjects would take place, with regard to trade and
public order. British subjects were hence to have access to markets,
just as German subjects could.

CONCLUSIONS

In the early stages of colonial expansion, there was hardly any
clear-cut distinction between commercial and political objectives of
colonization. As the Permanent Court of International Justice put it,
"that period was an era of adventure and exploitation."[9] From the
end of the 16th century until the 19th century, companies comprising
individuals and engaged in economic business (chartered companies)
were invested by states to whom they were subject with public powers
for the acquisition and administration of colonies. The chartered
companies thus formed establishments and exercised sovereign jurisdiction in what were considered to be "uncivilized countries."

The colonial companies, as they were also called, governed
colonial territories under concessions or treaties obtained from local
rulers. In many instances, the existence of the tribal chiefs was completely ignored in law, and their territories (countries) were treated
simply as "no-man's territories." Thus treaties concluded between
the companies and tribal chiefs were not regarded as international
conventions but rather as contracts of private or public municipal law.

The form of legal relations established was that of suzerain-and-vassal, or of the so-called colonial protectorates. The royal charters granted the companies what were known as charter rights: assurances of royal imperial protection, trading privileges, and wide administrative powers.

The Imperial British East Africa Company had four main interests in East Africa: abolition of slavery and the slave trade; colonization of the Africans, training them in laws and morals, encouraging their interpersonal contacts, and acquainting them with improved living standards, culture, and all forms of development; addition of new lands to the British Empire; and acquisition of individual wealth under cover of "legitimate" commerce, that is, fighting the slave trade by developing other competitive forms of trade and opening up Africa to European commerce.[10]

The Anglo-Bugandan agreement of 1900 was the most important agreement that the British government ever concluded with the various Ugandan kingdoms during the colonial times. The salient provisions of the 1900 agreement were as follows:

1. The number of the traditional Bugandan counties (sazas) was increased to 20.

2. The Bugandan Kabaka renounced all claims to sovereignty over, and tribute from, the kingdoms of Bunyoro, Busoga, Toro, and Ankole.

3. The Bugandan protectorate was divided into four provinces so long as they did not conflict with the 1900 agreement.

4. The Kabaka of Buganda would be recognized as the native ruler of Buganda, provided that he, his chiefs, and the Ganda people —his subjects—would agree to observe the protectorate laws and cooperate loyally in the administration of Buganda.

5. The Kabaka would have a guaranteed annual salary, and his courts could pass death sentences on his subjects only after obtaining permission from the chief British officer.

6. The Lukiko (parliament of Buganda) would comprise 32 members. It would have three main functions: to appoint the Kabaka's successor from the descendants of Kabaka Mutesa I, to discuss all matters pertaining to the native administration of Buganda, and to serve as a court of appeal from the courts of the county chiefs.

A new system of land tenure was provided for. Previously, the chiefs had not, by tradition, owned lands but had instead exercised jurisdiction, at the Kabaka's pleasure, over those people who had chosen to live in their territory. Now, land grants were given for private holding of about half of the land by the chiefs and subchiefs. The other half, consisting of swamps, forests, and uncultivated land, became Crown land in the domain of the king of England.

A gun tax was imposed, and Bugandan revenue was made part of the Uganda protectorate's revenue.

Unfortunately, discriminatory tendencies started to crop up among the colonial administrators and European settlers (colonists). These two groups of people wanted the best lands of East Africa—the highlands—to be preserved for European settlement only. At first, the British government (Foreign Office) backed mixed settlement. Later, the Foreign Office gave in to the demands of the colonial administrators and the European settlers.

The German, Belgian, Portuguese, Spanish, and Dutch colonizers applied more perfidious and brutal methods of rule to the colonized peoples than the British and French colonizers. The latter built schools, cities, roads, hospitals, and the like. They genuinely wanted to "civilize" their colonial peoples and territories. The Portuguese, Belgians, and Germans aimed mainly at the exploitation of their colonial peoples and territories and at the ammassing of wealth for their mother countries and for themselves. It was not surprising, therefore, that African reactions to these colonial policies and practices were extremely negative, as we shall see in Chapter 5. In the next chapter, we shall discuss the racial problem in colonial East Africa.

NOTES

1. For a useful account on the colonization of East Africa, see Sir Harry Hamilton Johnston, A History of the Colonization of Africa by Alien Races, 2d ed. (London: Cambridge University Press, 1913). See also Lord William Malcolm Hailey, An African Survey (London: Oxford University Press, 1957).

2. For further information on this question, see A. B. Herrick, Area Handbook for Uganda (Washington, D.C.: U.S. Government Printing Office, 1960).

3. See Zanzibar Treaties, British Foreign Office, 1910, p. 82.

4. A. J. Hughes, East Africa, Kenya, Tanzania, Uganda (Harmondsworth, Eng.: Penguin Books, 1969), p. 160.

5. Judith Listowel, The Making of Tanganyika (London: Chatto and Windus, 1965), p. 20.

6. See for instance Marjorie R. Dilley, British Policy in Kenya Colony (New York: Thomas Nelson and Sons, 1937; reprinted, London: Frank Cass and Co., 1966).

7. Quoted in British Order-in-Council of March 1926.

8. See Sir Edward Hertslet, Map of Africa by Treaty, 3d ed., vol. 3 (London: Frank Cass and Co., 1967).

9. Permanent Court of International Justice, Document A/B53, p. 47.

10. See generally P. L. McDermott, <u>British East Africa: A</u>
<u>History of the Formation and Work of the Imperial British East Africa</u>
<u>Company</u> (London: Chapman and Hall, 1893).

4

THE RACIAL PROBLEM IN PREINDEPENDENCE EAST AFRICA

The imposition of colonial rule in East Africa resulted in, inter alia, a very serious conflict between Europeans and Asians. The main cause of the struggle, established between 1890 and 1914, was racial discrimination by the Europeans against the Asians.[1] Whereas the main demand of the Asians was equal treatment of all the Asian peoples with the Europeans, the main demand of the Europeans was to classify Asians as "dangerous aliens." This was particularly the case in German East Africa, where it was believed that all Asians in East Africa were British subjects. In German law, however, Asians were classified as "natives" in East Africa. The Asians strongly resented that classification, but to the British, the prevention of East Africa from becoming an Indian colony was a matter of life and death. The racial struggle assumed legal, political, economic, and other aspects. As British subjects, the Asians had the legal right both to enjoy all the benefits and privileges enjoyed by British citizens and to demand equal treatment with the other subjects of the United Kingdom.

The British project for "closer union" in East Africa embraced racial differentiation in an East African context and provided for "partnership." The expression "partnership" was used to describe the relations between the Europeans and the other communities, which the British government wanted, as a matter of colonial policy, to establish in East Africa. The notion of "partnership" replaced that of "trusteeship," which had hitherto indicated the nature of British responsibilities toward her dependencies.

Ironically, the essence of the British colonial policy of racial differentiation through "partnership" was twofold: Each racial community in East Africa was to have a voice in the political process, and "partnership" seemed to depend partly on the measure of African, as well as Asian, representation in legislatures, and partly on Britain's

being willing to surrender a substantial measure of political influence
to the European unofficial residents.

THE EURO-ASIAN STRUGGLE IN COLONIAL
ZANZIBAR, TANGANYIKA, AND UGANDA

Zanzibar and German East Africa offered less economic opportunity to Asians than did the East African Protectorate (EAP). Zanzibar could not compete with the East African mainland areas, mainly
because of Zanzibar's limited resources and small area. German
East Africa was not attractive to British Asians, since it was German
and not British. Also, the German administration was not favorable
to Asian business. For example, the harsh German colonial administration, the long military campaigns by the Germans, the German
restrictions on Asian immigration to the German colony, the concentration of a plantation economy, and the neglect by the German administrators in constructing railway and other communicational facilities
and works all had a negative effect on the Asian population in what is
now Tanzania.

As from 1890, the Asians found themselves in changed circumstances in which their hitherto economic prosperity and influential
position in East Africa were to depend entirely upon the goodwill of
Germany and Britain. In Zanzibar, political and economic changes
favorable to Asians occurred after the British creation of a protectorate over Zanzibar in 1890; the Asians multiplied and prospered on
the island. Asian dissatisfaction with the European administration
in Zanzibar can be traced to shortly before World War I, when Asians
began to feel that their position had been harmed by the development
of British control: They realized that they could not now hold their
traditional high administrative and commercial posts. Indian commercial laws introduced in Zanzibar were repealed in favor of other
laws designed specifically for the island's new situation. Trial by
jury for Asians was abolished, no religious processions without permits were allowed, and the Asians had no right of appeal to India.
In 1909, the Asians staged the first organized protest against the British administration in Zanzibar. Soon they formed a political organization called the Committee of India, whose first president was Yu-
safali Alibhai Karinje.

In subsequent years, the Asian role in the economic sphere of
the island grew in significance. The prosperity of the Asians, especially in the 1920s, was felt mainly in the copra and clove industries,
which provided 98 percent of the island's exports; the Asians had a
major share in the marketing of those crops. Their prominent position in the economic life of Zanzibar was envied by the Arabs. The

Asians, in turn, envied the privileged position of the Arabs in the political and administrative activities of Zanzibar. Subsequently, the Asians launched protests, via their Indian National Council Association, against what they regarded as the inadequate recruitment of Asians for administrative services, the immigration restriction imposed upon the Asians, and the land legislation that controlled the alienation of land rights by Africans and Arabs. These three main Asian grievances were, in reality, prompted by the growing Arab consciousness and endeavors to stress the position of Zanzibar as an Arab state. Despite the Arab-Asian differences, however, no serious racial conflicts existed between the two ethnic groups in Zanzibar.

As for the position of Asians in Tanganyika, the report of the British government to the League of Nations on the administration of Tanganyika was probably the most impartial and authoritative opinion on the contribution of Indians to the economic development of the mandated territory of Tanganyika.[2] In that report, the valuable services of the Asians to the Tanganyikan society as a whole were outlined. The services gave every encouragement to the natives to utilize the "products of civilization" brought to their doors by the Asians and to engage in trade. Thus the international community recognized the useful and essential functions the Asians performed in the economic life of the territory. The report also pointed out that it would be difficult to replace Asian traders, and that native and nonnative trade were "complementary, not antagonistic."

The resentment of Asians over their legal status in German East Africa seems to have been the main reason for the formation early in 1914 of what became known as the Tanga Indian Association. The association was the first nonsectarian Indian organization on record in German East Africa.

However, before the imposition of the abovementioned immigration restrictions on the Asians, the declared German policy had been to admit Asians freely into that colony. It was only in the later period of German rule that the Asians were deprived of a privileged status— similar to the one enjoyed by the Europeans—and subjected to high and oppressive taxes, particularly on houses and businesses, besides import/export duties. Further, the Asians were menaced with discrimination in practice and legislation patterned on that of Natal in South Africa.

The position of Asians in the Tanganyikan trust territory presented the fewest problems in the region. The reasons for this included the value of Asians as traders and the terms of the trusteeship agreement.

Zanzibar had the smallest number of Europeans. Their position in Zanzibar and in Tanganyika was far less significant than that of the Europeans in the neighboring EAP. However, Europeans in Zanzibar

and Tanganyika suffered, like those in the EAP, from a superiority
complex. As in Zanzibar, racial conflicts between the Asian and European communities in Tanganyika became more serious during and after World War I.

The reasons for greater alien predominance in Kenya than in
Tanganyika included the mandated status of Tanganyika; the wealth in
natural resources in Kenya; the climatic conditions in Kenya, favorable to Europeans; the remarkably high number of tribal divisions very
bitterly opposed to one another in Kenya; and the daring, warlike, and
organized African resistances in Tanganyika in the very early days of
colonial rule in East Africa.

After World War II, the tendency was to transfer power from
the colonizer to the colonized African. Tanganyika was made a trust
territory under a UN trusteeship, by the Tanganyika Trusteeship
Agreement. Britain—the administering authority—had the duty to promote the development of free and suitable political institutions in Tanganyika. Under the new arrangement, Tanganyika's inhabitants—the
majority of whom were Africans—were to be assured of a rapidly increasing share in the administration and other services of their country.

As in German East Africa and in Zanzibar, the Euro-Asian rivalry in Uganda was not as acute as it was in Kenya. Uganda was remote from the thriving coastal settlements and was inhabited by Africans whose comparatively well-developed social, economic, and political systems served as impediments to alien settlements. Uganda
also offered a natural impediment not only to Asian but to white settlement. Basically, Uganda's climate was unsuitable for alien settlement. As James Hayes Sadler put it, "the climate is not conducive to
European colonization."[3] Moreover, it was provided that no nonnative could buy land from Africans without the governor's consent.[4]
As a result of this policy, the European population in Uganda did not
grow rapidly. Furthermore, a motion was made in the Ugandan legislative council to restrict the "free" entry of Asians into Uganda. And
all the African and European members of the council supported the
motion.[5]

A few Asians cultivated land; they mainly owned cotton and sugar
plantations. Their economic power improved at the expense of the Africans. The latter consequently adopted negative and envious attitudes
toward the Asians, whom the Africans accused of monopolizing Uganda's
commerce and trade.

The position of the Asians in Uganda was, however, tempered
by the new policies both in Tanganyika and Kenya. The policy of native paramountcy, for instance, first applied to Kenya only, was extended to Uganda, Tanganyika, and Zanzibar. The position of the
Asians in Uganda was ultimately bettered by both the decrease in em-

phasis on European development and the combination of the 1923 Devonshire Declaration and League Covenant Provisions.

As in Tanganyika, the Asians in Uganda in the interwar period
directed their protests at the government, rather than at the Europeans.
In Uganda, as in Tanganyika and Zanzibar, the European community
prospered at the expense of the Africans. The minority communities
could live side by side in harmony and peace, and neither segregation
nor reservation was necessary in Uganda and Tanganyika to prevent
racial friction. Consequently, there was no significant racial discrimination in landholding or in residential conditions.

THE EURO-ASIAN STRUGGLE FOR
DOMINANCE IN COLONIAL KENYA

In the preamble to the royal charter signed on September 3,
1888 and granted by Queen Victoria of England to the Imperial British
East Africa Company, a provision was inscribed that read: "The possession of the coastline . . . would be advantageous to the commercial
and other interests of our subjects in the Indian Ocean who may otherwise become compelled to reside and trade under the government or
protection of alien powers." In Article 17 of the same charter, it
was stipulated that "there shall be no differential treatment of the subjects of any power as to trade or settlement, or to access to markets."[6]
The charter thus favored Asian settlement in East Africa.

After 1913, the Asians of the EAP were, unfortunately, socially
subject to a color bar that denied them access to first-class restaurants, hotels, clubs, and resorts; and required them to use separate
and inferior hospital, prison, education, and transportation facilities.
The color bar extended to the civil services, and to the military and
police institutions in that Asians were never appointed to higher posts.
Professional degrees from Indian universities, particularly in medicine
and law, were not recognized. In 1910, there was a concerted European endeavor to exclude the Indians even from the Nairobi market-
place.

The Asians were far superior in numbers, and it was hence understood that, if they ever received full civic equality, the EAP would
be, in all but name, an Indian colony. However, martial law and arrests of some of the key Indian leaders curtailed Asian efforts for
revolution. Asians could not own land in the highlands, and no highlands property could be leased to them. In 1915, a policy of commercial and residential (municipal) segregation was adopted in the protectorate. On February 24, 1919, Edward Northey, the new governor
of the EAP, openly rejected the demands of Asian leaders for equal
representation in the central and municipal government: "British
European preponderance in the Government is essential."[7] Asians,

according to Northey, had an incurable repugnance to sanitation and
hygiene, an antagonistic philosophy, and a moral depravity damaging
to Africans.

Discrimination against the Asians in the EAP began to intensify
after 1919, with Europeans calling for residential and commercial
segregation; expulsion of Asians from the highlands; a maximum of
two nominated Asians on the legislative council; restrictions on Indian
immigration; and full recognition of the existing Asian rights in property and security of tenure. [8] These demands were categorically rejected by the Indians in the EAP and in India, where Mohandas Gandhi
was a staunch supporter of the Indian cause in East Africa.

In the later years of colonized Kenya, the causes of racial tensions still included the European objection to the Asian demand of a
franchise based upon a common political roll; the general disagreement between the Asians and Europeans on economic matters; the
notorious European doctrine of reservation of the "White Highlands"
for European occupation; the African grudges against the Asian economic superiority in the territory; and the Asian demands for a bona
fide implementation of the policy of interracial partnership, a move
totally unacceptable to the Europeans, according to whose policy the
colored man had no place in the region.

But in a correspondence in 1905 from then EAP High Commissioner Frederick Jackson to Alfred Lyttelton, then colonial secretary
of state, Jackson noted,

> The conditions are such that the black man is essen-
> tially everywhere, and over the great portion of the
> land must always predominante. To endeavour by
> legislation or otherwise to make any portion of this
> country exclusively a white man's country is . . .
> doomed to failure. There is a great future before
> East Africa, but it is as a mixed race country. . . .
> It is the duty of His Majesty's Government to legislate
> for these special conditions and not to unduly favour
> one race before another. [9]

The endeavor to create a white man's country in the Kenya highlands involved the exclusion of "coloreds" from gaining a title to land
in the area. The Africans already in the area—such as the Masai,
Nandi, and Kikuyu—were therefore to be removed and "resettled" in
African reserves. The determination of the European settlers to exclude all the colored peoples from the areas reserved for the whites
was advocated for the EAP as early as 1904 by H. H. Johnston, as
part of a larger plan to divide the entire African continent among
Europeans, Asians, and Africans. [10] Johnston's plan was to award to

Europeans the plateau territory of South, Central, and East Africa, which was not already occupied by Africans, and award to Africans and Asians the tropical lowlands. According to the plan, the Asians were to be allotted the unhealthiest lowlands. Johnston's further plan was to secure self-government for the Europeans in their own area; the African reserves were to be treated as the "black man's legitimate domain," with self-government for the Africans in their own areas as a "safety valve for racial aspirations."

In this way, Johnston had anticipated in the EAP separate but parallel development along South African lines—which was the most favorable and essential doctrine of the 1920s and 1930s to be applied in the colonies. Unfortunately, the Foreign and Colonial Offices in London strongly supported the idea and practice of racial segregation in East Africa.

Britain, the sole colonial power in Kenya, maintained support for racial differentiation, while in East Africa itself, the balance in race relations remained unaltered. In other words, racial conflicts continued to be great in Kenya, but only minimal in Zanzibar, Tanganyika, and Uganda. The fact is that nowhere else in East Africa did the position of Asians cause so much serious conflict as in Kenya.

ORIGINS AND DEVELOPMENT OF THE LEGISLATIVE AND EXECUTIVE BRANCHES OF GOVERNMENT IN COLONIAL EAST AFRICA

The British politico-colonial policy on representation was to split it into "equal" and "balanced" representation. According to the "equal" type, the same numerical representation was granted to each racial community. According to the "balanced" type, however, the community having predominant claims was granted a measure of representation equal to that granted to all the other communities taken together. The "balanced representation" doctrine was included in the project for "closer union" and applied in Uganda, where African unofficial representation equaled that granted to the Europeans and Asians. The same doctrine was also applied in Kenya, though in a different direction, and in Tanganyika.

In Zanzibar, the Sultan in 1926 created a legislative council and an executive council.[11] The latter's president was the Sultan, and its vice-president was the British "resident" (the representative of the United Kingdom in Zanzibar). The executive council also included the heir to the throne, four ex officio members, and three nominated officials. All these representatives were members of the British administrative or departmental services.

As for the legislative council in Zanzibar, the British resident was its president. Its other members were the four ex officio members of the executive council, five nominated officials, and eight "un-officials." The latter were nominated by the Sultan, with the advice of the British resident, and included three Arabs, two Africans, and one European.

The representatives of the Arab Association called for the insti-tution of self-government under the Sultan's sovereignty, but based upon a legislature elected on a common roll. Unfortunately, the Arab and African communities were not unanimous on this issue, while the Asian community mainly aimed at the retention of its prominent eco-nomic position. So the struggle to obtain balanced or equal represen-tation continued to be the main problem in Zanzibar; and it became worse as the influx of European officials into Zanzibar grew and the position of the Sultan became weaker.

It is notable that the Africans in Zanzibar were of two types: the Shirazis and the pure Africans. The Shirazi Africans were the descendants of Persians and coastal Africans, and were actually Swahilis. The Arabs were well organized politically, and their na-tionalism, based upon racialism, was very strong and radical. How-ever, the Shirazi and African Associations combined to form the Afro-Shirazi party, which competed against the Arab-dominated Zanzibar National Party. By comparison with the Africans and the Arabs, the Asians in Zanzibar were few in number. British colonial policy in regard to the three racial groups stressed both the maintenance of the principle of Zanzibari citizenship and the promotion of development on nonracial lines.

In Tanganyika, the first legislative council was set up in 1926. The council comprised 13 official and ten unofficial members, of whom two were appointed to the Asian community and one (European) to represent African interests.

In 1945, an amendment to the Constitution of the Tanganyikan trust territory brought about an increase in the number of legislative council members to 15 officials and 14 nominated "unofficials." Of the latter, seven were Europeans (including the one who represented the African interests), three were Asians, and four were Africans.

In 1951, the government accepted the argument that equal dis-tribution of the unofficial seats between the three groups in Tanganyika would be the only fair representation of racial interests in the terri-tory's Legislature. In the ensuing years, therefore, the idea of equal distribution of the unofficial seats was implemented.

With regard to Uganda, an order-in-council was enacted on May 17, 1920, which brought the executive and legislative councils into existence.[12] The executive council members were strictly official, while the legislative council had six members of whom four were of-ficials (that is, the four executive council members) and two were nominated unofficial members; all six were Europeans. The Asians

of Uganda boycotted the legislative council until 1926, on the grounds
that their demand for parity of representation was not being fulfilled. In 1926, the number of unofficial members on the council
was raised to four—the two Europeans and two newly nominated members.

The Africans had little or no interest in participating in the central councils (legislative or executive), particularly in Buganda, where
the Kabaka and his people concerned themselves more with the maintenance of their own traditional institutions and the preservation of
the Anglo-Bugandan agreement of 1900 than with central representation. It was not until 1945 that the Africans in Uganda were officially
represented for the first time in the Ugandan legislative council by
their own African members. Seats for unofficial representation in
the council had been distributed, as of 1934, equally among Africans,
Asians, and Europeans (three seats apiece).

In 1952, the legislative council was expanded to include 16 official and 16 unofficial members, of whom eight, four, and four were
Africans, Asians, and Europeans, respectively. From 1952 onward
also, Asians and Europeans on the council were to be appointed by the
governor. Africans were to be nominated by the governor from a
list of names submitted to him by the northern, eastern, and western
provincial councils and their equivalent in Buganda—the Lukiko. From
the list the governor would select two Africans each from the northern
and eastern provinces, and one each from the western province and
Buganda. One of the remaining two was to be nominated by the Kabaka
and the other by the rulers of the other three kingdoms.

In 1955, a ministerial system was introduced into Uganda's
executive council. The executive council would now consist of 13
ministers, eight official members of the legislative council, and five
unofficial members of the legislative council, of whom three would be
Africans. Also in 1955, the Kabakaship became a monarchy, and
henceforth the Kabakas would be constitutional monarch in Uganda.

In Kenya, attempts by the European community to secure a constitution of responsible government were made as early as 1913. The
Asians and Africans made desperate attempts, in the European-domi-
nated Kenyan society, to secure an adjustment of claims to a share
in the political organs of the colony. The fact of European domination
remained unaltered, and the electoral franchise was confined to British subjects of European extraction. The idea of a franchise based on
a common roll was totally rejected by the Europeans.

Kenya, at the same time, was the first East African territory
to include an African unofficial member in its legislative council.
That was in 1944, and in 1946, a second African representative was
appointed in Kenya on a temporary basis. In 1947, this seat became
permanent. In 1948, African representation was raised to four, these

being nominated by the governor from a list of names presented to him by African local government organs. Like the legislative council in Kenya, the executive council was established by a Kenyan order-in-council (October 22, 1906). The executive council was, originally, entirely official. The unofficial element was introduced into it in 1919.

Significant constitutional developments began to occur in Kenya in the early years of the 1950s. In 1952, for example, the unofficial side of the legislative council rose to 28 members: 14 European and six elected members; one Arab elected member, and six African representative members. The official side comprised 26 members: eight ex officio members and 18 nominated members. In March 1954, Lyttelton (the colonial secretary of state) announced, while on a visit to Kenya, important changes designed to create a multiracial system of government in Kenya. These changes have been commonly known as the Lyttleton Settlement.[13] The settlement was a racial arrangement by which the Europeans—the smallest of the major communities—were accorded a representation, both in the legislative council and, after 1954, in the council of ministers, which equaled that accorded to the Africans, Arabs, and Asians taken together.

The Asians in Kenya envied the position of the Europeans because of (1) what the Asians considered an unfair Asian representation in the legislative council; (2) the European proposal to segregate Asians in the urban areas; and (3) the continuing reservation to Europeans of the best and richest lands in the "white highlands."[14]

This discriminatory British attitude in fact represented a policy for the Kenyan highlands established by Charles Eliot. After Eliot's forced resignation from the post of high commissioner for the EAP in 1904, the initial tendency was to avoid segregation against the Asians. But, after 1905, the British policy of favoring Indian settlement in the highlands was reversed; the new governor of the EAP, Sadler, now adhered to the doctrine of granting land between Kiu and Fort Ternan to Europeans only.

In 1915, however, a Crown lands ordinance was enacted that did not prevent Asians from acquiring land anywhere in Kenya. It was, nevertheless, always the practice of the colonial administrations, when disposing of lands in the highlands, to stipulate that the purchaser be of European extraction and that transfers between persons of different races required government sanction. In 1912, legislation was passed to prohibit all non-Europeans from occupying certain urban areas.

British attitudes toward non-Europeans worsened over the years. In the period from 1923 to 1946, for example, it became a rule that entry into Kenya was permissible only to British subjects who were not considered as "undesirables," and who could support themselves in the colony. In 1949, Tanganyika, Uganda, and Kenya had identical immigration ordinances regulating the entry of new immigrants.[15]

BRITISH GOVERNMENT REACTIONS TO THE EURO-ASIAN CONFLICTS IN COLONIAL EAST AFRICA

The British government and politicians in London, as well as the colonial administrations and individual personalities in East Africa, helped solve and at the same time intensify the racial problem in the region. Because the problem was most evident in the EAP, the events that occurred there are examined below.

Eliot's Crown Lands Ordinance of 1902, for instance, alienated lands from Africans, excluded Asians from buying land in the highlands, and gave white settlers free grants of land. All that Eliot's policy could do was turn Kenya into another South Africa. Fortunately, the then British secretary for foreign affairs, Henry Lansdowne, together with the Foreign Office, the Colonial Office, and Eliot's deputy, Jackson, opposed Eliot and thus saved Kenya from becoming another South Africa. In July 1904, Lansdowne told Eliot's successor, Donald Stewart: "The primary duty of Great Britain in East Africa is the welfare of the native races."[16] At the same time, Lansdowne sought the opinion of Lyttelton on the reservation of the highlands for white settlement. Lyttelton's response was that any legislation reserving the highlands for European settlement would not be "in accordance with the general policy of His Majesty's Government" and that East Africa was "the natural outlet for Indian emigration."[17]

In February 1921, Winston Churchill became secretary of state for the colonies. Optimism now grew that the East African (Kenyan) problem of Asians would be solved more reasonably and justly. Outstanding British politicians became sympathetic toward the Asians in Kenya and demanded equal treatment of all His Majesty's subjects. In August 1921, Churchill had the following remarks to make to the Imperial Conference: "The British Empire could have only one ideal on this matter . . . no barrier of race, colour, or creed preventing any man by merit from reaching any station if he were fitted therefor. I am unable to adopt any lesser statement of principle in regard to the Crown Colonies."[18] Thus during his first year as secretary of state for the colonies, Churchill pursued a policy on Indians that was on the whole pro-Indian. He also rejected the discriminatory Kenya Public Health Ordinance enacted by the Kenya colonial legislative council in January 1921. Thanks to Churchill's initiative, furthermore, an agreement was reached between the British India and Colonial Offices regarding the Asian question. According to the agreement, equal citizenship for Indians was guaranteed, no segregation was to be practiced outside the Kenyan highlands, the highlands were to be reserved for Europeans, and an endeavor to meet the European claims was to be made.

These "concessions" were soon followed by another agreement between Churchill and E. S. Montagu, the secretary of state for India. According to the new agreement, there would be (1) an enfranchisement of about 10 percent of the Asian population; (2) a common electoral role for the Asians and Europeans; (3) three or four guaranteed Asian seats in the Kenyan legislative council; (4) no restrictions on Indian immigration to the EAP; (5) no segregation in the townships; (6) a definite area for Asian settlement between Mairobi and the coast; (7) an exclusive use of the highlands by the Europeans; and (8) a policy of "equal rights for civilized men." All these proposals were to be incorporated in a new constitution to appear at the end of 1922 or the beginning of 1923.

Again, the Montagu-Churchill proposals, like the agreement before them, retained the policy of European supremacy and privileged position in Kenya, especially in the highlands. Thus the very fact that Churchill retained the old doctrine of reserving the highlands for Europeans only, and granting full civic and political rights only to those Asians and Africans who were believed to have reached and conformed "to well-marked European standards" was clearly indicative of the British government's policy of remaining pro-European in East Africa. European opposition to Churchill's impending settlement was great and forced him to abandon his proposals made with Montagu. Thus Churchill's very controversial London statement of January 27, 1922 was a strong departure from his earlier proposals: "We do not contemplate any settlement or system which will prevent British East Africa or Kenya becoming a characteristically and distinctively British Colony, looking forward in full fruition of time to complete responsible self-government."[19] Churchill's change of attitude, caused by increased European pressure, was a complete departure even from what "racists" had adhered to in the past.

Churchill's statement was interpreted to mean a complete eradication of the idea of an Indian colony in East Africa and a complete subordination of African and Asian interests to those of the Europeans. The Kenyan Indians, and their supporters, were irritated by the statement and planned to retaliate. In turn, Montagu and other pro-Indian British political personalities were amazed and terribly disappointed. Montagu in fact resigned over the issue. Churchill was hence forced to initiate, again under pressure, a move to reinstall the Montagu-Churchill proposals. He also recommended an Asian municipal franchise and assured Asians of four members in the legislative council but imposed restrictions on Asian immigration and upheld the old highland doctrine.

Unfortunately, no solution was reached on the Kenyan Asian problem. But nevertheless the years from 1914 to 1922 were most important in Indian/East African relations. For it was within this

period that (1) the EAP was transformed into Kenya Colony; (2) the un-
changed highlands policy was fixed in legislation; (3) municipal segregation was implemented; (4) the spotlight on Asians overseas shifted
from South Africa to German East Africa (after World War I), and to
Kenya (after 1920); (5) both Europeans and Asians received elective
representation; and (6) for the first time India, on the belief that one
or part of one of the East African territories would become an Indian
colony, became a significant determinant of imperial policy in British
equatorial Africa.

After all, in 1858, Queen Victoria had declared, "There shall
not be, in the eyes of the law, any distinction or disqualification whatever, founded upon mere distinction of colour, origin, language or
creed. But protection of the law, in letter and in substance, shall be
extended impartially to all alike."[20]

In October 1922, Churchill lost his seat in parliament and thus
also his post of colonial secretary. He was succeeded by Victor Cav-
endish, the ninth Duke of Devonshire. He at first attempted to carry
on Churchill's policy by pressing for agreement to the Wood-Winter-
ton proposals that reaffirmed the Montagu-Churchill proposals. Lord
Wood and Lord Winterton at the time were principal assistants in the
British Colonial and India Offices, respectively; Winterton was under-
secretary of state for India. Between mid-April and mid-July of 1923,
negotiations on the Kenyan racial problem were held in London; these
were the so-called Devonshire talks and included representatives of
Indian and European interest groups and their supporters.

The Devonshire White Paper of 1923

The outcome of the Devonshire talks was Devonshire's decisions
that came to be known as the Devonshire White Paper of 1923.[21] The
core of the Devonshire White Paper was the policy of native paramountcy:

> Primarily, Kenya is an African territory, and His
> Majesty's Government think it necessary definitely
> to record their considered opinion that the interests
> of the African natives must be paramount and that if,
> and when the interests of the immigrant races should
> conflict, the former should prevail. . . . In the ad-
> ministration of Kenya His Majesty's Government re-
> gard themselves as exercising a trust on behalf of
> the African population, and they are unable to dele-
> gate or share this trust, the object of which may be
> defined as the protection and advancement of the
> native races.

The Devonshire decisions on Kenya consisted of 13 points:

1. A doctrine of native paramountcy;
2. Safeguarding of the interests of the other (nonnative) communities;
3. An offer to Asians of a lowland reserve
4. A guarantee to Europeans of an exclusive utilization of the highlands over an area of 16,696 square miles plus 3,950 square miles of forest reserve;
5. Abolition of segregation in the townships;
6. Establishment of a communal system of election rather than a common roll;
7. Asian and European community elective representation in both the central and municipal governments;
8. Eleven seats reserved for European unofficial representation in the legislative council;
9. A slight increase in Indian unofficial representation in the council to probably five seats;
10. One elective and one nominated council member granted to the Arab community;
11. One nominated missionary representing Africans;
12. Retention on the executive council of one Asian and one European appointed representative along with one African community representative;
13. No responsible government or unofficial majority to take place in the "foreseeable" future.

Hence Kenya was to be held in trust for Africans. For the same reason, some further immigration control was required, but no restriction would be imposed on immigration from one part of the British Empire to another. Hence the governors of Kenya and Uganda were to propose the amount of restriction required.

Devonshire actually achieved exactly what he wanted to evade—intensification of the racial problem in Kenya, especially between November 1924 and June 1929. In this period, the Conservative Party was in power in Britain. The new colonial secretary, Leopold Stennett Amery and the new governor of Kenya, Edward Grigg, were strong imperialists interested in establishing a firm foundation of European settlemen in Kenya, which was to be developed toward a responsible government and dominion status. The two men also hoped to unite all the East African territories in a federation dominated by Kenya. Thus the core of the Amery-Grigg doctrine was to bypass the Duke of Devonshire's arrangement of native paramountcy and perpetuate a policy of European paramountcy. This was reflected in a statement issued in London by a British member of Parliament, A. K. Keith, in 1927:

> It appears—the policy is to be inaugurated of subor-
> dinating the interests of the native population and
> the Indian immigrants alike to the welfare of the
> European settlers, regardless of the obligations
> of trusteeship affirmed so recently as 1923. The
> decision marks a distinct deterioration of British
> conceptions of fair play to native populations, and
> is an interesting illustration of the operation of
> Dominion modes of thought on Imperial statements.

When subjected to strong criticism in the House of Commons that he had intended to reverse the Devonshire doctrine, Amery denied this. He asserted that his Command Paper of July 1927 fully supported the Devonshire policy: "His Majesty's Government wish to make it clear, they adhere to the underlying principles of the White Paper of 1923—both in regard to the political status and other rights of British Indians resident in East Africa, and also as regards the Imperial duty of safeguarding the interests and progress of the native populations."[22]

Amery's aim was to ignore the doctrine of African native paramountcy. He wanted to apply the Tanganyikan trusteeship also to Kenya and Uganda. The responsibilities of trusteeship, according to him, had to be shared between Britain and the European community in Kenya, which was "the most advanced of all such communities in Britain's overseas possessions." Thus Amery and the Ormsby-Gore Commission were strongly in favor of European domination in East Africa. The Ormsby-Gore Commission comprised Frederick C. Linfield, then a Liberal member of Parliament, Archibald G. Church, a Labour member, and W. G. A. Ormsby-Gore, a Conservative member. This mixed commission promoted Amery's ideas. The Amery White Paper of 1927 was, like the Devonshire Paper, rejected by the Kenyan Asians and their sympathizers, because it neglected Asian interests. It even substituted Grigg's dual policy.

By Grigg's dual policy, native paramountcy was to be substituted by a new concept that would promote closer union. Grigg was also high commissioner of Transport for Kenya, Uganda, and Tanganyika. Thus by the dual policy, Grigg simply meant a combination of nonnative and native production and communities for these three territories, plus Nyasaland and Northern Rhodesia.

The purposes of Grigg's dual policy were to promote the well-being and development of the African peoples, bring about a political evolution of the territories, and prevent improper exploitation of Africans. Grigg's policy seems to have stressed equal rights for all, a policy initiated by Cecil Rhodes and later pursued by Churchill. However, the Grigg policy was in essence designed to bring about a European superiority and paramountcy in East Africa.

Passfield's White Papers of 1930

In 1929, the Conservative Party in Britain lost the election to the Labour Party; the Labour government then enacted two White Papers in connection with race relations in East Africa at that time. In the first of these papers, a Command Paper entitled "Statement of the Conclusions of His Majesty's Government in the U.S. as Regards Closer Union in East Africa" (London, 1930), Lord Passfield, the then colonial secretary, paid greater attention to the question of "closer union" than to any other issues. However, he proposed that African interests in the East African legislatures be represented by two African members. Passfield also provided for a common role for all races in future, equally on the basis of attainment in education and advancement in "civilization."

Passfield's second Command Paper (London, 1930) was entitled "Memorandum on Native Policy in East Africa." In this paper, Passfield reaffirmed the Devonshire settlement of 1923 and Grigg's dual policy. According to Passfield, "dual policy" and native paramountcy were complementary, not antagonistic. However, priority had to be given to native paramountcy as the central theme of British policy in Kenya.

ASIAN AND EUROPEAN REACTIONS TO BRITISH GOVERNMENT POLICIES IN COLONIZED EAST AFRICA

Reactions among the Asian and European communities in East Africa to the above British government stands can be summarized as follows.

Asian Response

The Duke of Devonshire's White Paper greatly disappointed the Indians, who rejected it. The declaration was, however, a turning point in Kenya's history, because by it, Devonshire rejected—through his doctrine of African paramountcy—Churchill's abovementioned argument (of 1922) that Kenya should be regarded as "a characteristically and distinctly British colony." The results of the new Devonshire approach were a departure from the belief by the Europeans in the "threat" of Asians and instead a consideration of the newly stressed African interests as the main impediments to European ambitions. The native problem thus replaced the Asian problem as the greatest concern of the British government in Kenya. In no way would Kenya become an Indian colony, as had very strongly been rumored. Henceforth, the Asians of Kenya were more united than ever before in a struggle for a social, economic, and political position equivalent to that of the Europeans.

Supporters of the Indian cause were also very disappointed by the Devonshire arrangement. H. Y. S. Polak, for example, said of it, "I fear the old evils will remain. . . . The stage is being set for a world-wide racial struggle between white and coloured peoples."[23]

Despite all these protests, the Duke of Devonshire was determined as ever to implement his paper. He therefore sent instructions to Governor Coryndon of Kenya asking him to act promptly, especially as regarded the regulation of immigration. Coryndon summoned the Kenyan legislative council into action and, as a result, the Immigration Regulation and Employment Ordinance of 1923 was enacted. This ordinance required every entering person other than a professional person or business partner to present a certificate from a prospective employer, who previously had convinced the immigration officer that it was impossible to find a suitable person locally. If the person had a certificate and could not convince the officer that the person's services were necessary for the economic development of the colony, and that he was assured of employment, he could, at the discretion of the officer, be either denied entry or allowed to enter on giving security toward the cost of his repatriation. An appeal could be made to the governor-in-council, but the 1923 bill in effect provided for the exclusion of immigrants "in the economic interests" of the natives.

The Kenyan Asians and their supporters voiced their complete rejection of the 1923 bill. The usual mass protests were held in Nairobi and other big towns.

The Indians disclosed their grievances at the 5th Annual Session of the East Africa Indian National Congress held on January 19, 1924. Discrimination was their main regret: Indians were still denied trial by jury; they had no government hospitals of their own; they were still excluded from the highlands; they could not possess firearms; government expenditure each year was about £24 for a European child and only £1 for an Indian child; segregation was still prevalent; representation in the central legislature was disproportionate; there was no common roll; and, finally, Indians could ride on the railway only with Africans in cars marked "For Non-Europeans Only."

Sarojini Naidu, one of the delegates to the 1924 congress invited from India, was made president of the session. She told the congress:

> East Africa is, therefore, the legitimate Colony of
> the surplus of that great Indian nation. . . . I stand,
> therefore, today before you as an Indian speaker on
> Indian soil—soil that your forefathers have built in a

land which your ancestors gave to the citizens of
your country—citizens by the right of heredity, citizens by the right of tradition, citizens by the right
of patriotic love which has been nurtured, fostered,
and developed by the sweat of the brow and the blood
of the heart, of the pioneers exiled from India, so
that Indian interests may grow greater.[24]

Asian reactions to the Passfield White Papers of 1930 were generally good, for in the papers the Asians found, for the first time, a
British policy highly favorable to them. However, the absence of
points opening the highlands to Indian settlement and raising Indian
representation in the territorial legislatures to that of Europeans,
were exceptions that the Asians regretted. Passfield, unfortunately,
gave in to criticism, like his pronative predecessors, and announced,
in November 1930, that the Command Papers would be submitted to a
Joint Labour-Liberal-Conservative committee for approval. That
meant that the doctrine of native paramountcy, trusteeship, and the
dual policy would be subject once more to review and alteration. In
principle, then, the Asians were bitterly opposed to the racial segregation doctrine and demanded equal treatment of all British subjects.
Their complaints were directed at the restrictions of the colonial administration on the acquisition of urban and suburban land, and at the
reservation of the most desirable commercial and residential areas
for Europeans. Remembering the treatment of their fellow kinsmen
in South Africa, the Asians of East Africa looked to India for support
and inspiration. Unfortunately, their demands were largely ignored
by the European colonizers. In East Africa, as indeed in South Africa, the British government only paid lip service to the ideal of equal
rights for all British subjects irrespective of color or creed, while
continuing to accept the practice of discrimination. In fact, the concern of the Asians over their position in the EAP had begun to be shown
as far back as 1900, when they formed an Indian Association at Mombasa. L. M. Savle and his supporters were always conscious of their
great economic contribution to East Africa's development. Three of
Savle's supporters were the wealthiest and most influential Indians in
East Africa: Allidina Visram, A. M. Jeevanjee, and his brother,
Tayabali Jeevanjee. The lack of European appreciation of the Asians'
contributions to the development of the region greatly irritated the
Asians, whose leaders organized anti-European activities and encouraged the formation of further Asian associations to resist European
domination in the region. A. M. Jeevanjee emerged as the toughest
and most prominent Asian in the protectorate. He built the Nairobi
Public Market; owned most of the land in what became the Indian ba-
zaar; had the distinction and honor in 1909 of being named the first

Indian nominated to the Kenyan legislative council; presented Asian
grievances to the local, British, and Indian governments; and publicized
the grievances in the newspapers of Britain and India. Unfortunately,
the Europeans were dominant politically, and thus the Asians could
have little hope for a change in their favor. The pro-British colonialists who had brought Asians to East Africa reduced them to a secondary social and political position, and denied them access to the best
agricultural land. The Asians had no alternative but to go into business. The British accusations that the Asians monopolized the economy of the region hence could not be justified.

European Response

The European reactions in East Africa to the British government's policies on the Kenyan conflict were mixed. When Europeans
started to settle in the EAP, they bitterly opposed the then British
policy of combining European and Asian settlement. That was pre-
cisely why 22 of the European settlers met in Nairobi to form the "Society to Promote European Immigration." The main object of the
group was to discourage all Asian immigration and foster European
settlement in the EAP.

As noted previously, the European community in Kenya was very
shocked and alarmed at Churchill's statement made in August 1921 at
the Imperial Conference. The Kenyan Europeans, therefore, in fear,
formed a Reform Party to oppose any possible ascendancy of the
Asians in the EAP. They also bitterly opposed the Passfield White
Papers of 1930; the papers made the Europeans turn against the idea
of closer union they had so enthusiastically welcomed previously.
From then on, the idea of closer union could be acceptable to them
only if they were allowed an unofficial majority in the legislative council. Rejections and protests aimed at the new British (Passfield)
stand, especially on native policy and paramountcy, were echoed everywhere in Kenya, Uganda, Tanganyika, Southern and Northern Rhodesia,
and even South Africa. The Convervatives in England, staunch supporters of the whites in East Africa, sharply repudiated the Labour
government's new policy. For example, Grigg, the staunchest of all
the critics of the new policy, attacked the move to distribute the Passfield "Memorandum on Native Policy in East Africa" to district officers along with instructions to explain the policy to Africans at tribal
meetings.

At the same time, the Devonshire White Paper (of 1923) was received by Kenyan Europeans with mixed feelings; they did not favor
the paper's provisions on responsible self-government, segregation,
and administration of the trusteeship but were pleased with the provi-

sions concerning the highlands, immigration, and the communal franchise.

Among the factors leading to European dominance in East Africa, the following were particularly striking.

1. The post-World War I period had brought world economic depression.

2. There were European conflicts at that time in various parts of Africa.

3. There was a growing struggle for independence in India in which Jawaharlal Nehru was playing a prominent role.

4. There was a general awareness everywhere that the troublesome conflict among the immigrant communities in East Africa was actually less significant in the long run than the problem of reconciling these communities with those of the Africans.

5. The Europeans in East Africa started to realize the futility of trying to raise immigration barriers and impose other restrictions to drive Asians "home," and they were no longer so fearful of what they had formerly called the "Asian menace."

6. The Asians in East Africa were also becoming reconciled to the fact that British administration meant, in practice, European supremacy, and they increasingly realized the folly of striving for proportional political representation, a common roll, and free access to the highlands.

7. There was widespread acceptance in India of the concept that Africa belonged to the Africans, and a new generation of political leaders was convinced that India had to become independent before the position of her peoples overseas could be measurably improved.

8. British humanitarians who had backed the Kenyan East African Asians were not retired.

9. There was the menace in the 1930s of an income tax, plus the delimitation of the highlands and African reserves by orders-in-council.

By 1939, the European position in Kenya was at the top, the Asian position in the middle, and the Arab and African positions at the bottom. At the same time (1931-39) in Zanzibar, Tanganyika, and Uganda, measures detrimental to Asian economic interests were taken, as an outcome of the world economic crisis. Despite those measures, however, harmonious relations generally prevailed among the Europeans in the three territories.

CONCLUSIONS

Interracial contacts in East Africa have resulted in clashes of peoples and races—whether native or alien—based on radically contrasted forms of life: regional or tribal groups versus national or parent groups; national law versus local custom; written versus oral law; liberty versus authority; and innovation versus tradition.

On the eve of African independence, European civilization with its "dictates of modern life" was unpalatable to Africans. Tribal languages and other traditions are still major dividing forces in the multilateral societies of East Africa. In Kenya, for example, Kikuyus are still envied by the other tribes as the single dominating group in the country. The Luos, however, also occupy an ascendant position as the second largest group. It seems that the right solution to this tribal problem is a combination of democracy and national unity.

The Asians in East Africa sided emotionally with the Africans against the Europeans. Economically, however, the Asians leaned toward the Europeans, their central aim being to safeguard their economic prosperity against the possible menace of Africanization and thereby maintain their traditional position as middle men par excellence. Asians had claimed all along that they had assisted in much of the region's economic and political development.

Meanwhile, there were false European accusations that Asians had contributed little to the development of East Africa. The fact is that Asians were willing to and did perform duties in East Africa that the Europeans refused and the Africans were unable to do. On the other hand, Afro-European accusations that East African Asians had taken capital out of East Africa were quite justified.

In addition, the Europeans were not willing to drop their claim of exclusive superiority over all other races in East Africa. They feared, for example, that African nationalism, when translated into existing standards, could be quite dangerous to the European community. Further, it was feared that the attainment of independence and power by Africans would end European domination and influence. The Europeans also feared that democracy in East Africa might establish autocratic government. This, in the view of the Europeans, would lead to tyranny, corruption, and bribery, which would, in turn, stultify the development of the region. Apart from these political fears, the Europeans had also the cultural fear that their whole life might be swamped by people of a completely different culture and the economic fear that land expropriation through nationalization might deprive Europeans of their historically established land rights.

The issues of land, commerce, the vote, ethnic group rights, tribalism, and education still stand out today as the main causes of racial and communal tensions in East Africa. Already in the preindependence era of East Africa, a discriminatory system of education had been established. Better educational standards were given to the Europeans and Asians, while Africans were not fully aware of the need for education in the modern world. The language problem—teaching in the African schools was for a long time done in vernacular—plus the differences in class, wealth, and culture, were terrible obstacles to educational integration.

The so-called nonracialists were a group of people found in small numbers but in every racial group. The nonracialists believed in the good of the whole nation, rather than of any one section of it. They thus wanted to advance toward nationhood, which undoubtedly would involve a sharing of certain advantages with the majority of the people. Movements like the Capricorn Africa Society and establishments such as the United Kenya Club gave the nonracialists an outlet for their ideas and the opportunity to associate. In 1956, the Capricorn Africa Society held, in Nyasaland (now Malawi), its convention of delegates from five multiracial territories of East and Central Africa; for the first time, controversial political issues were tackled by all races together. The outcome of the meeting was the signing of a multiracial contract.

The Capricorn Africa Society had been founded around 1949 by Colonel David Stirling of Britain, a progressive nonracialist who advocated a federation of Kenya, Uganda, Tanganyika, Nyasaland, and Northern and Southern Rhodesia. In essence, Stirling urged Europeans to develop the Eastern and other African regions jointly and thereby make possible a true partnership between Europeans and Africans.

Stirling called for a combination of the increasing Western immigration to East Africa and technological skill with the concealed capacity of the African and other races. No European, according to Stirling, was to possess land in the African areas, and no African was to own land in areas to be developed, barring houses, in urban centers. European presence was necessary in territorial as well as federal government. Franchise must be granted to Africans who had acquired the necessary social and educational standard. The policy of race relations had to be flexible enough to meet the special requirements of each territory.

Reactions to these so-called Stirling Capricorn declarations were mixed; most Europeans in East Africa execrated them, while the British public and a few Europeans in East Africa supported them. The British government dropped the old democratic principle of equal racial representation—in any multiracial society—and favored the doctrine of European superiority. As a result, race relations in East Africa remained strained.

What must now be done is to build up harmonious societies in East Africa in which racial integration, trust, and goodwill will be promoted. The old slogan "Africa for Africans" is no longer relevant. Nonracialists are still found in every racial community in the new East Africa. The group's outlook is still above the issue of race. Its people have a common purpose and an understanding of the interdependence of the inhabitants of each of the new East African states.

Africans in preindependence East Africa believed that the fight against racialism should be one of the main occupations of the European missionaries. But the missionaries did not oppose the discriminatory policies and practices of the colonial officials and settlers. The Africans started to be skeptical about the missionaries and to doubt their converting and "civilizing" mission.[25]

NOTES

1. See Norman Leys, The Colour Bar in East Africa (London: Hogarth Press, 1941).

2. See Colonial Office, no. 148 (London, 1938), pp. 72-73. See also General Correspondence of the East African Indian National Congress (EAINC), November 18, 1923, Nairobi.

3. Quoted in Britain, Command Paper no. 2250, London, March 31, 1904, p. 28.

4. See Land Office Leaflet no. 2, of March 19, 1913 (Kampala), pp. 1-2.

5. See Africa Digest 2, no. 8 (March/April 1955), p. 20 et seq.

6. See P. L. McDermott, British East Africa or IBEA (London: Chapman and Hall, 1893).

7. Quoted in Northey to Colonial Office, June 5, 1919, in Colonial Office, 533/210.

8. For detailed information on this question see, "Indians Abroad: Kenya," Bulletin, no. 6, July 1923 (Bombay).

9. Colonial Office, 533/5, Jackson to Lyttelton, November 11, 1905.

10. For a fuller discussion on this topic, see "The White Man's Place in Africa," in 19th Century and After 328 (June 1904), particularly pp. 937-46.

11. See "Zanzibar Colonial Decrees, 1926," in Laws of Zanzibar Protectorate, 1934, chap. 28.

12. Lord Hailey, An African Survey (London: Oxford University Press, 1957), p. 284.

13. For details see Britain, Command Paper no. 9103, 1954.

14. See Command Paper no. 9475, 1908, pp. 19, 169; and Command Paper no. 4117, 1908, pp. 25, 33.

15. For a fuller account of the immigration problem, see "Kenya: Immigration Control (Amendment) Ordinance No. 20, 1949," in Kenya

Laws, 1949; Tanganyika Laws, chap. 251, 1949; and "Uganda Immigration (Amendment) Ordinance no. 18, 1949," in Uganda Laws, 1949.

    16. Foreign Office, 2/833, Lansdowne to Stewart, July 8, 1904.

    17. Colonial Office to Foreign Office, August 15, 1904.

    18. Command Paper no. 1747 (London, August 1921), pp. 8 and
34-39.

    19. See Indian Annual Register 2 (1922), pp. 282-83.

    20. McDermott, op. cit.

    21. See Command Paper no. 1922, Indians in Kenya: Memoran-
dum (London, July 25, 1923).

    22. Command Paper no. 2904 (London), p. 3 et seq. See also
Command Paper no. 2387, 1924, The Ormsby-Gore Commission, pp.
21-27, 71.

    23. See Indian Review (October 1923), p. 645.

    24. Quoted in Indian Quarterly Register (Nairobi), January 1924,
pp. 312, 315-16.

    25. See, for details, Roland A. Oliver, The Missionary Factor
in East Africa (London: Longmans, Green and Co., 1952).

5

AFRICAN NATIONALIST RESPONSE TO ALIEN RULE IN EAST AFRICA

ORIGINS AND GROWTH OF AFRICAN
NATIONALISM IN EAST AFRICA

The definition of "nationalism" as quoted in a study by S. S.
Goodspeed has value for our discussion: Nationalism is

> a sentiment or determination to create a separate
> political entity, free from alien control, for the
> preservation and cultivation of common ideals, loy-
> alties, and traditions. It is a strong force for incur-
> ring tensions, inflaming hatreds, and augmenting the
> sovereign ideal of a strong, independent, national
> state. . . . It represents a feeling of belonging, a
> spirit or sentiment of loyalty, a group-conscious-
> ness of the nationality which is held and defended by
> the nation from attacks launched by the foreigner.[1]

Nationalism thus has the following characteristics: It is a set
of ideas, whether tolerant, relevant, or not; it is a collection of ideological assertions and claims of national solidarity—a sense of belonging; and it serves social needs, for example, how to live together,
how to realize aspirations, or how to overthrow a rejected system or
order. The satisfaction of these social needs leads to the satisfaction
of the individual.

At the same time, the notion of nationalism suggests three types
of movement. First, there is the movement seeking to build, or con-
solidate, state systems on the basis of preexisting cultural ties (for
example, of language, race, religion, and the like) by encouraging
greater consciousness of these ties. Emphasis is here placed upon

the development of a common culture and on the consolidation of political and socioeconomic institutions—existing within delimited boundaries. Nineteenth-century nationalism in Europe was a good example
of this concept of nationalism. Second, there is the "pan" movement
within established state borders, with wide cultural affiliations. Thus
Pan-Arabism has cultural and linguistic affiliations; Pan-Islamism has
religious affiliations; Pan-Africanism has continental affiliations;
Negritude and Garveyism have physical affiliations; and so on. And
third, there is the movement establishing, or seeking to establish,
independent states on the basis of common citizenship among entirely
new political and cultural ties. Although this type of movement may
not necessarily have the same traditional cultures and values, it is
united by a common colonial fate. Thus such movements and the people they represent share the following (common) features: regions
formerly colonized by aliens; a common colonial past; common interests resulting from their confrontation with the "common other"—the
colonizer; and a common dependence on the colonizers. East African
nationalism belonged to this third category of nationalism.

In this classification, African nationalist response, that is, African reactions to alien colonial rule in East Africa, appeared in two
phases. In Phase 1, African reactions were unorganized and were directed against the Portuguese in East Africa. The question of Portuguese rule in the region does not fall under our present analysis, which
is mainly concerned with British and German rule in the region. This
is why the expression "African nationalism" will, in this chapter, be
used only in relation to British and German rule in East Africa. However, the African opposition to the Portuguese in the pre-nineteenth-
century period conditioned the African opposition to the British and
Germans in the nineteenth century.

In Phase 2, African reactions to alien colonial policies and practices became more orderly, and produced the struggles that culminated
in independence for East Africa. The origins of organized East African
nationalism can be traced back to 1919; in fact, it began with a report
issued by the Economic Commission in Kenya. The report, whose aim
was to play off Africans against Asians, stated, inter alia:

> It is a distinguishing peculiarity of this country that
> here the Indian plays the part of clerk, artisan, car-
> penter, mechanic, etc., functions which the African
> is capable, with training, of performing and does
> elsewhere perform satisfactorily. The presence of
> the Indians organized as they are to keep the African
> out of every position which an Indian could fill, de-
> prives the African of all incentives to ambition and
> opportunities of advancement. Physically, the Indian

is not a wholesome influence because of his incurable
impugnance to sanitation and hygiene. In this respect
the African is more civilized than the Indian, being
naturally cleanly in his ways; but he is prone to follow
the example of those around him. . . . The moral depravity of the Indian is equally damaging to the African, who in his natural state is at least innocent of
the worst vices of the East. The Indian is the inciter
to crime as well as vice.[2]

This in effect was an accusation that the Indians were the natives' worst enemy. The Indians hit back hard by holding up to public
ridicule the pretensions of the white settlers to be trustees for "the
native," and by cultivating allies among the small group of literate
Africans (elite nationalists) in places such as Nairobi. Africans
promptly and positively responded to the Asian appeal for unity
against the whites. The reasons for the prompt African alliance with
the Asians against the whites included the African grievances against
the Europeans, repeatedly voiced over the years, which had arisen
from (1) the imposition of fresh taxes on the Africans, which should
have been paid by the Europeans; (2) the introduction of identity cards
for Africans only; (3) the intensification of the cheap but forced African labor on European farms; (4) the alienation of African lands to
Europeans without compensation; (5) the refusal to pay bonuses and
compensation to African exservicemen after World War I; and (6)
the improvement of the privileged social position of the Europeans at
the expense of the Africans.

Thus already in the early days of the 20th century, when imperialism was being replaced by modern colonial nationalism, East
Africa had elite nationalist groups that initiated strong resistance to
alien rule. They fostered enhanced awareness of African traditional
values, and organized anticolonial and antiimperialist movements.
Anticolonialism, and for that matter antiimperialism, was actually
anti-Europeanism, for it was a new challenge to European imperialism.
Indigenous groups of educated men in East Africa nurtured new ideas
and became a very strong operative factor throughout the region. The
new elite, the "emergents frontier," demanded freedom and self-
government, greatly influencing (and convincing) the hoi polloi.

Independence movements were vigorously staged by emergent
nationalists such as Jomo Kenyatta and Oginga Odinga of Kenya, Mil-
ton Obote and Benedicto Kiwanuka of Uganda, Julius Nyerere of Tanganyika, and Abeid Karume of Zanzibar. These nationalists opposed
discrimination on the grounds of sex, religion, race, language, or
color. They favored the development and realization of the idea of
"trusteeship." They fought for the right to form multiracial organiza-

tions and political parties and demanded proper education for the Africans, self-rule, and ultimate independence.

East African nationalism grew and matured only after World War II. "Liberal" nationalism was buried for good, and was succeeded by organized mass nationalism that had violent elements. This strengthened the already established elite nationalism, and the resulting militant African nationalism, together with the existing international interest in East Africa, shortened the road to independence for the East African colonial territories. The period of organized mass nationalism actually began in the late 1940s and matured in the 1950s. Violence and antiimperialist resistance was organized through legal and underground methods. Killings, imprisonments, detentions, deportations, and brute force became the order of the day. Thus the nationalist movements in East Africa took the same direction. New African parties were formed, and they, together with the old African political associations, presented African interests before the colonizers.

MAJOR CAUSES OF THE NEGATIVE AFRICAN REACTIONS TO ALIEN RULE IN EAST AFRICA

The hostility of the African local tribes, besides their refusal to cooperate or compromise, led the Europeans to impose indirect rule upon the indigenous Africans. As a method of imposing control on the colonized peoples, indirect rule in some cases unified and in others divided the subjected peoples. To any political unit, anyone not belonging to that unit is an alien. Therefore the negative African reactions to alien rule in East Africa must not only be seen as having been directed against Europeans. Alien rule in the region must also be taken to mean any rule that was imposed, or attempted to be imposed, by an alien group. Arabs on the East African coast were an alien group, for instance, who imposed their alien rule on the coastal East Africans. Incidentally, one of the reasons the coastal Arabs launched strong resistance movements against European rule in East Africa was to uphold their (Arab) rule on the coast of East Africa. Similarly, the Nandi raids on the Kavirondo Luos and Luhyas, the Masai invasions of Kambaland, the Buganda raids on Bunyoro in Uganda, the Wahehe and Wanyika raids in Tanganyika on other comparatively weak tribes, and the counterraids of the invaded tribes, were all attempts to impose alien rule by some tribes on other tribes and resist alien rule.

In Kenya, where the burden of European rule was heaviest, tribal politics were encouraged by four factors: the colonial administration's hostility to African nationalism; the demarcation of tribal land units; the limitation of political organization to district level; and the famous principle of divide-and-rule, from which sprang the indirect rule system. Whereas alien rule was imposed on the East Africans gradually and with little or no clear warning, the Africans responded to that rule promptly and with full and open violence.

As for the African response to the Euro-Asian struggle for dominance in East Africa, the overall tendency was to be neutral and keep aloof, because the Africans knew very well that "where two elephants fight," as the famous Swahili proverb says, "it is the grass that suffers." The Africans therefore preferred to press for the realization of their demands rather than side with either of the rivaling racial minority groups in that region.

With regard to the Afro-Asian relationships in the region, the Africans were not, initially, worried about the Asians because the Africans believed the Asians were not an immediate menace to African interests. The Africans also believed the Asians did not belong to the ruling class. However, a sufficiently great friction existed between these two racial groups in the later part of the colonial period. Two reasons can be given in this regard: the economic position and power of the Asians became "dangerous" and too strong for the Africans to bear, and the spirit of African nationalism gained greater momentum.

Taken in broad terms, there were four main causes of the negative African response to colonial rule in East Africa:

1. European colonial policies and practices had included restrictions on the movements of the Africans, the loss of their stock, and the closing of forests to them; fines imposed on Africans for the slightest trespass; excessive and inhuman physical abuse of the Africans; summary dismissals of the Africans, after they had done dirty work; and encouragement of disrespect among African youth for the traditional and customary ways of African life.

2. The Euro-Asian struggle for dominance was in complete disregard of African interests and aspirations.

3. The overall position of aliens in East Africa was continually improving.

4. The position of Africans vis-a-vis the position of aliens in the region was deteriorating.

African Reactions in Zanzibar and Tanganyika

In Zanzibar, the Arabs revolted against the British in 1895, following the assumption by the British of direct rule over the coastal zone and along the EAP. Ironically, the Arab Zanzibari nationalist movement claimed to be nonracial, spontaneous, democratic, and not

Arab-dominated. The African Zanzibari nationalist movement, on the
contrary, opposed the views of the Arabs and asserted that the Arab
party was racialist and anti-African. The Afro-Shirazi Party rejected
the idea of self-government for Zanzibar, because of the fear that the
Arabs might dominate Zanzibar and restore the historical Arab superiority on the island. The Afro-Shirazi Party opposed the demands of
the Arab Association for universal suffrage, on the grounds that it was
undemocratic to guarantee equal (democratic) rights to a minority.
The Africans in the Zanzibar legislative council vehemently attacked
Arab demands for elections for all. Racism was particularly acute
during and after the June 1961 elections. Of the 68 persons killed
in election riots, 64 were Arabs. Some Africans belonged to the Arab-
dominated Nationalist Party and opposed the Afro-Shirazi Party. Africans were also found among the Independents. Similarly, Asians were
divided into the three (abovementioned) political groups. And so were
a few Arabs. The result of the groupings was a serious weakness in
party politics and a great promotion of intraracial conflicts, which
prevented Africans from forming a strong united front against the imperialists. In this way, African nationalism was immensely handicapped, and when the British decided to grant independence to Zanzibar on December 10, 1963, it was the Arab (Nationalist) Party that
formed the first government. The Afro-Shirazi party came to power
only after an armed uprising in Zanzibar on January 12, 1964. The
armed revolution was the result of the failure of the British colonial
policy to bring about a bloodless independence to the island. Abeid
Karume, leader of the Zanzibari Afro-Shirazi Party, signed an Act of
Union with Tanganyika in April 1964. Karume became the first vice-
president of the newly formed United Republic of Tanzania but was
assassinated in April 1972; he was succeeded by Aboud Jumbe.

The Germans became known to the Africans as the "people of the
25" because the common sentence for the most insignificant offense
was 25 lashes from the hippopotamus-hide whip. In 1895, Karl Peters
had to be removed as commissioner of Kilimanjaro District by dint of
his notorious practices. The German colonial administration forced
the Africans to plant cotton and, until 1907, followed a policy of forced
African labor for European plantations and for public works.

In the interwar period, African resentment burst into flames
as land transfers to aliens kindled the fire of African rebellion. The
German colonizers were thus faced with even greater African resistance than that experienced in Zanzibar. The Africans, Arabs, and
Asians in German East Africa united and acted against the German
colonizers. German military forces and even British warships were
sent to East Africa and utilized to suppress the native uprisings.

Both Arabs and the various African tribes, notably the Wachagga
of Kilimanjaro, the Wanyika, and the Waheke, staged strong anti-Ger-

man resistances. A very dangerous revolt was launched by the Hehe
tribal leader and ruler, Mkwawa. He, like his father, Bwana Munyi-
gumba, was a fighter, military organizer, and liberator of his tribe,
which consisted of about 100 clans. Under the strong, merciless, and
brutal leadership of Mkwawa, the Wahehe continued to harass the Germans as well as other tribes and their leaders who refused to join
forces with Mkwawa to raid the German colonialists. The Mkwawa
raiders and supporters started to lose the battle in 1894, but they remained loyal to their leader. In 1898 Mkwawa shot himself near his
beloved capital—Kalenga—and fell into a fire specially prepared by
his page (whom he had shot previously) so that the German intruders
could not reach and capture him even in death.

The Maji-Maji Uprising

The greatest African resistance to the German colonial rule in
East Africa was the so-called Maji-Maji uprising of 1905. Maji-Maji
was, as translated by the witch doctors living in German East Africa
at that time, sacred water that a snake god called Koleo, living in the
Pangani Rapids of the Rufiji River, had used to break magic. From
that, the belief became widely developed that a water strong enough
to break magic must also be powerful enough to break European rule;
bullets would hence be turned into water. The central aim of the Maji-
Maji rebellion was to expel all foreigners, starting with the Germans,
and restore the tribal chiefs to their old splendor.
There were five immediate causes of the Maji-Maji uprising:

1. The Germans had suppressed the African rulers and ruling
tribes, and made them work with their slaves and serfs.
2. The Germans had introduced in the German East African
Protectorate in 1897 a hut tax of two or three rupees per year in cash.
That taxation angered the Africans who believed that hard cash was a
higher price to pay than would have been payment in cotton.
3. The German colonial administration had endeavored to force
the growing of cotton with a view to export revenues.
4. There had been a loss of trust in Germans on the part of
Bwana Chaburuma, the powerful Ngoni ruler (sultan), because the
German district commissioner, Hauptmann von Richter, refused to
condemn Chaburuma's wife whom Chaburuma believed to have been un-
faithful; the German district commissioner rejected Chaburuma's al-
legation because the chief could not produce any evidence. The rejection enraged Chaburuma, who henceforward execrated Germans.
5. The German administration introduced a poll tax in 1905.
The policy of subjecting the East Africans to taxation of one type or

another was introduced throughout East Africa by the German and
British colonial administrations. Thus, in 1900 and 1901, Kenya and
Uganda were also subjected to hut taxes.[3]

The Maji-Maji rebellion was extreme in its cruelty. All Europeans were murdered in the area between North Nyasa and the Kilwa
Coast; even the missionaries were killed. The Germans finally sub-
dued the rebellion in 1907, after 120,000 Africans had been killed, including a large number as a result of famine and disease connected
with the German suppression.

Mandates and Trusteeships in East Africa

The mandate system of the League of Nations and the trusteeship
system of the United Nations both had a positive impact on East Africa.
The League Covenant of 1920 graded the League's mandates into three
groups—A, B, and C. Tanganyika was placed in Group B, and the
mandatory power—in this case, Britain—was required to maintain an
administration spearate from its other colonial possessions. (Group
B was an intermediate group of territories that would eventually become independent, after long preparation.) The duties of the mandatory power were to ensure and be responsible for peace, a good government, and order within the mandated territory; to avoid establishing military bases in the territory; and not to use the territory's inhabitants for military service except in defense of the territory; to
promote the material and moral welfare of the indigenous inhabitants;
to prohibit slavery and/or forced labor; to endeavor as much as possible to guarantee equal economic rights for all the nationals of the
League's member states; and finally to control the traffic in ammuni-
tion, arms, and liquor.
When the trusteeship system was introduced after World War II,
the United Nations took over the old mandate system and integrated it
with the new system.
International interest in Tanganyika therefore was launched in
1919, when the League of Nations bestowed upon Britain, at Britain's
suggestion, a mandate over former German East Africa, which was
renamed Tanganyika. Horace Byatt became Tanganyika's first governor and commander-in-chief on July 22, 1920. However, Britain
started to implement fully the mandate provisions over Tanganyika
only in 1922. When Tanganyika was placed under UN trusteeship,
Britain retained her administrative status over the territory, which
she started to administer as a trust territory in 1947. The Constitution of the Tanganyikan trust territory differed from that of a protectorate only insofar as, under international law, Tanganyika's adminis-

tration was subject to the degree of international supervision formerly
exercised by the League of Nations via the agency of the Permanent
Mandates Commission, and later by the UN General Assembly via the
agency of the Trusteeship Council. [4] In domestic law, however, the
administration of the territory was, as in the case of the protectorates,
based upon what were known as "Crown instruments" issued under the
terms of the U.K. Foreign Jurisdiction Act of 1890.

Contacts between Tanganyika and the United Nations were established through UN visiting missions. In 1948, a UN mission reached
African opinion via African chiefs. That mission's report criticized
the exclusion of Africans from the Tanganyikan executive council and
their inadequate representation in the legislative council. The report
also criticized the virtual exclusion of Africans from the middle and
upper ranks of the civil service. The United Nations strongly backed
the doctrine of racial equality, and the educational, social, political,
and economic advancement of the trust territory and its inhabitants,
until the time when they would speedily attain self-determination and
eventual independence.

The United Nations continued to send visiting missions to Tanganyika and to support the Africans. In this way, the dominant position
of aliens was terribly jeopardized in the territory. Also, Tanganyika's
special position was one of the strong forces that prevented the growth
in East Africa of a settler-dominated political association on the lines
of the Rhodesia-Nyasaland Federation. It also prevented the introduction in East Africa of the policy of "separate development" on the pattern of South Africa.

In 1954, a third UN visiting mission arrived in Tanganyika.
The Africans voiced the following demands:

1. Britain must accelerate the decolonization process.
2. Britain must alter her method of creating a multiracial society in Tanganyika.
3. There must be no color bar in education, hospitals, employment, hotels, and the like.
4. Britain must shorten Tanganyika's road to independence and
transfer power to the Africans at once.
5. There must be equal representation in the legislative council on the territorial basis: the nine provinces and Dar-es-Salaam
must each possess one member of each race.

On March 7, 1955, Nyerere and other Tanganyikan African politicians presented petitions to the UN Trusteeship Council in New York.
As the chief petitioner, Nyerere outlined African demands as follows:

1. Nomination must give way to election in the legislative council.

2. Democratic representation in Tanganyika must be introduced at once; there must be an African majority in all public representative institutions.

3. Racial segregation, and alien immigration and dominance, besides expropriation of land in Tanganyika, must stop at once.

4. The African majority community must not be subjected to the exploitation of the European and Asian minority groups.

5. Tanganyika should attain self-determination at once and be assured of an early independence.

6. The future government of Tanganyika must be primarily African.

Certain politicians in Tanganyika were known as black racists. Their aim was to turn independent Tanganyika into a purely black man's country. The "black racists," all members of parliament, were Said Mtaki, Aron Msindai, John Mwakangale, Christopher Tumbo, and Richard Wambura. The black racist doctrine expounded by these men consisted of three central points: all Europeans and Asians were foreigners, whether born in Tanganyika or not, and whether their parents and grandparents had been born there or not; no foreigners should occupy any key positions in the country, and those in such positions should unconditionally resign; and all aliens wishing to become Tanganyikan citizens should be put on a seven-year probation first or be examined by a committee.

The multiracialist group in Tanganyika could not accept the black racist doctrine. This view was expressed particularly by the Tanganyika National Society (TNS) and the United Tanganyika Party (UTP), which had been formed in November and December 1955, respectively, as the first multiracial organizations in Tanganyika. The main purpose of these groups was to advance the ideas and ideals of the Capricorn Africa Society—essentially that no one racial group should dominate the others. In its program, the UTP emphasized racial equality; racial independence; and a detestation of the color bar in the country.

When the UTP accused Nyerere's Tanganyika African National Union (TANU) of racism, Nyerere and his TANU followers rejected Stirling's multiracialism, because they believed strongly that the Stirling doctrine would perpetually uphold the white minority dominion in Tanganyika and elsewhere in East and Central Africa. The main problem with the Stirling doctrine and its future effect in East Africa lay in the fact that the doctrine was conceived at a time when African nationalism was extremely strong, and Europeans were beginning to realize their privileged position in that region could not last long. African nationalists were, on the other hand, also beginning to realize that they would need European and Asian assistance even after independence. This situation meant European and Asian participation in the economic and political development of the region.

The British colonial doctrine of balanced representation in East Africa was categorically rejected by the Africans. Racial parity was reached in the executive council of Tanganyika in 1954. From that year onward, however, the Africans made it clear to the colonizers that the Africans would not accept the idea of parity. Thus no doctrinaire enforcement of multiracialism would exist. In parliament and in government, an African majority would predominate.

In the meantime, UN missions continued to pour into Tanganyika and to submit their (pro-African) reports in the ensuing years, including 1957. During this period, party politics were reactivated everywhere in East Africa. In Tanganyika, the African National Council (ANC) appeared on the scene. And the UTP comprised all the unofficial members—Africans, Asians, and Europeans—of the legislative council.

TANU, formed in 1957, consisted of nationalists who opposed, and were in turn opposed by, the UTP. Almost all of TANU's members were Africans. The ANC was a racial political group. When a general election was held in 1958, the UTP and the ANC very heavily lost to TANU. The UTP and the ANC hence had no alternative but to disintegrate. By 1960, the UTP had disappeared, but the ANC still survived as a party. And when Richard Turnbull became governor of Tanganyika, the Africans were assured of predominance in Tanganyikan politics: Nyerere became their leader, and Turnbull their friend.

A final UN visiting mission was sent to Tanganyika Trust Territory in 1960, the year general elections were held in the territory, with TANU winning. On September 1, 1960, Turnbull summoned Nyerere to form a government. On May 1, 1961, Tanganyika achieved full internal self-government. That meant that the governor of Tanganyika would, from that day onward, no longer preside in the cabinet/ Nyerere, the prime minister, would preside. Tanganyika at last attained full independence on December 9, 1961. On April 26, 1964, Tanganyika and Zanzibar united (Union Day) to form one state, which was renamed Tanzania on October 29, 1964.

African Response in Uganda

Anti-British revolts in Uganda were launched by the kingdom (tribal) rulers, including King (Kabaka) Mwanga of Buganda, King Kabarega of Bunyoro, King Kyebambe I of Toro, and King Ntare of Ankole. Busoga was probably ruled by strong chiefs like Chief Lubwa, since Busoga was not a kingdom but, for a considerable period, a tributary of Buganda Kingdom. Busoga became a district under the Protectorate of Buganda. All the affairs of Busoga were managed through a district council. As elsewhere in East Africa, the central purpose of the African revolts against the colonizers in Buganda was to force the latter to transfer power to the Africans.

Believing strongly in separatism, the Ganda people, led by their successive kabakas, determinedly fought against every alien attempt to impose control on Buganda. That was the case, for instance, when Kabaka Mwanga of Buganda rebelled against the British in 1897. The African response in Buganda to the concept of closer union was extremely negative. The Bugandan peasants (Baganda) and clans (Bataka) could neither tolerate European expropriation of Baganda's land nor forfeit their privileged position and that of their province in Uganda. The other genuine concerns of the Africans in Buganda Kingdom—and indeed elsewhere in the protectorate—included the fear of political dominance by the settler population; and the fear that the (European) economic arguments for closer union, if implemented, would not alter the economic status quo.

The Kingdom of Bunyoro, alias Kitara Empire, or Bunyoro-Kitara, was the largest of the Ugandan kingdoms of the lake area. Of all the anti-British rebels in Uganda, King Kabarega of Bunyoro was the greatest. He revolted against the British in 1894-96. British troops were, however, too strong for Kabarega to conquer. He was subsequently forced to surrender and flee northward across the Nile.

African resistance to British rule was also staged in Ankole Kingdom. Here, however, the British did not experience many serious problems, and, by 1898, they had firmly established themselves in Ankole. In Busoga, the British were opposed both by the Basoga and the Baganda. The latter claimed to exercise dominion (hegemony) over Busoga.

In Toro, the opposition to the British was also not as great as that of Buganda and Bunyoro. The main reason for the "favorable" reception of the British colonizers in Toro was that the British restored the independence of Toro from Bunyoro and set up a Toro confederacy under a restored Toro mukame (king).

The main impediments, then, in the struggle for independence in Uganda included the clash between modern nationalism and the privileged protagonists, that is, the champions and advocates of traditional value; hereditary kings; long-established tribal forms of government; religious rivalries; and the tribal struggles for supremacy over the largest part of Uganda. Taking advantage of the kingdom rivalries, the British sought to extend their rule everywhere in Uganda.

In 1955, an agreement called the Namirembe Agreement was concluded between Buganda and Britain. It democratized Buganda, which thenceforth would be regarded as an integral part of Uganda and would send representatives as before to the Uganda legislative council. However, the Baganda disagreed with the agreement, and demanded independence for Buganda by December 31, 1960. Britain reaffirmed that there should be only one Ugandan state with a strong central government, in which Buganda would be granted a federal status based on the superiority and special position of Buganda in Uganda. One salient feature in Ugandan politics was the active participation of religious groups in political discussions. For example, in 1956, the Catholic bishops of Uganda requested the Anglicans to join in sponsoring a Christian Democratic Party. The Anglicans declined, but the Catholics went ahead on their own and managed to get the new (Catholic) Democratic Party (DP) to work closely with the UNC for Catholic action. In 1958, Kiwanuka, a Kampala Catholic lawyer, assumed the leadership of the DP, and became its second president general.

Countrywide elections in Uganda were held in 1961 and 1962. Difficulties over the semiindependent Kingdom of Buganda were resolved at the London Constitutional Conference of September 1961, when Buganda was given a semifederal relationship with the rest of the country. On March 1, 1962, Uganda attained internal self-government with Kiwanuka as prime minister. In the general election that followed, however, Kiwanuka's Democratic party government was defeated by the Uganda Peoples' Congress (UPC), in alliance with the Kabaka Yekka Movement of Buganda. Obote, UPC president, took office as prime minister on May 1, 1962. A further series of constitutional talks was held in London in June 1962, to pave the way for complete independence for Uganda later in the same year. Under the new constitution, known as the Constitution of Uganda (First Amendment) Act of 1962, Uganda at last became independent on October 9, 1962, with Obote as prime minister.

THE KENYAN EXPERIENCE

The Kenyan case was the most sensitive in the East African region. In addition, African resistance to British rule in Kenya was, as in the other East African territories, staged right from the beginning of alien rule. In December 1894, for instance, the Bukusu, or the Ketosh as they were called at that time by the British, attacked a mail party in the Kavirondo area. The Bukusu strongly resisted British pressure until their resistance was foiled in 1895.

African resistance to alien rule in Kenya was also intensified after 1900. The Masai opposition, besides the Nandi and Kikuyu resistances, were the greatest obstacles to British colonial authority in Kenya. The sensitive land question sparked off a series of tensions and clashes between the natives and the aliens.

Unfortunately, distance, the fear of domination by one tribe over another, the different traditions, customs, and tastes among the tribal groups in the colony, and the white man's superiority in weapons were great impediments to a united and omnitribal resistance to alien rule in Kenya.

After 1900, in Kenya and throughout East Africa, prophetic beliefs (millennarian cults) were revitalized. In Buganda, it was believed that the one most powerful way to get rid of the alien intruders was to beseech the gods to expel the intruders. Millennarian cults were thus native African responses to European maltreatment and dispossession of lands from the Africans. On the other hand, European church organizations were acceptable to some Africans who believed the organizations played leading roles in the advancement of social justice, progress, stability, and equality among the East African inhabitants.

The Kamba and Luo tribes of Kenya were very good at the prophetic cults. Near Machakos in Kambaland, for example, a movement (cult) was started in 1911 by a widow called Siotune, who claimed to be possessed by a ghost. Siotune became very famous. She later had a young follower called Kiamba, a man who predicted that the European administrator in Kisumu would very soon be lifted up to heaven, and all the other Europeans would flee the country. Later, however, the EAP government banned the Siotune movement, after arresting all its organizers.

Among the Luo, an atavist movement called Mumbo also arose against the Europeans and their Christian religion, which the cult described as "rotten." The Mumbo movement was also an endeavor to reject all Europeans and their activities. The cult was founded by Onyango Dunde in 1913. Dunde affirmed that he had been instructed by a sea serpent from Lake Victoria to reject Christianity and Europeans and to maintain the African traditions and customs of the Luo people.

At the coast of East Africa, the Giriama people in August 1914 also strongly revolted against the Europeans. The Giriama proved to be very tough, stubborn, and extremely disobedient in the face of European aliens and their government in the EAP.

Harry Thuku was the leader of the East Africa Association in Kenya. He was a shrewd Kikuyu leader who organized regular meetings of the association to discuss African grievances. Thuku became famous and acceptable among the Africans throughout East Africa.

African and Indian nationalism had similarities. Thuku was a kind of Kenyan Ghandi. In fact, it was after Thuku had come into contact with the Indians that he broke away from the Kikuyu Association (led by Kikuyu chiefs) to form the Young Kikuyu Association, which on July 1, 1921, became the East Africa Association. The idea of the new association was to allow for non-Kikuyu membership. Thus Asians were admitted to the association, and on July 10, 1921, the association passed a series of resolutions, one of which declared:

> This mass meeting of natives of Kenya puts on rec-
> ord that in its opinion the presence of Indians in the
> Colony and Protectorate of Kenya is not prejudicial
> to the advancement of natives as has often been al-
> leged by the Convention of Associations and some
> of the writers in the press and is of the further
> opinion that next to Missionaries Indians are their
> best friends. [5]

When Jeevanjee went to London to air Asian grievances, the East Africa Association requested him to present the African case to Churchill and to Prime Minister Lloyd George, as well as to the India Office and pro-African British members of parliament. The branch of
the Young Baganda Association in Nairobi aired the Baganda's views
in their monthly newspaper Sekanyolya. The Baganda called on East
Africans to ignore the Asians and lay more stress on the education
of native Africans.

     The Kenyan European leader Delamare described the abovemen-
tioned East Africa Association resolutions, at the joint meeting of the
Convention of Associations and the Nairobi Political Association on
August 22, 1927, as "evidently inspired by the Indians." He noted:

> Gandhi and the political agitators in India are said to
> be receiving some money from the Bolshevists. . . .
> If we fail to prevent this injustice [of racially mixed
> government], then it means the Government of Kenya
> by Indians because no one else could take part in the
> ineffectual unjust and corrupt government which must
> result from dual control. . . . It is quite certain
> that [if India rules after the British are gone] she
> will be unable to control the native populations un-
> less she has European officers to help. And are
> those gentlemen to be asked to lead their men against
> natives to repress revolt raised against this govern-
> ment by a corrupt race? [6]

Delamare and other European settlers in effect confused and divided
Africans in Kenya Colony. Thuku was subsequently arrested after a
riot (where the University of Nairobi now stands) in 1922, in which
15 Africans were killed.

     In 1926, the East Africa Association was reorganized as the
Kikuyu Central Association (KCA), and a new spokesman emerged:
Jomo (then known as Johnston) Kenyatta, general secretary and edi-
tor of the Kikuyu vernacular newspaper Muigwithania, now became
KCA's new secretary. Joseph Kang'ethe became KCA's president,

and other prominent members of the KCA included Senior Chief Mbiu Koinange.

The British colonizers were determined all along to smash the nationalist movements that were a menace to alien rule in East Africa. They consequently had intensified their "taming" methods; but no native tribe had been brought to full, administrative alien control by 1914. The Kikuyu political opposition to alien rule in Kenya was later voiced by the Kenya African Union (KAU). KAU was the greatest promoter of what became known as the Mau-Mau, a strong nationalist movement whose aim was to liberate Kenya Colony from colonial rule and to transfer power to the Africans.[7] The Mau-Mau anti-European movement in the 1950s was actually the outcome of African nationalism first recognized in 1947, and prompted by the grievances of the African Kikuyu tribe, which felt it had been subjected to the greatest injustices that humanity could ever be made to suffer. The Kikuyu were thus bound by oath to force the expulsion of the white man from Kenya. In 1952, the Mau-Mau movement began bloody reprisals against the European settlers, particularly in the "White Highlands," which had, for a long time, been claimed by the Kikuyu as tribal lands. The settlers retaliated; the Mau-Mau in turn hit back hard; and casualties grew; Kikuyu who refused to join the Mau-Mau were murdered by the terrorists.

By 1956, however, British forces had driven the Mau-Mau into the mountain forests, where they were killed or eventually captured. Later, the entire Kikuyu tribe was resettled within a guarded area, and Kenyatta, suspected to be the leader of the movement, was imprisoned. The state of emergency that had been declared in 1952 was lifted in 1960. Kenyatta was released in 1961. The British had spent more than £50 million on the war by the time the whole business was over.

The Maji-Maji and Mau-Mau

An examination of the Maji-Maji and Mau-Mau rebellions reveals that the two revolts had more dissimilarities than similarities. Thus, both had a common end—the expulsion of aliens and abolition of alien rule, and the restoration of traditional values and institutions; the methods, however, of attaining that ideal were quite different. In addition, the Maji-Maji rebellion was suppressed after a shorter period than the Mau-Mau revolt. The African resistance in the Maji-Maji uprising was not accompanied with as much African cruelty as was the case in the Mau-Mau rebellion. And yet the German treatment of the Africans in the Maji-Maji uprising had been far more brutal than the British treatment of the Kikuyus in the Mau-Mau revolt. Furthermore, only a handful of European civilians were murdered by the Maji-Maji African rebels. The Mau-Mau rebellion, on the contrary, saw far greater brutality and ruthlessness. The rebels mercilessly murdered more than 2,058 civilians in Kenya, most of whom were innocent children, women, and men. Of these, about 2,000 were African Kikuyus that had been loyal to the colonial administration, while 26 were Asians and 32 were Europeans. The Mau-Mau also murdered 591 security troops in Kenya, of whom 525 were Africans, three were Asians, and 63 were Europeans. All in all, the Kenyan colonial government lost 2,461 people in the struggle against the Mau-Mau revolt: 2,357 Africans, nine Asians, and 95 Europeans.

The So-Called Masai Treaties

Both the colonial government in Kenya and the Colonial Office in London questioned Masai rights in the Rift Valley, which was the strategic key to the Kenya highlands. It hence became clear that it was absolutely essential to remove the Masai people from the Rift Valley to provide room for white settlement. Masai reaction to that colonial land policy was extremely negative. The Masai hence continued to claim land rights in the highlands, as did the European settlers. The European colonists insisted that a Masai reserve be established at the Laikipia Plateau. Treaties were consequently signed with the Masai in 1904, 1910, and 1911.

The purpose of the 1904 treaty was to move the Masai and their flocks from the Rift Valley to the Laikipia Plateau. The treaty was to be enduring as long as the Masai as a race should exist. Out of this deceptive policy, two reserves actually emerged: one on the Laikipia plateau, about 4,770 square miles, and the other to the south of the Uganda Railway and Ngong, about 4,350 square miles.

The treaty of 1910 was signed by Lenana, the Masai expert and paramount chief, the two main leaders of the northern Masai—Legalishu and Masikondi—and 11 others. The main aim of the 1910 treaty was to bunch the Masai tribe into one reserve, and to ask them to accept the government-favored Lenana as their paramount chief. The move had been initiated by the governor, Sir Percy Girouard, who wanted to preserve the highlands for European settlement only, against the instructions of the Colonial Office in London. The Masai consequently rejected the 1910 treaty, and the government representative did not sign it.

Governor Girouard nevertheless continued with his treaties and finally succeeded, after Lenana's death on March 7, 1911, for Legalishu signed the 1911 treaty, though he regretted it later.[8]

A question arises as to the validity and legal force of the agreements signed between the natives and colonial administrations. When cases regarding the agreements were brought to the East African Court of Appeal, the court held that such agreements were not contracts, but treaties concluded with foreign subjects, which were not cognizable in municipal courts. Such an opinion of the Court of Appeal could only be favorable to the colonial government, in the case of the treaties with the Masai, because the treaties had a binding force, even though the Masai were cheated and threatened by the local colonial administrators. The treaties were thus excellent instruments for promoting colonial interests.

Party politics in Kenya were already active before the British Conservative government's "winds of change" policy was started in 1959 by then Prime Minister Harold Macmillan. Of the older political groupings, the abovementioned KAU proved to be the most active and demanding. The union demanded, for example, freedom of movement and assembly for Africans, African election, instead of nomination, to the legislative council, and a legal prohibition against racial discrimination. The later African political parties formed in colonized Kenya included the Kenya African National Union (KANU), dominated by the Kikuyu and Luo tribes, the Kenya African Democratic Union (KADU), dominated by the Luhya and coastal tribes, and the African People's Party, formed on the eve of independence by the Kamba leader Paul Ngei; of these, KANU and KADU, formed in 1960, emerged as the greatest. The main difference in policy between the two parties was that KADU was for regionalism, that is, regional representatives in authoritative regions and in the central government, while KANU was for national unity and a unitary government. Further, KADU supported a two-party system of government. KANU, on the contrary, was "extreme" and noncommittal, and advocated a one-party government system. Unfortunately, these newly formed African parties in Kenya imported the bitter rivalries of tribes, with all their ancient antagonisms, into the sphere of politics. Party politics continued to be activated in Kenya. The usual constitutional conferences were held in London between the years 1960 and 1963. In May 1963, an election was held in Kenya that produced a KANU government, which would lead Kenya into independence. On December 12, 1963, Kenya attained full independence with Kenyatta as prime minister.

THE RESPONSIBILITIES OF COLONIZATION

The colonization of East Africa resulted in moral as well as legal and material responsibilities on the side of the colonizers toward the colonized. Thus the resistance and waging of wars by the East African indigenous peoples against what they deemed to be harsh, irresponsible alien rule over them were both natural and justifiable acts.

For indeed, there can be no greater impertinence than that of one
country imposing its ways upon another country and expecting the
other country to live according to those ways. And yet this was, no
doubt, the implication in the imposition of alien rule in East Africa.
Not only morally, but legally as well, it is absolutely wrong for one
people to impose its rule on another. Colonization is therefore a direct violation of human rights and fundamental freedoms, for it
raises discrimination on linguistic, sex, racial, and color grounds.
Colonial rule is further a great violation of the universally accepted
principles of human equality and self-determination as stipulated in
the 1948 Universal Declaration of Human Rights. Colonization is a
tool for the advancement of superiority exercised by a minority who,
being different from the local majority in culture, history, beliefs,
and often race, impose social, economic, political, and other considerable measures on the majority population. Colonization therefore
is against the law of nature, which conforms to the supreme triumph
of the human person, and stands for the existence of purpose in law.
This purpose in law requires, in matters of government and the governed, that the former not only be responsible to the latter generally,
but also that governments take decisions and make laws specifically
for the realization of certain ends, and for the benefit, and not exploitation, of the governed. Thus natural law like divine law has an
authority superior to that of any merely positive law of human ordinance
as the one imposed by colonizers upon the colonized. In this way,
colonial rule is against the rational nature of man.

The law of nature, however, is one thing, and the law of deter-
minism another. And where the two collide, the latter must prevail.
That is, if it had always been true that European powers had colonized
other parts of the world—and it was true that they had done so for 400
years—then it was not surprising that East Africa was later to be colonized by the same alien powers.

The introduction in East Africa of the alien colonial notion
sparked off a series of native hatreds of aliens in that territory. Before the advent of alien rulers to East Africa, the natives there had
developed their own ideas and ways of life. They had employed different methods of rule. Political and tribal organizations had ranged
from tyranny in some areas to extreme democracy in others. Much
had depended on the ability of individual leadership or on tribal traditions. Thus the stronger the individual leader or tribe, the better
had been the chance of subjecting others.

The indigenous East African peoples would perhaps have been
more friendly toward the aliens if the latter had endeavored to convince the Africans that they would have been at peace and happy with
their neighbors, even were the Africans to refuse to adjust themselves
to the changed circumstances they found themselves in. For the col-

onizers, however, happiness simply meant gratification of their desires alone. On the other side, the ruled refused to adopt alien methods and ideas, and instead staged rebellions. To the British officials, their "punitive expeditions" were justified both by the depredations of "offending" Africans, and by the need to inflict a "severe lesson" to secure the final pacification of a recalcitrant area. After pacifying the recalcitrant Africans, the British began to develop the African areas; they built roads, bridges, railways, towns, hospitals, schools, and other public works as required by the Pax Britannica.

During the period of colonial rule, the Africans formed political parties aimed at creating independent welfare states, in which all citizens, irrespective of color, creed, class, language, or tribe, should possess equal opportunity, and be assured of the basic needs of life in a modern society. The African political parties also aimed to establish and maintain the social and economic foundations of welfare states, through the processes of a planned economy.

In all the East African colonies, the British government retained, after the attainment by the colonies of self-government, control over their external affairs, defense, and internal affairs. The control was exercised by the British governors, until the colonies were granted full independence. After Uganda's independence, Buganda Kingdom achieved a federal status, whereas all the other former kingdoms achieved a semifederal status. The traditional kingdom rulers or kings became constitutional monarchs.

The division of the colonial territories into smaller portions (native states) could only enhance disobedience to the central government. It got the tribes at loggerheads with one another. It was a system of government that had been nonexistent in Africa, and hence was unknown to Africans. The indirect rule method had, therefore, the following disadvantages:

1. The indigenous peoples were convinced that indirect rule advanced imperialism, which destroyed indigenous cultures by introducing foreign ways. This belief was rejected by the foreign rulers.

2. Indirect rule changed the already established social order and thereby encouraged conservative, gradual change and impeded rapid change. The outcome of that situation was revolutionary change and violence among the colonized peoples, especially during and after World War II.

3. The indirect rule method further introduced a system of closed society where government was not by politicians but by the elite who were demagogues: civil servants, intellectuals, lawyers, the bourgeoisie, artists, militiamen, and so on.

4. Indirect rule also encouraged excessive exploitation and subsequent impoverishment of the native peoples. Thus the central pur-

pose of imperialism was extraction by the colonizers of maximum
profit from the cheap labor of the indigenous peoples.

The indirect rule system, however, also had its advantages,
which were sometimes on the side of the native, but in most cases
favored the alien. The system (1) promoted and developed the divide-
and-rule principle, which favored the colonizers; (2) impeded nationalist unification by establishing and upholding numerous petty centers
of power; (3) weakened the indigenous peoples by, for example, making
them enemies of one another; (4) provided a very easy maintenance of
the status quo; and (5) enabled the colonial administrators to manage
their colonies cheaply. The system was thus an excellent tool for
colonial ruling.

In both colonization and decolonization processes, the use of
force was a common instrument. Thus independence was attained
either by violent means, that is, by revolution, as was the case in Al-
geria and East Africa, or by peaceful means, as was the case in India.
The Europeans further believed not only that Africans were primitive,
unable to learn, and backward, but that they were murderers, canni-
bals by nature—"submen." The Europeans consequently nurtured the
thought that imperialism was the best tool to "civilize" Africans.

The Africans, on the contrary, suffered from an inferiority complex, poverty, ignorance, dependence, and fear. To them, the Europeans were terrible people, man-eaters, "heartless gods." In this
way, revenge and guilt were worked out mutually between the colonizers and the colonized, and the outcome of this was antagonism and
alienation of the one group from the other. Nationalism meant Africanism. The spirit of Africanism varied in force and objective from
one country to another, and from one community to another. Africanism was spurred by the hatred of racial segregation (such as
apartheid) and by eventual independence.

The needs of the East African nationalism were decolonization,
independence, and development. The colonized East Africans feared
lest Asians might be grouped together with the Africans and thus suc-
ceed in winning a share in economic-political control of the region,
which would badly affect the position of the Africans.

Although in the eyes of some critics, alien rule innovated too
little and too slowly, the colonial contribution in East Africa was too
enormous to be ignored. Britain's main contribution lay in her efforts
to expand parliamentary institutions and set up modest five-year development plans.

The realization of the falsehood of the prophecy of indefinite
white domination in East Africa gained greater momentum in the 1950s,
when the prediction of African paramountcy began to be realized.

The year 1945 in fact marked the beginning of the transitional period—of rapid and numerous constitutional changes—that transferred power in the Crown colonies. This constitutional evolution saw the development especially of the institutions of the legislative council, the executive council, and the judiciary. Changes in the institution of the executive council included the limitation or split of the governor's combined key functions of sovereign, prime minister, speaker, permanent head of the civil service, and chief liaison officer between the mother country and the colony. The executive council system was also evolved into a cabinet-like system, in which the governor was first among equals, assisted by a sort of "inner cabinet" of senior officers. The later executive council system also included the leaders and representatives of the unofficial majority, who were normally more experienced and successful older statesmen and would correspond to ordinary ministers in a cabinet system. This entire body of administrators was known as the "principal instrument of policy" for the government of the colonial country. The heads of departments were responsible to the governor through the colonial secretary.

When the ministerial system proper was introduced, the colonial administration was organized in a series of departments under one minister, a permanent (or principal) secretary, and the various department heads. That was the beginning of the ministerial system in East Africa as we know it today.

Similarly, the so-called member system was introduced and applied with considerable success in East Africa. Any selected person became a member of parliament for a particular aspect of administration, such as agriculture; though not a head of a department, he spoke for that department in the legislative council. He was a specialist in a particular field. In this way, token representation in the colonies gave way to genuine self-rule, and nationalist movements were transformed into well-organized political parties with mass support throughout East Africa, until independence was granted to them. Constitutional evolution in East Africa reached maturity in 1959, when the "winds of change" really started to blow in the opposite direction with maximum force and speed. The long process in the melting away and unscrambling of the British Empire reached a climax. The "winds of change" policy introduced in 1959 by Macmillan involved a new colonial policy whose central purpose was to prepare the East African and other British colonial peoples and territories for early independence. The reasons for the decision to change British colonial policy included, first, the desire to concentrate on, and settle, Britain's own pressing problems at home and in Europe before getting involved in the problems of others. To do this, Britain had to liberate her colonies at once. Second, the new policy was a response to the reactivated strong spirit of nationalism and liberation movements in the colonies.

East Africans bitterly condemned—and still condemn—the alleged isolationism that runs through Asian culture and thought, plus their virtual lack of interest in, or responsibility for, the African people, their advancement, or the development of East Africa as a whole. These African accusations against the Asians are partly true and partly untrue. True, in the sense that Asians are, by nature, an isolated community that always wants to remain intact and pure; and untrue, in the sense that the contribution of the Asian community to the development of East Africa has been too immense to be disregarded.

However, to the Africans, multiracialism could not and cannot be an alternative to the racial problem in East Africa. Nothing is acceptable to Africans except racial equality. Nyerere of Tanganyika, for instance, has rightly argued that the problem of race in East Africa is one of living together in harmony and mutual respect. The majority of Africans did not question the right of Europeans and Asians to stay in East Africa, but the Africans demanded, and rightly so, to be masters of their own fate. This is still the case today. Africans reject the idea that the power to shape the destiny of their countries should be exclusively vested in the hands of alien and minority groups that aspire to uphold their own privileged positions and keep the African majority community in a state of inferiority in their own countries.

On the international level of responsibility, a comparison of the previously described mandate and trusteeship systems reveals that, first, the League of Nations Mandates Commission comprised private individuals (experts) who were not politicians representing their respective countries, while the UN Trusteeship Council comprises representatives of states that hence deal with political issues. Second, the trusteeship system contains a provision that facilitated the submission of petitions from the inhabitants of the Tanganyika Trust Territory, or from any other source, and a provision that a petitioner may appear in person to present his case orally before the Trusteeship Council or the General Assembly. Third, the UN system also provided for visits by UN missions to the trust territory, about once every three years. Each mission was normally composed of nine or ten persons: two from administering states, provided they were not nationals of the country administering the territory visited; two from nonadministering states; and five or six officials of the UN Secretariat. The missions normally spent three to six weeks in the trust territory, visiting hospitals, schools, and industrial institutions and meeting with native groups living in the various parts of the territory. The missions were also empowered by the Trusteeship Council to receive written and oral petitions later scrutinized at UN headquarters in New York. The reports submitted by the members of a mission were not binding upon the respective governments, although the Trusteeship Council attached great importance to the reports. These reports, plus an annual report by the administering power, and the information received from the petitioners, served as the basis for Trusteeship Council discussions and recommendations.

The basic similarity between the trusteeship and mandate systems lay in the common provision that Britain was to carry out the administration of Tanganyika, whereas the international community, through the Mandates Commission, and later the Trusteeship Council, would exercise supervisory functions. Britain's main responsibility was hence to prepare the "backward" peoples "to stand alone" in Tanganyika, while international supervision was intended to help the administering power improve its management and in any case to prevent that authority from exploiting the territory to its own advantage or neglecting its responsibility to advance the territory's welfare, that is, the political, social, economic, and educational prosperity of the territory. All in all, therefore, the trusteeship system came much more closely to grips with actual situations in Tanganyika than was possible under the more limited terms of the mandate system.

In the transfer of power to the native peoples of East Africa, the years 1960 to 1962 were what one might call the "vintage years" of British colonial constitution making. The British colonial secretaries who were keenly and greatly involved in the transfer of power were Ian Macleod (Conservative), 1959-61; Reginald Maulding (Conservative), 1961-62; Duncan Sandys (Conservative), 1963-64; and Anthony Greenwood (Labour), 1964-66.

It is notable also that the newly independent states of East Africa became republics on the first anniversary of their independence, except for Zanzibar. Moreover, the three East African Territories, like Nyasaland (Malawi), were not yet well prepared for independence when they got it. Racial and tribal problems were still acute at the time of independence. The lack of fighting was mainly due to the fact that almost every African in East Africa craved independence. So, when it came, the Africans preferred to have it, despite their lack of preparedness for it, rather than lose the golden opportunity. But even so, the state of unpreparedness was not suppressed completely, and thus in Zanzibar, a revolution was staged against the government of the newly independent island within a month of independence. Where colonial rule therefore collides with nationalism and unpreparedness for independence, the former should prevail. Perhaps it would have been better to uphold alien rule in East Africa until such time as the territories and their peoples would have been really ready for independence. At any rate, the blame for the state of affairs in East Africa certainly goes to Britain, which failed to prepare its East African colonies properly before the granting of independence to them.

The only territory that seemed ready for independence—when it got it—was Tanganyika. Apart from its international status, which we

have touched on above, there were other reasons why Tanganyika
achieved independence first in the region:

1. At Tanganyika's independence, its population was 98 percent
African, with only 3,000 European-owned estates, no white highlands,
no native reserves, and much less racial tension than, for instance,
in neighboring Kenya.
2. Tanganyika has 127 tribes, not one of which dominates the
country as do the Kikuyu in Kenya. Nyerere had thus to fight on one
front only—against the British—whereas the Zanzibari, Kenyan, and
Ugandan nationalist leaders had to fight on two fronts—against the
British on the one hand and versus competitive tribes on the other.
3. There were no language problems in Tanganyika. Tanganyikan tribes can understand one another, because Swahili—thanks to the
early history of Tanganyika and the educational system devised by
Stanley Rivers Smith, and Travers Lacey in the early 1920s—is Tanganyika's lingua franca.
4. In Tanganyika, a peaceful and headlong road to independence
via constitutional advances was quickly established already in the early
days of alien rule.
5. Nyerere had the integrity, intellect, organizing talents, and
ability to translate his idealism into popular and practical terms.
6. Nyerere had an excellent personal relationship with Governor
Turnbull.
7. Nyerere is a Zanaki. The Zanaki are one of the smallest
tribes in Tanganyika. Hence Nyerere's rise to great prominence did
not arouse tribal jealousies.

CONCLUSIONS

Britain, Belgium, Germany, France, and Holland certainly had
a revolutionary impact on their colonies. And although the degree of
this impact differed from one colony to another, European powers ruled
their colonies aggressively and ruthlessly. Unlike the Portuguese,
whose dependencies were not colonies but overseas "provinces" of
Portugal, the British accepted the idea that colonial territories that
were held in trust must be led toward independence. Colonial dependence must be only a temporary phase. Although the strategy of decolonization was sound and generally acceptable, the tactics tended
to proceed crookedly. The errors that were made could, to a very
large extent, be attributed to the lack of preparation and the lack of
thought, both in turn owing to the lack of time as the pace of change
hastened, and to the steady evolution, which finally became a headlong rush. The colonial secretaries and officials had far too many

things on their hot plate at once. The result of this surfeit of immediate problems to be dealt with by the same small group of people was
the neglect of matters that did not cry out so urgently for attention.
Now, therefore, that the British Empire has melted away, it is necessary to build new relationships between Britain and her former East
African (and other) colonies. The problems that now remain are those
of race and geography. To solve them, it is essential to regain
quickly a sense of mission and purpose.

The reasons for the refusal to grant a speedy independence to
the East African colonial territories and their peoples included (1)
their "backward" economy; (2) their lack of skills and industrial experience; (3) the problem of managing the affairs of the fairly large
region inhabited by diverse and warlike native communities; (4) the
fact that Kenya and the other East African territories were heterogene-
ous societies (mixed societies with racial and communal tensions and
antagonisms); (5) the lack of educated native administrators; (6) the fact
that special colonial interests had to be satisfied first; (7) injured
pride, deeming the opponents of colonialism to be hypocritical, ig-
norant, and worse than the colonizers; and (8) the desire not to leave
people whom one has taught to care for freedom to their own devices
before they are ready for it.

Freedom is not easy to establish. It depends on institutions and
habits that do not emerge of themselves as soon as a colony gets independence. Thus subjects striving for independence may get it, but
fail to get freedom, because they got independence too quickly. Thus
the capacity for freedom is an important condition for independence.
Also, the would-be independent peoples should be able to afford security of person and good government and produce native rulers strong
enough and sufficiently responsible to respect international law.

The division of East Africa into white and colored peoples is
merely an outcome of European conquests and the spread of European
civilization. It can be argued that if the Bantu were overwhelmingly
the wealthiest and most powerful race, East Africa, and for that matter the world, might be divided into the black and the "pale" peoples,
the Chinese and Asians being reckoned with the Europeans among the
"pale" peoples. The difference in color is an outward symbol of other
differences: white peoples have ruled colored peoples, but not the
other way about. The whites are generally richer than the "coloreds"
and have usually moved a good deal further in the direction of advancement.

Kenya, Tanganyika, and Uganda belonged to those unfortunate
colonies whose boundary delimitations were mere "geographical expressions." Each tribe, particularly in Kenya and Uganda, regarded
itself as a "separate or little nation," because of the diverse traditions, customs, cultures, and languages that existed in the tribal re-

gions. The grave mistake, therefore, that the colonizers made was to amass, divide, or separate all these territories into one nation, whether by treaty or on paper. The results of this colonial blunder were tribal conflicts, and even wars, and problems arising from the new different laws, traditions, tribal rulers, and obligations, which were quite dissimilar to the former ones, under which the native peoples had been brought up. The evils and negative repercussions of that colonial error are felt even today. The colonizers were determined to create sovereign nations within the very "geographical expressions" they had demarcated in East Africa 70 years earlier. Perhaps the greatest outcome of the imposition of alien rule in the East African region was the transformation of that region not into a white man's country or an Indian colony but a multiracial society in which the various ethnic, racial groups, whether citizens of aliens, black or "pale," could live together and play their various roles. The place and role of aliens in independent East Africa will be the topic of analysis in the next chapter.

NOTES

1. See S. S. Goodspeed, The Nature and Function of International Organization (London: Oxford University Press, 1954), pp. 18-20. See also Hans Kohn, The Idea of Nationalism (New York: Macmillan, 1945).

2. Quoted in Transition 27 (1966), p. 16.

3. For a detailed discussion of the Maji-Maji uprising, see Judith Listowel, The Making of Tanganyika (London: Chatto and Windus, 1965), p. 34.

4. For details see Britain, Command Paper no. 7081, 1946.

5. Transition, op. cit., p. 18.

6. Ibid.

7. See Fred Majdalany, State of Emergency: The Full Story of the "Mau-Mau" (London: Longman, 1962).

8. Attorney General's Office, 5520: "Hemsted to J. W. T. McClellan," March 21, 1913. Lane was nicknamed "Maji Moto" (hot water) because of his hot temper.

6

**PLACE AND ROLE
OF ALIENS IN
INDEPENDENT
EAST AFRICA**

STATE SUCCESSION AND "CIVILIZATION"
IN EAST AFRICA

Any real and exhaustive study and thorough understanding of the role and position of aliens in the new East Africa must be based on extensive, original academic research into the deep and primary sources of information available on this topic. The complex international legal implications of state succession in East Africa or the transfer of power or change of sovereignty from Britain to the newly independent states of East Africa will not be examined in detail here. Emancipation from the mother country was the way of transferring power from the predecessor states to the successor states in East Africa. The issue of acquired rights of aliens, which every successor state has a duty, under international law, to protect, will be examined at a later stage. Britain, which as the predecessor state concluded treaties with other powers, had an option—in international law at least —to conclude either what one might call "personal" treaties, that is, those essentially contractual treaties presupposing reciprocity between Britain and the other states with a view to an agreed end, or "impersonal" treaties, that is, those that would impress the East African colonial territories with some special legal status, and thus curtail the (British) element of sovereignty upon them. Britain chose the "personal" type, and therefore the new states of East Africa were not bound by the "personal" treaties. What, however, the newly independent states of East Africa have done is to maintain all treaty relationships for a fixed period after independence. They have also declared that, at the expiration of this period, all treaties the East African states did not affirm will be regarded as having lapsed, except those succeeded to under customary international law. Needless to say, this practice has the advantage that the East African states can discontinue treaty relationships at their option. However, the disadvantage of the East African practice is that any optional discontinuance on the part of an East African state would be a unilateral declaration. Also, it is administratively difficult to establish the position of any of the three states vis-a-vis each other in the fixed time in the declaration.

As for multilateral treaties, the emergence of the ex-colonial East African territories to full sovereignty presented the secretary general of the United Nations with the difficult problem of deciding whether to record the new states as parties to multilateral treaties, whether law-creating or not, or to require them to deposit instruments of accession. The practice adopted was the usual one: to treat the assignment of treaty rights and duties—as agreed with, or arranged by, the mother country—as effective at least when the successor state has communicated its acceptance to the UN secretary general and in the absence of objection from the other parties.[1]

The practice of the UN secretary general is to send to each new state a list of multilateral treaties of which he is depository, and to which the parent state was a party, asking the new state to declare its attitude. Each of the East African states decided to join, under Articles 4 and 102 of the UN Charter, the United Nations very shortly after independence: Tanzania joined the United Nations on December 14, 1961, Uganda on October 25, 1962, and Kenya on December 16, 1963. By deciding to join the United Nations, the East African countries voluntarily joined the so-called civilized community of states.

The expressions "civilized community," "civilized nations," and "civilization of states" are ambiguous. The concept appears only once in the UN Charter. In Article 38 of the Statute of the International Court of Justice (ICJ)—an integral part of the UN Charter—Section 1(c) reads: [The Court shall apply] the general principles of law recognized by civilized nations." The term "civilized nations" can be interpreted in a variety of ways. It may be interpreted, first, to mean any technologically advanced nations. It may further mean, according to one observer, "running contrary to the rules governing the interpretation of treaties to ignore it,"[2] that is, ignoring "civilized" and just "general principles of law recognized by the nations." The term "civilized" nations may also be interpreted to mean the principle behind Article 9 of the ICJ Statute, which reads:

> At every election, the electors shall bear in mind not
> only that the persons to be elected should individually
> possess the qualifications required, but also that in
> the body as a whole, the representation of the main
> forms of civilisation and of the principal legal systems
> of the world should be assured.

On this reasoning, the main forms of civilization and the principal legal systems of the world may be equated.[3] In a primitive area or nation, no settled body of legal principles to regulate relations between modern advanced societies can be expected to exist.

Finally, "civilized" nations may be contrasted with "savage" or "barbarian" nations, but the distinction is not always clear. This difficulty makes the question of civilization of states very complicated and controversial. It can, for instance, be argued that two kinds of states belong to the international community. The first includes states that are full members of international society because they are "civilized." The second consists of states that are semicivilized and hence can and do belong to the international community only insofar as they are bound by treaty to civilized states. In the international community, therefore, both civilized states and uncivilized or semicivilized states (that is, those not absorbed, or half-absorbed, into the ways of life of the civilized states) with different cultures, international structures, and economic and social philosophies, voluntarily agree to be united in a legal order and to share a common civilization, and to be bound by certain rules of international law that are common to all states, but that fix conditions within which states exercise their jurisdiction. The purpose of these common rules is to achieve a standard for "civilized" behavior. The expression "civilized" states originally meant European (Christian) nations only. When these European nations forced their way of life on other nations, which had their own civilization and cultures, the term "civilized" nation was extended to include all states that accepted, practiced, and developed the standard of European civilization.[4]

In East Africa, the "period of transition" (transferring power to the states) has been characterized by numerous errors and problems; East Africans could not be expected to achieve, in 13 years (1945-58) what took the "old" nations 13 centuries to achieve.

For one thing, lack of well-trained local staffs is a problem of public service, which became more serious over the years because the organization of the British colonial service failed in preparing the East African colonial territories adequately for independence in the foreseeable future. After independence, the East African natives were still faced with the same problem of finding competent staffs to carry on the work left behind by the colonial administrators. Who was to blame in the circumstances? Both the colonial power and the emerging independent state were to blame. A solution to the staff problems in the would-be independent countries of East Africa would perhaps have been found, if only the British Colonial Service had been reorganized in time. The African nations must also bear responsibility for the resulting situation, because they pressed for independence and got it prematurely. According to the British government's esti-

mate following the "winds of change" policy, East Africa was not to
become independent until after the 1960s. Tanganyika's independence
was set for 1970. Uganda would follow Tanganyika's independence,
and Kenya's independence was calculated for 1975 or thereafter. It
would therefore certainly have been better for the East Africans to
press for a more accelerated preparation for independence. If this
had been done with success, many of the problems—including those
of aliens—facing the newly independent nations of East Africa today
would have been reduced. But with the attainment of independence
prematurely, the new East African states were forced to enter into
treaty arrangements with Britain—the ex-colonial power—for the retention of the latter's overseas service in East Africa. Whereas,
therefore, the new East African governments were faced with the crucial problem of maintaining, on contract, former experienced colonial
staffs whose services the governments still needed, Britain was faced
with the major problem of assisting the East African governments to
find staffs from outside until they could recruit their own locally.
These treaty arrangements are still carried on by the East African
governments not only with Britain but also with other foreign governments.

LEGAL POSITION OF ARABS IN EAST
AFRICA: A RESTATEMENT

Racial minorities in present-day East Africa are divided into
citizens and aliens. Arabs in East Africa, who, like Asians and Europeans, are distinguished from Africans culturally and physically, are
not regarded as aliens. They are classified as citizens not so much
because they have resided in East Africa longer than any other racial
minority group, but mainly by legal definition. This is a point that
must be emphasized again and again. An authoritative local newspaper, for instance, has noted, in regard to the legal position of Arabs
in Kenya: "Locally born Arabs who have lived at the Coast for several
generations did not really have citizenship problems, as all of them
were automatic citizens under the Kenya Constitution."[5]
In another instance, the Community Relations Committee of the
National Christian Council of Kenya (NCCK) followed up on a debate
in the Kenya Parliament on April 17, 1973, which came after a motion
by S. M. Abdalla, the member of parliament for Mombasa North, for
the creation of a special commission on the eligibility for Kenya citizenship of a number of people, mainly at the Coast, who were born of
mixed marriages between Africans on the one hand and Arabs or Asians
on the other; the NCCK committee concluded that the assumption that
such persons had to apply for and obtain citizenship "was plainly false,

as a look at the relevant section of the [Kenya] Constitution clearly
shows." The committee noted further:

> The situation was further confused by statements sug-
> gesting that automatic citizenship applies only when
> the father is a citizen, and not when the mother is a
> citizen. . . . No one [during the debate] understood
> that the people being talked about were automatic
> citizens—that is to say, they became citizens by vir-
> tue of law on December 12, 1963, if born before that
> date. The relevant section of the Constitution is Sec-
> tion 87 (i). . . . Applications could also be made for
> citizenship under Section 88. The Constitution makes
> no distinction with regard to the sex of the parents born
> in Kenya for Section 87 to apply, as suggested by some
> participants in the debate. . . . Section 89 provides
> for automatic citizenship except only in special circum-
> stances, such as for example if the father possesses
> diplomatic immunity. . . . [This is] the correct legal
> position [of such persons, which was] not understood
> by the Members of Parliament. The correctness of
> this position has been verified with the appropriate
> legal authorities. [6]

COMMUNAL AND RACIAL CONFLICTS IN
INDEPENDENT EAST AFRICA

The origins of racial and communal tensions in East Africa can
be traced to the establishment of caravan routes by the Arabs to secure
trade in ivory and slaves. British interests, involving Europeans and
Asians, followed in the second half of the 19th century. The causes of
racial conflicts in the new East Africa are centered on two significant
factors: the economic gap between Africans and non-Africans, and
social impediments between Africans and non-Africans. Thus the
causes of the conflicts include: (1) the adherence by the racial minorities to their own racial, linguistic, and religious differentiations; (2)
the failure by the East African states to create an identification of
political and national divisions; (3) the resentment of, or the tendency
by the East African majority to resent, the presence of the racial
minorities—who are an unassimilated mass—in its body politic; and
(4) the feeling of the African majority that it possesses a national
characteristic in which the minority groups do not, and perhaps cannot, share.

It is extremely difficult to define such terms as "race" and "race relations." It is therefore probably better not to use them at all. However, it seems too much to hope for that the use of the terms "race relations," "race," and, for that matter, "racial" will be limited to those things that are genetically determined. Those who use the term the "Polish race," for instance, probably use it quite vaguely and would be able to justify it only by thinking of linguistic or political unity. Anyone who imagines that the inhabitants of Poland represent a single physical type is quite wrong. In Kenya, for instance, we may attain political unity, but if linguistic unity is not achieved, the creation of a homogeneous society will surely be frustrated. We cannot, even if linguistic unity is achieved in Kenya, claim in all conceivable circumstances to belong to a single race. The idea of "purity of race" is a concept of political propaganda, not based on any scientific description of human groups today. The main reason why many politicians pseudoscientifically classify peoples is to maintain a distinction between various groups in society, thereby perpetuating their monopoly of certain "good things" in society.

Race is thus very often used as a political weapon. Basically, there are two kinds of racial discrimination: discrimination practiced by a racial majority toward a minority; and discrimination practiced by a racial minority toward a majority. Four subcategories of discrimination stem from these major categories: discrimination approved by a state (as in South Africa); discrimination practiced by a racial group (or section of a population) in a multiracial society; discrimination practiced by a dominant group belonging to a particular race or religion (as in Northern Ireland or prepartitioned India); and discrimination based upon traditional prejudices, ignorance, and lack of mutual understanding.

East Africa has experienced the above types of discrimination in one form or another. Postindependence East Africa has experienced more discrimination by the racial majority (Africans) against racial minority groups than the other way around.

Racial attitudes in postindependence East Africa are found in every racial group, although politicians and other people say there is no room for racialism in East Africa. Government policy is one thing, and actual practice another. It is not uncommon to hear an African, for instance, say "this Asian," when an Asian drives along the road at a very high speed. Thus one whole racial group is singled out and condemned just because of a mistake made by an individual belonging to that racial group; it is an error resulting both from irrational generalization and racial attitudes. Furthermore, race relations in East Africa have always been influenced by many factors—such as politics, religion, race, skin color, and cultures—but the main influence on these relations has come from two forces: economics and law. This is still the case today. On the economic impact on race relations, problems of intraracial relations arise whenever movements of populations occur from one part of the world to another, because of economic reasons.

At independence, the East African society still was characterized by (1) residential segregation, (2) occupational segregation, that is, members of a community restricting themselves to certain occupations vis-a-vis the rest of the population, and providing a measure of self-sufficiency by having a fuller range of occupations, (3) group isolation, that is, a member of the community not becoming a part of the rest of the population, and vice versa, and (4) the roles of the members of the community being defined in such a way as to have two interpretations, one of which constitutes an ingroup behavior, and the other an outgroup behavior.

Outgroup and ingroup categories of people still exist in East Africa. By "outgroup" is meant all those social groups in East Africa whose way of life sets them apart from the mainstream of thought and action. Thus not only are racial minorities embraced but also those tribal groups like the Karamajong of Uganda, which are socially and geographically isolated. Thus outgroups in East Africa comprise both aliens and citizens. Of the ingroups, the most basic is the family.

Although Afro-Asian relationships in East Africa have, generally speaking, changed in the postindependence era, the popular conception, especially among the African population, is that Asians still stick to many of their isolationist and other characteristics of the caste system. These characteristics, it is argued, continue to cause racial and even communal tensions in the region. However, evidence of this assertion has still to be established, since neither accurate reasons nor statistics have so far been given in support of the African argument.

ASIAN ROLES IN INDEPENDENT EAST AFRICA

In postindependent East Africa, the main contribution of Asians has been in the economic field.[7] Thus despite outcries against Asian "exploitation" and despite government plans for transfer of the economy to Africans, Asians in independent East Africa continue to play vital roles in the economic field of the region.

The strong economic position of Asians is one of the major causes of racial tensions in present-day East Africa. The problem is so huge that it culminated in the expulsion of Asians by the East African states.

One further Asian role that needs to be mentioned here occurs in the political field. The racial stereotype of Asians being dishonest, crafty, and out to exploit the poor Africans was, like any other racial

stereotype, essentially a function of a given power structure. The acquisition of power by East Africans has clearly changed their attitudes.
Asians in East Africa never had the backing of the political power to
carry out cultural or political expansion. What Asians in East Africa
did—and continue to do—was to preserve their indigenous cultures.
The reason for the persistence, therefore, of the Asian racial stereotype is the fact that Asians have no political power in postindependence
East Africa. Whatever the rights and wrongs of the matter, no East
African nation seems able to tolerate—and for that matter no other
nation in the world seems able to tolerate—a culturally alien, relatively
affluent, and physically distinct minority in its midst. This is a fact
that Asians and other similar racial minorities in East Africa must
realize and face.

However, effective Asian integration at the political level would
certainly nowadays facilitate a sympathetic and successful ending of
many of their economic and social problems in East Africa. Also,
the trend in the same region toward one-party systems bodes well for
Asian survival, because it provides security from the fear of being
subjected to criticism or persecution by a party the Asians do not back.

It would, however, be quite wrong to say that Asian political involvement in East Africa is totally lacking. Asian participation in
East African politics in quite lively, especially in Tanzania. For instance, in the general election in Zanzibar in 1965, three Asians
were elected to parliament, all of them in overwhelmingly African con-
stituencies. If Asians continue to show absolute loyalty to their host
East African state and genuinely support, participate in, and maintain
uniformity in the political life of the country, there is no reason why
they should not play important political roles in East Africa.

Political activities among the Asians of East Africa are pursued
through associations such as municipal councils, town and district education boards, celebration and fund-raising committees, local branches
of major political parties, and in some towns, employers' associations.
In these associations, Asian leaders represent the entire Asian community, on the one hand, and the wider Afro-Asian community, on the
other. Thus, although no Asian politicians now exist to represent
Asian interests in the East African parliaments (except one in Tanzania) political activities in the three countries are still interpreted to
Asians by their own fellow Asian leaders. The same can be said of
religious and other denominational activities and interests of Asians
in East Africa.

EUROPEAN ROLES IN INDEPENDENT EAST AFRICA

The spheres in which the roles of Europeans have changed in independent East Africa are political, economic, educational, military,

religious, technical assistance, women's programs, and voluntary organizations. The political sphere was the most important field that the Europeans controlled completely before independence. After independence, most of the posts were Africanized, although a few were Kenyanized, Ugandanized, or Tanzanianized. In the field of administration, Europeans have really no role to play in present-day East Africa. The complete replacement of the colonial doctrine of communal roll by that of common roll mainly accounted for the absence of aliens in the legislatures and governments of three states.

Immediately after independence, trade was still largely in the hands of Europeans and Asians. Of late, especially following the intensification of the Africanization and/or nationalization programs, the process of transferring trade and the economy to the Africans has reached a climax. Expatriates, however, still hold key positions in some of the key specialized branches of the economy. Expatriates now work on contracts normally for two years each, and these are renewable. Therefore, the presence of aliens in these key positions of the economy is likely still to be felt for a long time to come.

In the educational field, the European role was played by missionaries and European expatriates, especially at secondary and university levels. Though Africans are taking over, foreigners are still maintained on contracts. The terms of contract in the three universities of East Africa—in Nairobi, Kampala, and Dar-es-Salaam—call for very high academic qualifications and extensive experience. Except in a few cases, the minimum requirement for acceptance as a teacher in the universities is now a Ph.D. degree.

Before independence, European representation in the military was very high. Since independence, Europeans have been replaced by Africans, but some European citizens in the region are still in military employment. Also, foreigners still train Africans in military jobs. East Africans are also trained abroad (including China). In Tanzania, for example, Chinese military advisers and technocrats are still in existence in large numbers.

The role of Europeans in the religious field is still played by European missionaries. However, the church has been considerably Africanized in East Africa, and Africanization of the church is still growing at a rapid speed. The great overall missionary contribution to the development of East Africa has been recognized and is still likely to be felt in the region for a long time to come.

In the sphere of technical assistance, many European expatriates are still found in the technical departments of government in East Africa. Terms of contract are usually laid down in agreements.

The UN technical (and other) assistance programs launched in the East African states also involve personnel, but their case is different, because they work in East Africa as international officials

whose legal position, privileges, and immunities in East Africa are
regulated by special UN conventions that we need not elaborate on
here. Thus it is in the field of technical assistance that the contribution of expatriates in East Africa is greatest. The ministries most
affected are economic development and planning, works, agriculture,
power and communications, education, health, justice, and natural
resources. Training and research institutions are also still filled
with expatriates. Africans cannot acquire the required qualifications
and expertise overnight. The number of African professionals in the
above fields is growing, but the point of saturation in all the fields
is still remote. The present writer does not share the views of some
East Africans, notably ordinary politicians and even ministers, that
the field of arts is already saturated with qualified Africans. Education, then, still needs to be stepped up in all the fields of life in East
Africa. Women's programs, in which many Europeans used to dominate, have been Africanized, but there are still a few women advisers
from UN bodies in the area. More local women's organizations have
been formed.

During colonial times, voluntary organizations like the Red
Cross were filled with Europeans. Nowadays, Africans occupy the
top executive jobs in the local branches of these organizations. However, even in their policies of Africanization, the East African governments can localize their industries only to a certain point. No country
in the world can be completely independent of other countries. The
East African states depend on foreign expertise and foreign people to
stimulate the East African economies.

A particularly remarkable change in the position of Europeans—
and Asians—in East Africa occurred in the field of law. The revised
laws of Tanganyika (1947), Kenya (1948), and Uganda (1951) clearly
show that the laws enacted specifically to regulate race relations in
East Africa included the African Authority Ordinance in Uganda; the
Compulsory Labour Regulation Ordinance in Kenya; and the Penal
Codes and Prisons Ordinances of the East African territories. There
were also laws that enabled separate courts to be set up, such as the
native courts (in Uganda and Tanganyika) and the African courts (in
Kenya under the 1951 ordinance). All these courts dealt with criminal
cases in which the accused was an African, and civil cases in which
the defendant was an African (and, in Uganda, in which all parties
were Africans). Non-Africans went before a magistrate or the high
court of the territory concerned. Europeans enjoyed, particularly in
Kenya, the significant privilege of trial by a jury that was composed
of Europeans only. The high courts heard such cases with a jury.
In Kenya and Uganda, the Prisons Ordinances distinctly called for the
separation, wherever possible, of African, Asian, and European pri-
soners, while different diets were provided for each by what was de-

scribed as "administrative justice." In Tanganyika, the Prisons Ordinance made no mention of race and did not specifically call for racial
segregation. The prison regulations in that territory, however, laid
down three different diets: English potatoes and butter, suited to the
Europeans; curry powder, ghee, and rice, suited to the Asians; and
beans, maize, and sweet potatoes, the usual food of Africans.

With independence just around the corner, the above laws were
repealed (in 1960 and 1961) and replaced by those currently in force.
For example, Section 159 of the Kenya Penal Code, which had made
sexual commerce between a white woman and an African man an offense, was repealed in 1961. However, the East African territories
entered independence with a good number of laws still in force that
distinguished between people on the basis of race. Race distinctions
in East Africa are now made—legally at least—not on the basis of
color (the laws of the independent East African states are now actually
color-blind) but on the basis of citizenship and alienage. Citizenship
is now a matter of residence and allegiance, and not of skin color.

THE LEGAL POSITION OF ALIENS IN
INDEPENDENT EAST AFRICA

The legal position of the European—and the Asian—changed considerably following independence in East Africa. The two systems of
courts that had existed under the colonial regime simply vanished:
the native courts in which minor offenses had been tried by native
law and custom, and in which it had been impossible to arraign a non-
African; and the central courts in which it had been impossible either
to try persons of any race for offenses against territorial code or to
hear an appeal from the native courts. This arrangement, though discriminatory on racial grounds, had actually been intended to protect
African interests. However, discrimination cannot and should not be
accepted in an independent state, and thus in Tanganyika, from January 1964, for example, a new system of local courts was created in
which persons of any race could be tried.

THE POSITION UNDER INTERNATIONAL LAW

The rules of international law concerning the position of aliens
are mainly general principles of customary international law, because
they are mainly derived from state practice, which obviously varies
from one state to another. Written international law, however, which
is treaty law, also often contains general principles that regulate the
status of aliens abroad. Thus bipartite or multipartite treaties of co-

operation, mutual assistance, friendship, and so forth often contain detailed provisions for the admission, exclusion, or deportation, for instance, of aliens. Apart from the spheres of admission, exclusion, and deportation of aliens, international law regulates the rights and duties of states and aliens in five other basic areas: the rights of aliens; the duties of aliens; expropriation of alien property; asylum; and the status of the refugee or stateless person. Foremost among the rights of a state in its dealings with aliens is the right to legislate over aliens. Modern authorities on public international law are unanimous on this view. [8]

The exercise of territorial or domestic jurisdiction over aliens represents one of the logical repercussions of the possession of sovereignty or independence by states.

In the sphere of admission, no state is under a duty to admit aliens into its territory. Every state has the power and right to forbid the entry of aliens into its territory or to admit them in such cases and on such conditions as it may deem proper to prescribe. In most cases, the classes of aliens that are freely admitted are those of students and tourists. Foreigners who come as immigrants are usually subject to relatively severe regulation. The criteria that states take into account when admitting aliens into their territories include safety, health, public order, and morals.

Aliens who are excluded from entry or residence are normally sent back to the country of last residence. If, however, that country refuses to accept them, aliens are then sent to the country of their nationality.

The legal position of aliens once admitted within the territorial jurisdiction of states thus depends, in the first place, on the judgment of the host government. It is the latter that decides what rights, other than protection of life and property, shall be conceded to aliens. Most states have been willing, in the more recent decades, to grant to aliens civil rights substantially the same as those enjoyed by the nationals of those states, while at the same time denying to aliens the political rights and privileges enjoyed by those nationals.

As regards ownership of property, aliens are, in certain countries, prohibited from owning or operating specific types of business subject to grants of licenses by the national government, grants that by law are available only to citizens of the state in question.

One of the more controversial aspects of domestic jurisdiction over aliens involves their induction into the armed forces or labor services of the host state. For very obvious security reasons, only "friendly" aliens, that is, neutral citizens or citizens opposed ideologically or in some other manner to a hostile government, are conscripted in time of war. Most countries reward military service by citizenship, often through a greatly accelerated procedure of naturalization.

Thus on the rights of aliens in general, international law requires that aliens once lawfully admitted to a state's territory should be granted certain minimum rights essential for the enjoyment of ordinary private life. International law prohibits states from depriving aliens of rights of contract, of acquisition of personal property, or of marriage and family rights.

The political rights denied to aliens under the approval of international law include the rights to vote, hold public office, or engage in political activities. Those rights allowed to aliens are frequently prescribed in treaties of commerce. In contemporary international law, the trend is toward the assimilation of the rights of aliens to those of citizens by virtue of the national treatment clause inscribed in many treaties, by which the citizens of each contracting state enjoy the same prescribed substantive rights in the territory of the other as its citizens. Further, the so-called most-favored-nation clause—by which one party grants to the other automatically any right or benefit it extends to a third state—tends to give equal rights to aliens of different nationalities in a given state.

Some states impose specific controls and restrictions on the acquisition by aliens of interests in, or management of, public utilities or enterprises engaged in such areas as water or air transport and the exploitation of land and other natural resources.

The state authority must pay due respect to the liberty, life, and property of resident aliens. The state is responsible for any failure to exercise due diligence in affording protection to aliens against any eventual act wrongfully committed by any person. The state authority must detect and identify any persons committing an act wrongfully against aliens in order to give the latter full opportunities to recover damages from the former. The state may also be responsible for failing to take reasonable measures to apprehend and punish the offender in order that offenses of a similar nature against aliens should not occur in the future. The question of state responsibility for aliens will be examined in greater detail in Chapter 7.

Aliens have the right to leave the state of their residence, and this is unqualified unless their local duties, such as payment of taxes, private debts, fines, and so forth, have not been cleared. Departing aliens must be allowed to take their possessions with them on the same conditions as citizens. As for state jurisdiction over alien corporations, international law requires states to allow alien corporations to carry on business within state territorial jurisdiction, but such discretionary permission entails adherence by the enterprise concerned to all regulations issued for them by the state in question.

A state exercises an exclusive, sovereign right in the field of expulsion of aliens. The right to expel aliens is not limited even by treaties guaranteeing the right of residence to the citizens of other

contracting states. Every state is free to determine, by its own criteria, the grounds for expulsion of an alien. However, this does not
mean that a state is at liberty to abuse the right of expulsion. The
state of nationality of an expelled alien may assert the right to inquire
into the reasons for the alien's expulsion, and into the sufficiency of
proof of the charges on which the expulsion is based.

In time of war, a belligerent state is entitled to expel all enemy
aliens within its territory. In time of peace, however, aliens may be
expelled only in the interests of public order, or welfare, or for reasons of state security, whether internal or external.

The judiciary may sometimes have power to interfere in the case
of an abuse of discretion by the executive, but aliens, especially in
the new nations and in the communist world, are not always given the
right to challenge the decision of the executive before the judiciary.
Furthermore, deportation should not be carried out with violence or
hardship or unnecessary harm to the expelled alien. There should be
no compulsory detention of an alien under an expulsion order, unless
in cases that warrant that. Also, an alien should be given enough time
to settle personal affairs before leaving the country and should be
allowed to choose the country to which he may apply for admission.

Thus every sovereign and independent state has an exclusive,
inherent, and inalienable right to admit, prohibit, exclude, prevent,
deport, or expel aliens who have neither been naturalized nor have
taken any measures toward becoming citizens of the state. This right
is essential for the state's independence, safety, and welfare. The
right is inscribed in the constitution of every country.

With regard to asylum, no state is, by international law, obligated to surrender an alien to a foreign state, or to expel him from
its own territory, unless some particular restriction or obligation has
been accepted in this regard. Also, the state of which an alien is a
national is not entitled to exercise physical control over him during
his residence in the territory of another state, despite its competence
to exercise jurisdiction over him through its domestic courts for offenses committed by him abroad, when he returns to his national territory. Hence a state can be an asylum for an alien who has been deported from, or has fled, the state of his origin or residence.

Asylum is usually granted to political offenders or political
refugees who are aliens or stateless persons. A political refugee may
be defined as an alien who has left, or has been forced to leave, his
country because of persecution for religious, ethnic, or political reasons.

The granting of asylum to political refugees and offenders is a
humanitarian and peaceful act. No international responsibility arises
for the state granting such asylum. Because international law does
not guarantee the right of asylum to anybody, and thus the right is ex-

ercised solely at the discretion of the state, it has been generally argued that the asylum is not a right at all. Hence the alien may not demand it from the foreign state in whose territory he seeks to reside.

Closely connected with asylum is extradition. The latter was defined in the Harvard Research Draft Convention on Extradition as "the formal surrender of a person by a state to another state for prosecution or punishment."[9] Extradition treaties and international comity often condition the right of the state to grant asylum. In cases of extradition, the need arises to punish offenders who have escaped from one state to another. The question of extradition falls wholly within the domestic jurisdiction of the state to which the fugitive offender has escaped.

As for refugees and stateless persons, their legal position has been outlined in a number of international conventions. A particularly noteworthy convention on the subject was the Convention Relating to the Status of Refugees, unanimously adopted at a conference convened by the United Nations in 1951.[10] In 1954, the UN Economic Council (ECOSOC) also convened a conference, which eventually adopted the so-called Convention Relating to the Status of Stateless Persons.[11] These two conventions contain excellent provisions on the rights and duties of refugees and stateless persons.

Refugees and stateless persons have duties to the country in which they find themselves. They are required to conform to the country's laws and regulations as well as to measures taken for the maintenance of public order. The contracting state must accord to them at least the same treatment accorded to its nationals, with respect to their freedom of religion and the religious education of their children, and at least the same treatment accorded to aliens generally concerning the acquisition of movable and immovable property; the right to engage in agriculture, industry, and the like, and to establish commercial or industrial companies; the practice of the liberal professions; housing; higher education; and so on. For the ordinary purposes of municipal law, therefore, refugees and stateless persons fall under the category of aliens. These two categories of people legally in the territory of a contracting state are not to be expelled save to preserve national security or public order, and their expulsion must follow a due process of law. Furthermore, a refugee is not to be expelled or returned in any manner whatsoever to the frontiers of territories where his freedom or life would be menaced, on account of his religion, race, nationality, political opinion, or membership in a particular social group.

THE EAST AFRICAN LAW OF ALIENS

The East African states have a common area of laws of aliens, although some laws are more detailed in one country than related laws are in another. The laws appear in the form of acts or decrees adopted at different times after independence, or before independence but amended in the postindependence era.[12] The legal position of aliens in East Africa is regulated by constitutional provisions and other laws, which, although they appear under different titles, are common in the three states. These laws affect aliens in the fields of citizenship; immigration (including work permits); business (licensing and transfers); nationalization; public order and security (police functions); civil, criminal, and penal cases; extradition; and marriage.

The scope of application of the immigration laws of the East African states is confined to aliens. However, the Uganda and Tanzania Immigration Acts of 1969 and 1972, respectively, state that the laws may be applied to citizens of the two countries if their immigration authorities deem it necessary to do so in order to determine the status of such persons. Also, a citizen of Tanzania or Uganda is liable to be proceeded against, convicted, and punished, for any offense he may commit against laws that the minister responsible for immigration matters may make, requiring that person (if an employer) to furnish information with respect to the persons he employs. Required in particular is information regarding citizenship, the nature of employment, qualifications and experience needed for such employment, and training programs for such employment.

Of special significance are the legal provisions pertaining to the work permit system. "Work permit" is actually the commercial expression for "entry permit" (as it is called in Uganda and Kenya, or "residence permit" as it is known in Tanzania), which is the legal term of the system. Any alien who intends to enter an East African country must possess (1) a valid entry certificate of residence normally issued to a permanently resident alien; (2) a valid entry permit —issued normally to an alien who desires to take up some sort of employment; (3) a valid pass—issued normally to an alien who desires to enter or reenter and remain in an East African country temporarily, that is, during the validity of the pass; or (4) any other legal authority, for example, an exemption or exclusion certificate. Aliens must, before they are issued with the above documents, fulfill any conditions that may be laid down by the minister, or under the immigration laws.

In Tanzania, a work permit issued to an alien is valid within such time as the principal immigration officer may specify. In Uganda, it is valid within one year after the date of its issue. But the Immigration Control Board—whose functions are similar to those of the principal immigration officers of Tanzania and Kenya—may in its absolute discretion extend the said time limit of one year for such period, but not exceeding two years, as it may consider expedient. The Uganda Immigration Control Board, comprising a chairman and six to eight other members all appointed by the minister in charge of immigration, has power to delegate, in writing, any or all of its functions relating to dependants' passes, visitors' passes, and special passes to the principal immigration officer. The latter is the secretary to the board; members serve for two years and can be reappointed.

The Work Permit System in Kenya

In Kenya, a work permit is valid within six months only of the date of issue thereof. However, an immigration officer has power to extend, at his discretion, the validity of a work permit for a further period of six months. Kenya makes the following 12 classes of work permits available to aliens.

1. A Class A permit is granted to an alien who is offered specific employment by a specific employer, who is qualified to undertake that employment, and whose engagement in that employment will be of benefit to Kenya.

2. A Class B permit is granted to an alien who is offered specific employment by the Kenya government, the East African community or any other person or authority under the control of the government or community, and whose engagement in that employment will be of benefit to Kenya.

3. A Class C permit is granted to an alien who is offered specific employment under an approved technical aid scheme under the UN Organization, or some other approved agency (not being an exempted person, that is, as specified by the minister of immigration or a diplomat or consul and their wives and children), and whose engagement in that employment will be of benefit to Kenya.

4. A Class D permit is granted to an alien holding a dependant's pass who is offered specific employment by a specific employer, and whose engagement in that employment will be of benefit to Kenya.

5. A Class E permit is granted to an alien who is a member of a missionary society approved by the Kenya government, and whose presence in Kenya will be of benefit to Kenya.

6. A Class F permit is offered to an alien who intends to engage, whether alone or in partnership, in the business of agriculture or animal husbandry in Kenya; who has acquired, or has received, all permissions necessary to acquire an interest in land of sufficient size and suitability for the purpose; who has in his own right and at his full and free disposition sufficient capital and other sources for

the purpose; and whose engagement in that business will be of benefit to Kenya.

7. A Class G permit is offered to an alien who intends to engage, whether alone or in partnership, in prospecting for minerals or mining in Kenya, and whose such permitted engagement will be of benefit to Kenya.

8. A Class H permit is offered to an alien who intends to engage, whether alone or in partnership, in a specific trade, business, or profession (other than a prescribed profession) in Kenya; who has obtained, or is assured of obtaining, any license, registration, or other authority or permission that may be necessary for the purpose; who has in his own right and at his full and free disposition sufficient capital and other resources for the purpose; and whose engagement in that trade, business, or profession will be to the benefit of Kenya.

9. A Class I permit is granted to an alien who intends to engage, whether alone or in partnership, in a specific manufacture in Kenya; who has obtained, or is assured of obtaining, any license, registration, or other authority or permission that may be necessary for the purpose; who has in his own right and at his full and free disposition sufficient capital and other resources for the purpose; and whose engagement in that manufacture will be of benefit to Kenya.

10. A Class J permit is granted to a member (alien) of a prescribed profession who intends to practice that profession, whether alone or in partnership in Kenya; who possesses the prescribed qualifications; who has in his own right and at his full and free disposition sufficient capital and other resources for the purpose; and whose practice of that profession will be of benefit to Kenya.

11. A Class K permit is granted to an alien who is above 21 years of age, and who has in his own right and at his full and free disposition an assured annual income of not less than the prescribed amount, being an income that is assured, and that is derived from sources other than any such employment, occupation, trade, business, or profession as is referred to in the description of any of the classes of permit specified in this analysis, and being an income that either (1) is derived from sources outside, and will be remitted to Kenya; (2) is derived from property situated or a pension or annuity payable from sources in Kenya; or (3) will be derived from a sufficient investment capital to produce such assured income that will be brought into and invested in Kenya. The alien also undertakes not to accept paid employment of any kind should he be granted a work permit of Class K, and his presence in Kenya has to be of benefit to Kenya.

12. A Class L permit is granted to an alien who is not in employment whether paid or unpaid; who under the repeated acts was issued with a resident's certificate, or who would have on application been entitled to the issue of such certificate, or who has held a work permit

or work permits of any of the foregoing classes of work permits for a
continuous period of not less than 10 years immediately before the
date of application; and whose presence in Kenya will be of benefit to
Kenya.

The Work Permit Systems in Uganda and Tanzania

In Uganda, the classes of work permits available to aliens are
exactly the same as those in Kenya, except that Uganda does not possess corresponding classes for A, D, E, K, and L of Kenya. As for
Tanzania, it possesses all the classes of work permits existing in
Kenya, but Tanzania boils all the 12 classes down to three categories
only. They are issued, as in Uganda and Kenya, only to persons who
are not prohibited immigrants, and as follows:

1. A Class A permit is issued to an alien intending to enter or
remain in Tanzania and engage in trade, business, agriculture, a profession, animal husbandry, prospecting for minerals, or manufacture
—if he or somebody else on his behalf furnishes security by depositing
with an immigration officer such sum as is enough to cover the cost
of returning him, his wife or dependent children—if any—to his country
of origin, or to some other country to which he may be admitted; and
if he furnishes security by a bond with one or more sureties. An
alien holder of a Class A permit is subjected to conditions relating to
the area of his residence in Tanzania, to the kind of business or occupation (if any), to restrictions, prohibitions, or limitations subject to
which he may engage therein, and to the duration of his residence in
Tanzania as may be specified in his work permit by the principal immigration officer.

2. A Class B permit is granted to an alien who is offered a specified employment in Tanzania, and if the principal immigration officer is convinced that the person possesses the necessary qualification
or skill for such employment, and that his employment will be of benefit to Tanzania, provided that his employer gives such security for
such purposes as the principal immigration officer may direct, before
the granting to such an alien of a work permit. An alien offered a
Class B work permit is also subject to the conditions of a Class A
permit, and any others that the principal immigration officer may
specify.

3. A Class C permit is granted to an alien who does not hold a
Class B work permit. He is also subject to the conditions of the Class
A and Class B permits.

The principal immigration officer has the power to cancel, vary, or add to the conditions of any work permit, provided the cancellation of a work permit by the officer is subject to the confirmation of the immigration minister, whose decision is conclusive.

Tanzania issues work permits for a maximum period of three years. They can be renewed, but only up to five years. In Uganda and Kenya, no duration of work permits has been fixed, but practice in these countries has revealed that work permits are issued for periods of between 30 and 36 months, and are renewable.

Kinds of Passes in East Africa

The East African countries also issue a pass in common. Thus an immigration officer (the Immigration Control Board in Uganda, unless it delegates its power to an immigration officer) in any of the three nations is at liberty to cancel at any time any pass issued to a person and to vary any term or condition thereof. In Kenya, however, no dependent's pass may be canceled without the prior approval of the responsible minister. In all three countries, there are the following eight kinds of passes.

1. A Dependent's Pass may be issued to any person materially dependent upon the earnings of another, whether because of age, disability, incapacity, or for some other reason. Any person legally in, or entitled to enter, an East African country may apply for a dependent's pass.

2. A Pupil's Pass may be issued to any person seeking to enter or remain in an East African country for the purposes of receiving education or training in the country.

3. A Visitor's Pass may be issued to any person desiring to enter an East African state for the purpose of a holiday; temporarily engaging in a business, trade, or profession; or for any other temporary purpose that may be approved by an immigration authority.

4. An In-transit Pass may be issued to any person desiring to enter an East African nation for the purpose of traveling to a destination outside that country; possessing valid documents that may be required to allow him to enter the country of destination; and qualified under the law in force in the country of destination to enter that country.

5. An Interstate Pass may be issued to any person legally present in an East African country, who by reason of his business, employment, profession, or other calling, is required to make frequent visits to either of the other East African states.

6. A Prohibited Immigrant's Pass may be issued to a prohibited immigrant, permitting him to enter and remain in an East African

country temporarily for such period and subject to such conditions as
may be specified in the pass.

7. A Special Pass may be issued to any person who desires to
enter or remain in an East African state for a limited period for the
purpose of education and training; for applying for an entry permit or
pass; or for any other purpose that an immigration officer considers
suitable.

8. A Reentry Pass may be issued by an immigration authority
to any person who, being legally, or legally residing, in an East African state, wishes to leave the country temporarily, or who, having
left the country temporarily and having been at the time of his departure legally present in the country, failed for reasons, which an immigration authority is satisfied are good and sufficient reasons, to apply
for a reentry pass before his departure.

"Legally residing" does not mean "legally present." Furthermore, the periods of validity of the abovementioned passes are to be
specified in the passes themselves. Similarly, the terms and conditions under which pass-holders may enter, remain, or reenter an
East African country are specified in the passes.

The Tanzanian laws do not mention the Pupils, Interstate, and
Prohibited Immigrant's Passes. But there is no doubt that aliens
holding these kinds of passes in Tanzania are subject to the conditions
and requirements of the passes as in Kenya and Uganda.

EAST AFRICAN LAWS RELATING TO BUSINESS

Another area of life in which the position of aliens in East Africa
is regulated by law is the field of business. The immigration acts of
the East African countries currently in force[13] contain provisions that
are of direct concern to aliens. The Tanzania Immigration Act defines
"business" as "any form of trade, commerce, craftsmanship or specified profession carried on for profit or gain." "Auxiliary business"
is defined as "any business not specified in a business licence fee,
which may be lawfully carried on under such licence by virtue of the
provisions of section 4." Section 4 states that no person shall carry
on auxiliary business:

(a) In banking, shipping, lighterage, or stevedoring;
(b) Unless he is authorized to do so by licence issued
    in relation to such business;
(c) Which can be legally carried on only if a licence,
    permit or other authority granted by, or under
    any other written law;

(d) Unless the licence fee in respect of such business requires it to be so assessed on an annual turnover (profit);

(e) Unless a licence fee of a specified amount, if so required, is paid; and

(f) Unless the licence so held by the holder is in relation to a business in respect of which the same local authority is the licencing authority.

Similarly, no person can carry on any business without a valid business licence authorizing him to do so in the place specified therein.

An auxiliary business also means a business

(i) Which is not specified in the licence granted; and

(ii) If a separate licence had been applied for such business, the licence fee payable for such licence would not have exceeded the licence fee payable for the licence granted.

Although the above legal definitions of certain key expressions do not actually appear in the Kenya and Uganda Acts, the definitions also apply in the latter two countries. Similarly, the meanings of "trading center" and "general business area," although they appear respectively in the Uganda and Kenya business laws only, are equally applicable in Tanzania. Thus a trading center is legally defined as any area in Uganda so declared by the minister responsible for local administrations, by statutory order. In Kenya, a general business area is any area, or part of an area, city, municipality, or township so declared by the minister responsible for commerce and industry, by an order. And specified goods are any goods so declared by an order of the minister. Finally, by a "specified profession" is meant the following professions: medical practitioner, dentist, veterinary surgeon, optician, chemist, pharmacist, lawyer, auditor, registered or chartered accountant, tax consultant, management consultant, estate agent, quantity surveyor, or engineer. This category also includes any profession that no person can legally carry on unless he is registered by or under any written law; and any profession that the minister may, by notice in the Gazette, declare to be a specified profession.

Aliens are restricted in, and even prohibited in many cases from, performing business activities in certain East African areas. In Uganda, for instance, the minister may, by statutory order, declare from time to time any business area or trading center to be an area in which a person who is not a citizen of Uganda may not trade. The minister may also declare any particular good or goods of any particular class to be specified, and may declare goods that an alien is prohibited from trading. Thus an alien is not allowed by law to trade outside any city, municipality, or town; to trade in any trading center in respect of which an order is made prohibiting noncitizens from trading in that area; or to trade in any area of any city, municipality, or town that has not been declared a general business area.

Business restrictions are also extended to citizens of Uganda, who are forbidden to trade either directly or indirectly on behalf of any person who is an alien in Uganda, whether under a license granted to those citizens of Uganda, or in any other way. Also, no alien in Uganda is allowed to engage, or permit a Ugandan citizen to trade either directly or indirectly on his behalf, whether under a license granted to that Ugandan citizen, or in any other way, in any area or goods in which such person is prohibited by law from trading.

Exempted from the above restrictions are companies or firms comprising partly Ugandan citizens and partly aliens, if such companies or, in the case of firms, their first names, were registered as such in Uganda on or before January 1969.

An alien in Uganda may thus conduct a business or trade in the country only in accordance with the terms of a current business license, which may be held. The case is exactly the same in Kenya. In Tanzania, the case is straightforward: nobody is allowed to carry on trade without a business license.

In all three states, anybody who breaks the business rules is liable to a heavy fine of up to 10,000/= (East African shillings) or to an imprisonment of up to 12 months, or both. In Tanzania, any person who breaks the above laws after the revocation, suspension, and disqualification from holding a business license is liable, on conviction, to a fine of up to 30,000/= or to an imprisonment of up to five years or both. In Tanzania, general offenses against people who carry on trade illegally are punishable by a fine of up to 15,000/=, or an imprisonment of up to two years, or both. In Kenya, any person guilty of an offense to the business law where no penalty is specifically provided is liable to a fine of up to 5,000/=, or an imprisonment of up to three months, or both. In Uganda, where no penalty is specifically provided, any person guilty of an offense to the business law, is liable to a fine of up to 1,000/=. Where institutions are concerned, an offense by them calls for the joint conviction of directors or officers of the institutions unless these persons prove that the offenses were committed without their knowledge.

A provision in the Tanzania law stipulates that general offense to the law carries a maximum penalty of 2,000/= (instead of 15,000/=) if the offender satisfies the court that the date on which it is alleged he committed the offense was 21 days from the date on which the business license previously held by him expired or, as the case may be, the date on which he first commenced his business.[14]

OTHER LAWS RELATING TO ALIENS
IN EAST AFRICA

Apart from the immigration and business laws that impose specific restrictions and control on aliens in East Africa, there are other laws that impose general restrictions and control. The Kenya law, known as the Aliens Restriction Act of 1973, is entirely based on the Ugandan legislation enacted in 1949, and revised in 1964 as the Aliens (Registration) and Control Act. [15]

The Kenya act empowers the minister responsible for internal security to impose, whenever necessary (for example, during a state of war between Kenya and a foreign power, or when imminent danger or great emergency arises), restrictions on aliens by order. The burden of proving whether or not a person is an alien in either of the two countries lies entirely upon that person. In Kenya (alone), however, the minister may, also from time to time, make an aliens order to prohibit aliens from landing in, or otherwise entering Kenya either generally, or at certain places; and to impose restrictions or conditions on aliens landing or arriving at any port in Kenya. The minister may also by order prohibit aliens from embarking in, or otherwise leaving Kenya, either generally or at certain places. He may finally impose restrictions and conditions on aliens embarking, or about to embark, in Kenya.

The Kenya minister responsible for domestic security can, at any time, revoke, change, or add to any aliens order. Any of the above powers conferred on the minister, or any others he may exercise, are only in addition to, and not in derogation of, any powers regarding the expulsion of aliens, or their prohibition from entering Kenya or any other powers conferred on the minister or any other authority by any other written law.

The power to deport aliens is mentioned in the Ugandan legislation alone. But the deportation of aliens is a right that every sovereign state is free to exercise. In Uganda, an alien who incites sedition or disaffection in the Ugandan Armed Forces or the civilian population is liable, on conviction, to an imprisonment of up to ten years. Similarly, any alien who encourages or endeavors to encourage industrial unrest in which he has not bona fide been engaged for at least two years immediately preceding in Uganda, is liable on conviction to imprisonment of up to three months. Exceptions to these provisions are people legally entitled to diplomatic privileges. The minister may, by order, apply the act to Africans as well.

Whereas in Kenya any person contravening any provision or requirement of an aliens order is liable, on conviction, to a fine of up to 3,000/= or to an imprisonment of up to six months or both, in Uganda, such fine amounts to a maximum of 2,000/= or an imprisonment of up to six months, or both. Similar restrictions and control are imposed on alien refugees by the Ugandan and Tanzanian laws enacted in 1964 and 1965, respectively.

EAST AFRICAN AND INTERNATIONAL LAW
RELATING TO ALIENS: A SHORT COMPARISON

When examined against the background of the international law of aliens, the above East African laws conform, in general, to the international rules. However, loopholes in the East African laws exist, which are deviations from the international rules relating to aliens. Similarly, the practice toward aliens in East Africa greatly deviates from the requirements of international law, and even from the law of East Africa itself. A case in point is citizenship, which was one of the problems requiring solution by the governments of newly independent East Africa.

Among the implications of citizenship, first, any of the immigrant communities (whether Kenya Colony "British citizens" or Uganda Protectorate and Tanganyika Trust Territory "British protected persons") who did not become citizens of the country in East Africa within two years of independence would have the right to leave; however, the Kenya Constitution at independence guaranteed resident aliens in the country against expulsion. Second, any in the immigrant communities who did not become citizens of an East African state but remained British citizens would have the right to enter Britain. Incidentally, the British Commonwealth Immigration Act of 1962 did apply, as we shall see later, to British passport holders. The immigrant communities in East Africa were hence not affected by the British legislation. Finally, any in the immigrant communities who did not become citizens of an East African state would have the right to stay and work in that country. Aware of the rights to stay, leave, and enter, most Asians and Europeans opted to remain aliens.

The practice in East Africa, however, clearly indicates that the above legal provisions have been evaded. A good number of the immigrant communities applied for citizenship but were not granted it. Some of the policies adopted by the newly independent East African states are openly discriminatory. For example, the policies of Africanization, Kenyanization, Ugandanization, and Tanzanization, have been terribly confused. There seems to be no distinction between Africanization and Ugandanization, for instance, which are two distinct doctrines. The expulsions of Asians by the East African states have also represented some of the deviations from the understandings made at the independence of the countries. By expelling some of the Asians who were citizens of East Africa (as in Uganda, as we shall see), the practice was directly against not only the East African law relating to aliens but also the general principles of international law regulating the status of aliens. In 1960, it is believed, Uganda expelled 40,000 black Kenyans who had been gainfully employed and living in Uganda for many years. The same practice of expelling black Kenyans from Uganda was repeated, according to many commentators, in the late 1960s and early 1970s. When General Amin became president of Uganda, he revoked the citizenship of many Asian citizens of Uganda. Zanzibar imposed a number of restrictions on the rights of Arabs and Asians. Whereas Arabs were forced to intermarry with Africans, Asians in Zanzibar were restricted on their right to leave the island. In some cases, the right to leave is completely prohibited. In others, the right to leave is conditional on the payment of large fees. This restriction also applies to Africans. In fact, all citizens of Zanzibar intending, for instance, to visit mainland Tanzania, must get permission to do so. Otherwise, their departure would be illegal. Many Asians who were citizens of Zanzibar but were away from the island during certain periods of time were declared no longer citizens and are thus now not citizens of Tanzania. The above practice has resulted in categories of people, mainly Asians, becoming stateless persons. Kenya is believed to have expelled many of its citizens generally by first revoking their citizenship.

There is no doubt that the East African states violate the important (international law) doctrine of acquired or vested rights, which are, strictly speaking, legal rights. It is an important principle of international law that acquired rights of aliens must be respected. No change of sovereignty should work any effect on such rights; aliens should be accorded the protection given to citizens. This protection involves the provision of compensation for any nationalization or any other kind of seizure. The stress is on respect for property rights acquired or vested, which are an aspect of human rights. And yet the East African states have, in practice, regularly and stubbornly refused to accept the doctrine of vested rights of aliens, for example, to reside and carry on a business or profession in East Africa. Many of the Asians expelled from East Africa had lived in that region for many years. Some of them were even born there and knew no other place of residence except East Africa. Surely, this historical fact vested in such people the right to stay in East Africa. The East African countries, however, generally accept and implement the international rule that no state has a right to expel its citizens. Even President Idi Amin of Uganda was forced to withdraw his expulsion decree against the Uganda Asian citizens, as we shall see below. Also, every time Kenya has wanted to deport one of her citizens, she has first deprived him of his Kenyan citizenship.

The East African nations also recognize the principle of the right of entry of citizens. But the lack of clear protection in the re-

gion's countries against deprivation of citizenship has caused a situation and category of stateless persons. The root of the problem lies,
inter alia, in the "elements of discrimination" contained in some of
the laws of the three countries.

Although the citizenship laws of the East African states prohibit
deprivation of citizenship acquired through birth, they allow for deprivation of citizenship by registration or naturalization. This is a
weak and discriminatory legal provision, which enables the East African governments to deprive East African citizens of their East African
nationality by registration or naturalization, without giving any reasons
for such action. There also seems to be no machinery for appeal or
review. The governments have extensively exploited this legal loophole. The practice is certainly contrary to international conventions,
on the elimination of statelessness, for instance.

Aliens in East Africa are also sometimes deprived of rights of
contract, of acquisition of personal property, and even of marriage,
as has often happened in Zanzibar. In practice, nationalization has
taken place in East Africa without prompt, effective, and sufficient
compensation. In many cases, discrimination has been displayed in
the compensation rule.

No law has been enacted so far to regulate the crucial questions
of asylum and statelessness in East Africa. Tanzania and Uganda
have laws dealing with refugees. Kenya has none, although she has
the Aliens Restriction Act (1973). There is no such act in Tanzania,
although the Tanzania Immigration Act of 1972 generally deals with
the question of aliens. The Ugandan aliens restriction law contains
sections on aliens and Africans that are extremely vague: "This Act
shall not apply to Africans: provided that the Minister may by statutory instrument, apply any or all of the provisions of this Act to any
or all classes of Africans."[16] Elsewhere in the same law, it is provided that an "alien" in Uganda is "a person who is not a citizen of
Uganda or a Commonwealth citizen within the meaning of Section 13
of the Uganda Citizenship Act, or a citizen of the Republic of Ireland."[17]

The business law of Tanzania does not contain any element of
discrimination, for it is provided therein that nobody is allowed to
carry on business if: he has no valid business license; he is under 18;
he is disqualified by an order from holding business; and he is illegally present in Tanzania and not authorized to trade in the country.

The trade laws of Uganda and Kenya are discriminatory. Ironically, this type of discrimination is recognized in international law.
The fact, however, is that international law contains a considerable
number of rules that are terribly confusing on the legal status of aliens.
Perhaps the reason for this confusion is that there is a great variety
of issues, some of which are partly governed by international law
and some partly by municipal law. Other issues are solely governed

by municipal law, and others solely by international law. What, on the contrary, international law does not recognize is discrimination against citizens. And yet this is done in East Africa, where discrimination against non-African (nonblack) citizens is common.

CONCLUSIONS AND RECOMMENDATIONS

Race relations in East Africa have many aspects: cultural, social, economic, religious, political, and legal. In colonized East Africa, racial integration was disallowed by the colonial policy of racial isolation and segregation. Afro-Asian or Afro-European social relations were confined to the master-servant or shopkeeper-customer level. In independent East Africa, this social setup has been discouraged, and social mingling has been encouraged. Residential segregation, like segregation in bars, clubs, and restaurants, has, by law at least, been abolished. In practice, however, racial discrimination still exists in the region. It is evident especially in schools, employment, and business. The duty to eradicate discrimination rests with each and every individual in society, but with the East African governments rests the ultimate task to correct any social injustice that may exist in an East African society. A serious ingroup segregation in East Africa, particularly in Uganda, Kenya, and Zanzibar, still exists among the various tribes of East Africa. The tribal problem is least evident in Tanganyika. Tribalism not only impedes complete racial harmony but also obstructs the development of East Africa. The governments of East Africa, therefore, need to devise some methods of complete social integration. They should, for instance, check every practice of distributing loans unequally in the various parts of their countries. Development projects should be launched and distributed equally throughout the regions of the country.

It is encouraging that segregation or group consciousness is rapidly dying out, with the establishment of coeducational and multiracial institutions such as kindergartens, schools, hospitals, clubs, and universities, throughout the East African countries. All these, and other humanitarian organizations such as the Red Cross and National Services, are great melting pots whose numbers should be increased, as they are fundamental instruments of racial harmony.

Racial consciousness among the African people is no doubt a by-product of colonialism. The acceptance by the African that he is different from other people is a phenomenon that has occurred only after the attainment of independence. Endeavors by African leaders to institutionalize this African feeling have led to the charge of "racialism" by non-Africans. The non-African in East Africa is of the view that racial awareness and distinctions should be perpetuated even

though East Africa is a nonracial society. The white man viewed the
African as an inferior being; it is therefore not surprising that the
African wants to show the white man that the African is now the superior man—the master—and that the African can now develop the same
superiority complex that the white man had developed. Race relations
in East Africa also have legal aspects. In Tanganyika, for instance,
a law was enacted after independence which provided that no alien
(barring an African from a few neighboring countries) could enter or
remain in Tanganyika without an entry permit. Moreover, of the three
classes of entry permit introduced in the country, the Class A permit
may be granted without the requirement of security, while the Class
B permit can only be granted on the furnishing of security sufficient
to cover the cost of returning the holder of the permit to his country
of origin or, in the discretion of the principal immigration officer, to
some other country into which he may be admitted, together with a
further sum not exceeding 25 percent of such first-named sum.

People who receive Class B permits can apply for Class A permits, and indeed must obtain one after the lapse of the period specified
in their Class B permit. People who hold certificates of permanent
residence are given Class A permits on application within six months,
and these permits are valid for two years. The permits, except in
the case of the former holders of certificates of permanent residence,
are issued subject to the area within which the holder may reside, the
occupation or business (if any) in which he may engage, and the restrictions, prohibitions, or limitations subject to which he may engage
therein. The central purpose of this entire mechanism is to enable the
government to exercise effective control over the number, occupation,
and location of immigrants. It also means that aliens have little security regarding the right to reside in the country.

The corresponding legislations of Uganda and Kenya contain
similar provisions, but grave violations of the laws have occurred in
the two countries. In fact, Asians were expelled from Kenya in 1968,
despite a constitutional safeguard against expulsion. Similarly,
Uganda expelled in 1972 Asians ordinarily and lawfully resident in the
country for many years.

The East African states need to reexamine their practices toward
aliens, and respect their duties toward them not only under international law but also under the very laws that they themselves make relating to aliens. Government assurances and utterances given to
aliens are valueless unless they are fairly and justly implemented.
The government policies of Africanization have prevented every possible promotion of the fundamental international legal principle of equality of treatment. Whether, therefore, Africanization means "equalization," "localization," or "blackenization" is a matter to be clearly
determined not only in policy but in law as well. If Africanization

means "equalization," then equality of treatment should be ensured at all levels and to all citizens. As currently implemented, Africanization in East Africa means "blackenization"—that is, replacement in business and other areas of aliens and Europeans by blacks. This being the case, either a new expression should be formulated and substituted for the term "Africanization" or the latter should be given its right meaning (of "equalization") in practice and implementation and not just in stated policy.

The nonexistence of some of the essential laws, whether throughout East Africa or in some of the East African states, is a deviation per se from the international rules. Kenya has no separate law to control refugees. Tanzania has no law on vagrancy. Uganda has no clear law on nationalization, although she has laws on the transfer of Asian businesses and on participation in companies. Apart from a legislation on the nationalization of the Kenya Broadcasting Service, Kenya has no law on nationalization. Uganda has no general law on the transfer of business, which is an important aspect in the Africanization policy. Whereas in Kenya, nationalization may be done by the minister responsible, in Tanzania and Uganda, the power to nationalize is vested in the president. The duration of work permits is not specified anywhere in the laws. The understanding is that any offer of a job to an alien—whether on contract or not—is intended to make that alien prepare a citizen or citizens to take over. Even here, the law is violated in practice, as only African citizens take over and non-African citizens are discriminated against. And yet the laws state that working aliens in the Africanization programs have a duty to prepare all citizens to take over.

Kenya has two laws on extradition: the Extradition (Contiguous and Foreign Countries) Act of 1966, revised in 1967, and inserted by Act 65 of 1968, which became the Extradition (Commonwealth Countries) Act of 1970. The crimes enumerated in these acts are basically the same as those in the Extradition Acts of Uganda (1964) and Tanzania (1965).

To improve the position of aliens in the region, the East African states should respect the laws they make, and the principles of international law governing the status of aliens. The states should carry out bona fide their obligations arising from international law and their membership in the society of civilized states. Furthermore, the East African states must both accept the fact that they are multiracial and multicultural societies and live up to the "civilized" requirements (international and national standards) of such societies. Racialism must hence be vehemently rejected and completely eradicated wherever it exists or crops up.

It is most unfortunate that international law recognizes discrimination in certain fields. The East African countries are among the states of the world that practice discrimination in the field of business. International law is far from perfect. Some of its rules on aliens are still vague, confusing, incomplete, and even uncodified. This means that individual states, including the East African states, have a duty to work for the perfection of international law. What must be done is to develop the international law of aliens through international conferences and organs such as those of the United Nations. What is needed is to codify international rules that will regulate, in clear terms, the position of the individual in international, and even national, law, with full consensus.

It is essential also that Uganda and Kenya be specific in their laws relating to aliens; for example, the duration of work permits should be specified. This would help remove some of the ambiguities presently existing in the laws. The East African states must enact the "missing" laws of aliens. For example, there is an imperative need for a law on stateless persons. The purpose of enacting "missing" laws is to make the East African laws of aliens more uniform than they are today.

The improvement of the place and role of aliens in East Africa will also depend upon the attitudes of aliens themselves toward the governments and citizens of the three countries; the attitudes of East African citizens toward aliens in the region; and the politics that the East African governments will adopt, plus the manner in which the governments fulfill their duties, under international law, toward aliens.

NOTES

1. See for instance, United Nations, Document ST/LEG/7, 1959, p. 47; and U.N. Yearbook (New York: United Nations, 1963), p. 181.

2. See International Court of Justice Reports, 1949, p. 219.

3. For further information consult Current Legal Problems, 1955, p. 212 et seq.

4. For interesting remarks on this question see G. Schwarzenberger, A Manual of International Law, 4th ed., vol. 1 (London: Stevens and Sons, 1960), p. 29.

5. Quoted in Daily Nation (Nairobi), April 16, 1973.

6. Quoted in Daily Nation, November 6, 1973.

7. This and other points are discussed at length in Who Controls Industry in Kenya? (Nairobi: East African Publishing House, 1968). See also H. S. Morris, "Indians in East Africa: A Study in a Plural Society," British Journal of Sociology 7, no. 3 (1956).

8. For example see generally D. W. Greig, International Law (London: Butterworths, 1970).

9. See American Journal of International Law, supp. 15, no. 21 (1935).

10. See United Nations, Treaty Series, 137, 1951.

11. See ibid., 117, 1954.

12. For laws of the East African states relating to aliens see Uganda, Constitution, September 8, 1967, Laws of Uganda, 1964, vols. 2 and 4, Statutes, 1970, Statutes, 1971, Decrees, 1972, Decrees, 1973; Kenya, Constitution, 1969, Revised Laws of Kenya, 1970, Kenya Acts, 1964-73; Tanzania, Interim Constitution, 1965, Revised Laws of Tanzania, vol. 1-3, 5, 6, 9, Tanzania Acts, 1965-68, 1971, 1972.

13. Kenya, Trade Licensing Act, 1967; Uganda, Trade Licensing Act, 1969; Tanzania, Business Licensing Act, 1972.

14. Tanzania, Immigration Act, sec. 17(2).

15. See Laws of Uganda, 1964, chap. 63; and Republic of Kenya Acts, 1973.

16. See Uganda Aliens (Registration) and Control Act, sec. 6, 1964.

17. Ibid., sec. 2.

7

THE QUESTION OF STATE RESPONSIBILITY FOR ALIENS IN EAST AFRICA IN THE LIGHT OF INTERNATIONAL LAW AND DIPLOMACY

LEGAL DEFINITION OF STATE RESPONSIBILITY

The reasons why it is essential to hold states responsible for their acts or omissions of acts, whether unlawful or lawful, which they may impose on other legal persons, include the need to maintain a unified social and economic order for the conduct of international commerce and intercourse among different states; and to protect not only travelers and alien nationals and investments but also property interests and rights in the international field. All these interests and rights, besides aliens and alien investments, certainly require the diplomatic and judicial protection of international law. In short, therefore, it is necessary to have state responsibility because we live in a world of interdependence. Responsibility is the essential corollary of a right. Therefore, all rights (which are legal rights) of an international nature involve international responsibility. State responsibility in relation to international duties is thus a legal responsibility.[1] This means that any violation, whether by act or omission, of any duty created by a principle of international law automatically establishes a new legal relationship between the subject to which the act is attributable, who is under an obligation to respond by making adequate reparation, and the subject who has a claim to reparation because of the violation of duty.

It also means that every violation of an international legal duty constitutes what is known as international delinquency, that is, any injury—illegal act or breach of duty resulting in loss—to another legal person (normally a state) committed by the head or government of a state in violation of any international legal duty, or acts of the judiciary, officials, or other individuals commanded or authorized by the government or head of state.

State responsibility essentially comprises three constituent elements: an act or omission that violates an obligation created by a principle of international law in force between the state responsible for the act or omission and the state injured thereby; the illegal omission or act must be attributable to a legal person; and loss or damage must have resulted from the illegal act or omission. In other words, international duties or obligations arise when the following elements come into existence: the violation of any international duty must be ad invitum, that is, against the will of the complainant (volenti non fit injuria—that is, no injury is done to the willing); an act or omission must be unjustified; and a violation must be confined to acts or omissions that, in the light of ius aequum are both attributable to a subject of international law and voluntary. By ius aequum is simply meant the spirit of reasonableness and good faith. In the case of treaties, the ius aequum rule requires a party to a treaty to do everything in its power to avoid every violation of the treaty.

A question that arises now is whether injurious acts or omissions can, in any way, be justified. The response to this question must be given in the affirmative. Thus self-defense, sanctions, reprisals, and consent given because of force, deception, or error are justifiable even if they are injurious to legal rights and interests. The same goes for necessity, which may compel a legal person to save itself from a huge and imminent danger uninduced and unescapable by the legal person.

COMPENSATION AS A LEGAL DUTY
IN INTERNATIONAL LAW

A question of great significance is that of reparation. It is a fundamental principle of international law that any violation of an international duty imposes an obligation on the violating legal person to make reparation, for the injury caused, in an adequate form. The key expression is "compensation," and its purpose is to restore the status quo ante, that is, to eradicate all the consequences of the violation and to reestablish the situation existing prior to the commitment of the wrong.

Reparation or compensation may be made in three different ways: either in kind or restitution in money or indemnity, or in satisfaction. Compensation in kind has the aim of reestablishing the situation that would have existed if the wrongful act or omission had not occurred, by fulfillment of the obligation that the legal person failed to discharge. Compensation in money, the most normal form of reparation, is given especially for other than material damage. Satisfaction is not compensation, but any form of nonpecuniary or moral injury to a legal person. Satisfaction cannot therefore lead to restitution. Its primary purpose is to repair breaches of international duties in cases where, for instance, pecuniary compensation is neither appropriate nor sufficient.

Forms of reparation include apology and punishment of wrong-doers. State responsibility can either be internal, that is, toward its own subjects, or external, that is, toward other legal persons. Similarly, state responsibility can either be original, that is, for actions or omissions done at a state government's command or authorization, or vicarious, that is, for certain unauthorized injurious actions or omissions done by state legislative, administrative, executive, and judicial organs.

LEGAL PERSONALITY OF INDIVIDUALS IN INTERNATIONAL LAW

The question of legal personality in relation to individuals is tricky. It is, nonetheless, widely accepted that states, which are the normal legal persons, are responsible only to other legal persons, and not to individuals, who are normally objects of international law. What, however, is still disputed is the question as to whether individuals are, or can be, legal persons in the eyes of international law and diplomacy.

Individuals are not subjects of international law, and as such, they do not bear any responsibility for violations of international duties imposed by customary international law, because these duties can only rest upon legal persons—most notably states and governments. But there is no international rule that expressly stipulates that individuals cannot possess some measure of legal personality. In fact, individuals do have legal personalities, for certain purposes and in certain cases. For example, UN officials have brought disputes for settlement before UN administrative tribunals, and there is no doubt that they have done so not as legal objects, but indeed as legal subjects in the eyes of international law.

Thus although the assumption of customary international law is still that only states can make and bring claims before international tribunals, individuals also do have the capacity to do so, and many of the disputes brought before international courts for settlement quite often concern losses suffered by individuals.[2] Also, individuals can be held responsible, and in fact do bear (international) responsibility for any acts or omissions that constitute crimes. The right of individuals to bring claims against independent, sovereign states has been inscribed in several multilateral treaties.

STATE RESPONSIBILITIES FOR ALIENS
IN EAST AFRICA

We will now examine the responsibilities of the East African states, for aliens in the region, against the background of the theory and practice of international law and diplomacy.

The responsibility of the East African states for aliens in East Africa certainly includes the legal duties of the states that arise, or may arise, as a result of any violation, by these states, of any legal interest of any alien in East Africa. The question of state responsibility for aliens in East Africa, therefore, involves both the legal rights and corresponding legal duties of the countries toward aliens, and of the latter toward the former. The rights of the East African nations actually appear in the form of government policies toward aliens in the region. These include (1) the right to localize the various sectors of the economy; (2) the right to nationalize the various industries and resources or to expropriate the property of aliens; (3) the right to try aliens; (4) the right to punish aliens; (5) the right to detain or imprison aliens; (6) the right to deport aliens; (7) the right to extradite aliens; and (8) the right to self-defense.

Corresponding to the above rights are the duties of the East African states, inter alia, to compensate for any Africanizations or nationalizations of any alien properties; to offer aliens easy access to the courts; to prevent denial of justice to aliens and discrimination of any kind against aliens, whether in law or in practice; to treat aliens in accordance with the requirements of international law and to recognize and respect their right to self-defense and to their private property; to respect international conventions on, for instance, discrimination and statelessness; to protect the personal and property rights of aliens, which are their legal rights; to respect their own laws relating to aliens and to remove loopholes in these laws either by improving the existing laws or by enacting new laws. The primary duty of aliens in East Africa is to comply with the laws of the three states.

RIGHTS AND DUTIES ARISING FROM
AFRICANIZATION IN EAST AFRICA

"Africanization" is an expression that has been interpreted variously and confusingly. In the understanding of most people in East Africa, and the East African governments themselves, "Africanization" means transferring the country's economy and resources to black citizens. This interpretation is unacceptable particularly to those nonblack citizens of East Africa, such as Asians, who affirm that their possession of East African citizenship entitles them to the enjoyment of rights and privileges emanating from that citizenship, on an equal footing with any other citizens of East Africa. One Asian citizen of Kenya has emphatically remarked to the writer: "My problem is indeed an 'African' one. I was born here, am a Kenyan, etc. I was privileged as a child and we [the Asians] have had it good. I have tried to identify myself with Kenya but the Africans are not willing to accept me for what I am, a true Kenyan."

According to other people, "Africanization" means "nepotism" or "tribalism." Still others believe the expression means "localization" or "equalization," and thus the elements of nepotism and color are nonexistent. What exists, and must be borne by the claimant, is the burden of proof that the claimant is a citizen. Hence the call is for equality of opportunity and equal treatment of all citizens. In other words, "Africanization" should mean "Kenyanization/Ugandanization/Tanzanization." "Kenyanization" of the economy, for instance, means transferring the economy not merely to Africans but to all Kenyan citizens. Many people, including the Kenyan authorities, have therefore very mistakenly interpreted "Kenyanization" to mean "blackenization"—transferring of power to blacks. In this sense, "Kenyanization means "equalization" or "localization," or better still, "citizenization." Unless this point is properly understood and the present practice of "localization" adjusted, the charges of discrimination will continue to be made against the East African governments, and correctly so. The same can be said of "Ugandanization" and "Tanzanization." The above observations should help establish, both in policy and in law, generally accepted definitions of "Africanization" and "Tanzanization/Ugandanization/Kenyanization." Initially, "Africanization" meant administrative reconstruction, whereas political reconstruction meant, after independence, transferring political power and influence from the former colonial powers to the Africans. The results of the administrative reconstruction were employment of Africans mostly, if not solely, in the civil services of East Africa; replacement of many non-African civil servants by African civil servants; and performance of the "low-quality jobs" by the untrained and inadequately educated Africans. But that was a matter of government policy whose central purpose was to integrate Africans into the economies of the three countries and thereby improve their living standards. Economic establishments were formed for the realization of the policy; they assisted Africans in projects, loans, industrial and commercial ventures, and so on. Programs were introduced for training Africans both locally and overseas. Aliens greatly helped in the realization of the local programs. Thus close economic integration was a good condition of preventing racial isolation in East Africa.

Similarities exceed variations in the doctrine of Africanization in the three countries of East Africa. In Tanzania, however, emphasis

is put on the doctrine of socialization. But generally, the policy is
to strengthen the system of black capitalism introduced (to replace the
old colonial nonblack capitalism) soon after the political independence
of the three countries.

The colonial masters in East Africa introduced a work system
whereby Europeans were put into top decision-making places both in
the public and private sectors of the economy. Asians occupied the
middle ranks, and Africans were given the low, unspecialized jobs.
Such a situation of imbalanced opportunities gave rise to African resentment and nationalist demands for equality of opportunity and development. African nationalism thus stressed priorities for Africanization and black capitalist development.

As early as 1943, Kenyatta explicitly made African feelings
known to the Europeans on the topic of equal opportunity: "Let the Africans have equal educational facilities with the Europeans, and leave
them free to make the best use of them. Give them an equal chance
of economic enterprise, equal opportunity in business and the professions, and a say in the Government of the country. If they then show
themselves unequal to the strain of Western civilization, they will
have no right to resent being treated as a backward race."[3]

What the new East African governments have set out to do in
their Africanization policies has been to Africanize capitalism—that
is, to blend African opportunity with the continued operation of the
private enterprise system. A significant aim of the Africanization
programs has been to remove the remnants of the colonial racial imbalances that were carried over the colonial borders into the postindependence era. One of the fields greatly affected has been that of
income policies. At the time of independence in East Africa, Africans came to man most of the places in parliament and government,
besides the policy-making positions in the civil services. However,
the racial structuring of opportunity remained unaltered in the technical, scientific, and professional spheres, and in private industry and
commerce generally. Alien control over investment was thus too
complete to be shaken by the mere attainment of political independence
by the East African countries. The colonial status quo in postindependence East Africa was resented by Africans.

The idea of racial balance in independent East Africa is contra-
dictory to the maintenance of some form of economic efficiency. The
African demand for Africanization was part and parcel of the wider
nationalist drive for racial balance and equality. Africans demanded,
for instance, that Asian businesses be Africanized, that the East African governments should force Asians to leave and reallocate the
left-over Asian businesses to Africans. These demands were realized
after 1967 but in an irrational and racial manner. The aim of the Africans was to subject the Asians, and yet the real blame for the then

existing situation went to the European colonizers. In any event, there could be no justification for the violation of individual, human, property, and constitutional rights for the sake of racially founded African group rights. The demands for rapid Africanization were very much mistaken, since their implementation could only result in extensive harm to the economic development of the region.

Putting right past racial inequalities could not and did not mean introducing an Africanization policy based upon racialism. This was, unfortunately, the implication of the demands in Kenya and Uganda. The Africanization policies in these countries have not tallied with assurances of equality and fair policy. The utterances of the African leaders cannot alone guarantee a future for the immigrant communities in East Africa. Nor can they give the communities equal rights and opportunities with Africans, which should be the purpose of Africanization; not surprisingly, Julius Nyerere in Tanzania has revoked Africanization in favor of localization. Africanization should not be implemented at the cost of the required standards in East Africa. These standards include the right qualifications, experience, ability to do a job, and efficiency. Africanization should be accompanied by equal treatment under the law for all citizens, property safeguards, and recruitment policies stressing individual achievement and merit. Further, the Africanization policy should aim at eliminating the effects of the old racial imbalances in East Africa. The present trend of the policy clearly indicates that the clash between development demands and equity (that is, the fundamental revision in the priorities of colonial times) is widening, and is increasingly not simply one of racial interests but of class or tribal interests. Thus a properly experienced labor force is still scarce, and it will be a long time before, to use the late Tom Mboya's words, this "gigantic shortage"[4] of trained and experienced personnel can be completely removed. It seems that the duration of the "gigantic shortage" will depend on such forces as the sufficiency of the educational system to deal with future needs, the rate of the economy's growth, the level of wastage, the attitudes and contributions of the population, both citizens and otherwise, toward the region's economic development, and so on.

The policies of Africanization in East Africa—and indeed elsewhere in Africa—thus raise many complex problems. The cons are just as many as, if not more than, the pros of Africanization. The ideals of Africanization are excellent, but the methods of implementing it in East Africa are terribly erroneous. The Africanization policies are inconsistent in many ways and indiscriminant. Africanization should be defined, and applied accordingly, simply as "a policy of recruiting citizens for existing high-level positions both in the private and public sectors of the economy, rather than creating new opportunities." The crucial element in Tanzanization/Ugandanization/

Kenyanization should be citizenship and not color. However, the East
African governments have a legal responsibility to compensate promptly, effectively, and sufficiently where necessary for any take-overs
of non-African businesses; to avoid discrimination, both in law and
practice, and any other form of unfair or preferential treatment; and
to shun corrupt practices in their Africanization programs, which
should never be used as a pretext for government misfeasance or for
the practice of tribal or racial inequality in the region. Where equity
and development demands collide, however, the latter should prevail.

RIGHTS AND DUTIES ARISING FROM
NATIONALIZATION IN EAST AFRICA

The Kenyan Case

In Kenya, the ambiguity in the government's policy on land
makes it difficult to determine whether it is a policy of Africanization
or nationalization. It seens, however, that the central purpose of the
policy is to transfer land from aliens to black citizens of Kenya. If
this is true, and it would appear that it is, then the government's land
policy is one of Africanization of land. This is perhaps the reason
why parliamentary back-benchers in the Kenya National Assembly have
on several occasions demanded an immediate amendment of Section
75 of the Constitution (which deals with protection from deprivation
of property) to facilitate immediate transfers of land to Africans.
Some of the back-benchers have demanded that land should be given
to Africans free of charge; others have charged that a lot of unfair
land distribution, corruption, tribalism, discrimination, and the like
have characterized resettlements of Africans on land. It has also
been charged that the government's land policy has favored not only
big landowners but also aliens.[5] During the debate on the supplemen-
tary vote for the Ministry of Lands and Settlement, held in October
1972, the back-benchers strongly criticized the above land policy and
urgently called for its revision. Mbiu Koinange, however, the minister of state in the president's office, and other government spokesmen
rejected, as usual, the above allegations. Kenyatta said his government "had already given 1,000,000 acres of land, formerly occupied
by aliens, to the landless Wananchi [Africans]."[6] Kenyatta, however,
admitted that it would take some time before land transfers to Africans
would be completed. That statement indicated that land in Kenya was
being Africanized and not nationalized. Thus although the land policy
in Kenya is terribly vague, the above observations do not in any way
suggest that there have never been full-blown demands for nationaliza-

tions in the country. The only Kenya law that has called for nationalization was the Kenya Broadcasting Corporation (Nationalization) Act
no. 12 of 1964.

Government spokesmen have on many occasions expressed the
view that nationalization is not necessary in Kenya. Sheikh M. Balala,
for example, an assistant minister for finance, remarked in 1964,
"Nationalization would be merely [a pretext] to misuse scarce capital resources."[7] The Kenya Foreign Investments Protection Act of
1964 guaranteed that "no approved enterprise or any property belonging thereto shall be compulsorily taken possession of, and no interest
in or right over such enterprise or property shall be compulsorily acquired, except in accordance with the provisions concerning compulsory taking of possession and acquisition and the payment of full and
prompt compensation contained in Section 19 of the Constitution of
Kenya."[8] Hence this law has acknowledged Kenya's responsibility
to compensate for any expropriation and possible nationalization of
private property.

The Ugandan Case

In Uganda, the government's policy regarding nationalization
has never been ambiguous. Already in the first republic under President Obote, nationalization was a "great possibility." The country's
tendency toward socialization—perhaps under Tanzania's influence—
was apparent. In the second republic, under President Amin, nationalization has become a "great practicability." Thus in December
1972, just a year after his assumption of power after ousting Obote,
Amin decided to nationalize 15 alien companies, 14 of which had been
British-owned, and a major American-owned company, International
Television Sales, Ltd. The major nationalized British companies
were British-American Tobacco, Brooke Bond Oxo (Uganda), Killing-
ton Tool, Consolidated Printers, Securicor (Uganda), British Millers,
Uganda Transport, and British Metal Box.[9] The hitherto almost exclusively white Kampala Club was also among the companies taken
over by the Ugandan government. The club, now known as the Government Club, is used by the president and his cabinet for discussing
state affairs and entertaining visiting ministers. The presidential
decree also stated that 26 alien tea estates had been nationalized. Of
these, 20 were wholly or partly British-owned, and some others
were Greek-owned. Only one month after the announcement of big
company nationalizations, Amin informed the acting British high commissioner in Uganda, A. H. Briand, that Uganda would also nationalize another 500 British companies, representing about 90 percent of
British interests in the country.

The Ugandan government under Amin's leadership has also nationalized (acquired) businesses of many Asians expelled from Uganda
in 1972. Again, Uganda is also under a legal responsibility to compensate for its nationalization of the foreign firms.

The Tanzanian Case

As regards Tanzania, nationalization is a clear and major policy in the country's socialization system. Tanzania's Acquisition of
Building Act of 1972, for instance, expropriated properties from
landlords and thereby prompted the nationalization of more than 3,000
buildings. Whereas in Kenya, the parliament has been sharply divided
over the nationalization issues, in Tanzania, there has not been much
marked division. Thus the aforementioned act was unanimously
enacted by the National Assembly. The act empowered President Nyerere to acquire for the state the above properties valued at more
than £5,000 and rented by private individuals.

Apart from the nationalization of the Kenya Broadcasting Corporation in 1964 and apart from the steps of nationalization taken by
the Revolutionary Council in Zanzibar since the Karume-led revolution of 1964, there were no nationalizations in East Africa until
those in Tanzania of February 1967. At that time, Tanzania took a
conclusive step toward socialism with the adoption of the so-called
Arusha Declaration at a meeting of the TANU National Executive
Committee; this policy statement was later adopted by the party
conference. The declaration outlined a national policy of socialism
and self-reliance; TANU was described as a party of peasants and
workers; economic development of the country would be based upon
agriculture rather than on alien-supported industry; and the behavior
of leaders was subjected to stricter rules. On public ownership,
the declaration stated:

> The way to build and maintain socialism is to ensure
> that the major means of production are under the
> control and ownership of the Peasants and Workers
> themselves through their Government and their Co-
> operatives. . . . These major means of production
> are: the land; forests; mineral resources; water;
> oil and electricity; communications; transport; banks;
> insurance; import and export trade; wholesale busi-
> ness; the steel, machine-tool, arms, motorcar, ce-
> ment and fertilizer factories; the textile industry;
> and any other big industry upon which a large sec-
> tion of the population depend for their living, or

which provides essential components for other industries; large plantations, especially those which
produce essential, raw materials.[10]

The National Executive Committee's call to the government to
implement this policy was promptly responded to by the government.
Within a week, all the commercial banks were nationalized, besides
12 importing and exporting companies. Also, eight milling companies
with associated food-manufacturing interests were nationalized. The
National Insurance Corporation was brought completely under public
ownership, and was to acquire a monopoly of insurance. The government was to be empowered to acquire compulsorily up to 60 percent
of the shares in eight industrial companies.

The above decisions were given legal sanction after a two-day
session of the National Assembly, which unanimously approved the
bills without detailed scrutiny. Even outside parliament, the nationalizations were enthusiastically welcomed. The government then
stated that it had no further plans for nationalization and that within
the nonnationalized fields—such as the sisal estates—private investment would still be welcomed.[11] The main argument was that it was
essential to nationalize most of the alien-owned companies if Tanzania
was to conduct its own development properly. The nonnationalization
of the large private sector was indicative of Tanzania's sustained interest in receiving foreign capital and private investment.

Kenya and Uganda have not followed Tanzania's nationalization
strategy, but they also adopted policies of socialism. Their attitudes
toward nationalization were outlined in two white papers.[12]

As a legal institution, nationalization can be defined as the compulsory transfer to the state of private property dictated by economic
motives, and having as its purpose the continued and essentially unaltered explication of the particular property. A nationalization step is
hence one that sets in motion a legal process whereby private rights
and interests in property are compulsorily transferred to the state,
or to some organ established by the state, with a view to the future
exploitation of those rights and interests by and for the benefit of the
state. Nationalization may be distinguished from expropriation or
compulsory purchase of particular pieces of property, of which the
typical instance would be acquisition of land by a public authority for
public purposes.

Also, nationalization is distinguishable from confiscatory or
discriminatory measures that have a punitive or retaliatory aspect
and are aimed at certain individuals or groups of individuals. However, conceptions of nationalization and expropriation are related in
several respects.

The (Zanzibar) Public Enterprise Decree no. 1 of 1966 and the
National Transport Corporation Order of 1966 are good instances of
permanent legislation enabling measures extending the scope of nationalization to be taken from time to time. A total of five nationalization acts were enacted in Tanzania in February 1967.

Of these acts, only one expressly extends to Tanganyika and
Zanzibar; the rest apply only in Tanganyika. They all specify by name
the firms to be nationalized, and where businesses of named firms
are acquired, the firms fall into two groups: those companies registered under the companies ordinance currently in force in the country,
and those companies incorporated under foreign law. In these cases,
all the local assets and liabilities are taken over. Assets here include
all rights under contracts and agreements, besides rights, interests,
and claims in or to property. In relation to each of the companies,
the responsible minister was empowered to make, and did make, regulations modifying the provisions of the companies ordinance and the
various articles of association.

The directors of the nationalized companies were retired from
office, but they might be called upon to help in the nationalization process. For certain ends, the legal form of the limited company was
retained. But nevertheless there is recourse to the familiar device
of the public corporation for carrying on the businesses acquired. As
a result of the nationalization exercises, two new public corporations
were created: the State Trading Corporation (STC) and the National
Bank of Commerce (NBC). The existing public corporations—the National Insurance Corporation (NIC) and the National Agricultural
Products Board (NAPB)—received new statutory responsibilities.
These four corporations were assigned functions relevant to their
fields of activities. The compulsorily acquired shares of the eight
industrial companies were vested in the National Development Corporation (NDC).

EAST AFRICAN POLICY ON COMPENSATION

The question of compensation for nationalized private assets in
East Africa is significant, first, because of the immediate financial
effects of payment and, second, owing to the effect on foreign sources
of capital as regards future investment in the East African states.

The Arusha Declaration of Tanzania stresses that although plans
for development are not to be based on receiving foreign capital,
this does not imply or mean that all foreign investment is unwelcome.
On the contrary, by declaring that it had no further plans for nationalization, the Tanzanian government was, as we have explained above,
encouraging foreign investment in the sectors unaffected by the na-

tionalizations. In that way, the government was demonstrating that
its intentions were genuine in the question of compensation. But that
demonstration did not mean that the Tanzanian government was willing
to meet any and every claim for compensation that might be made.

All the nationalization acts—barring the one that created the insurance monopoly—provided, in agreement with customary international
law, for the payment of "full and fair compensation." In the case of
companies registered in Tanganyika, where all or part of the share
capital was acquired, compensation was to be in respect of the shares
acquired. In all other cases, compensation was to be in respect of
the net value of the nationalized assets. In every case, the responsibility to pay was imposed upon the United Republic of Tanzania.

Although the nationalization laws did not specify how compensation was to be paid, or to whom it would be paid, they made it clear
that no former director was to be compensated for loss of office. The
government would fix the amount of compensation; the finance minister would issue a certificate setting out this amount, which would then
be charged on, and paid from, the consolidated fund. Further, the
minister would determine the manner of paying, and installments of,
the compensation. No legal requirement for parliamentary or presidential approval was provided for. In cases of lack of agreement or
of compensation, the Tanzanian High Court and, on appeal, the East
African Court of Appeal would settle compensation disputes. The
Tanzania Government Proceedings Act no. 16 of 1967 repealed the
Government Suits Ordinance of 1921, under which ordinance the Tanzanian government might only be sued in the courts after permission
was first obtained from the minister of justice. The Government Proceedings Act of 1967 was not drafted in the same terms as the Government Proceedings Acts of Uganda and Kenya; the Kenyan and Ugandan
laws were modeled on the U.K. Crown Proceedings Act of 1947, which
provided that the government could be sued as of right wherever it
had formally been possible for a petition of right to be brought. The
Tanzanian act simply provides that "the Government shall be subject
to all these liabilities in contract, quasi-contract, detinue, tort, and
in other respects, to which it would be subject if it were a private
person of full age and capacity."

The nationalizations in Tanzania were carried out in pursuance
of a policy of socialization approved and implemented by the country's
political, administrative, and legislative institutions. Further, the
nationalizations did not seem to be discriminatory against alien private rights and interests. Also, the nationalization laws of Tanzania
provide for the payment of compensation that does not seem to fall
below the internationally accepted minimum standard of compensation. It would appear, therefore, that Tanzania did discharge her international responsibilities regarding the questions of nationalization
and compensation.

Even if compensation for the nationalizations in Tanzania was inadequate or delayed, the fact is that the nationalizations were legal, and they did not violate any treaty obligations. As noted by the Harvard Draft Convention on the Responsibility of States for Injuries to Aliens, payment of compensation may be by installment—that is, spread over a period of years—if and when nationalization is part of a general program of social and economic reform—a point wholly applicable to Tanzania. Also, there is no indication that Tanzania has violated the international principle that compensation for nationalized assets must be effective—that is, paid in some form that may be utilized by the former owners. Tanzania has fulfilled its obligation here by including the matter in overall agreements on compensation. Finally, Tanzania's Foreign Investments (Protection) Act protects certain of the nationalized businesses.

The act actually confers investment guarantees on investors. It stipulates that any nationalization or expropriation of a private enterprise or property must be followed by payment of compensation equivalent to the "full and fair value of the approved portion of the enterprise or property." In the event of a disagreement or dispute between an asset owner and a government authority, there should be recourse to arbitration.

As in Uganda and Kenya, a large variety of joint business ventures existed in Tanzania before the 1967 nationalizations. The Tanzanian government compulsorily acquired majority shareholdings in the industrial firms, and private buildings were nationalized, as we have explained above, by legislation passed in 1971. In August 1973, the government announced it would soon start paying compensation to the former landlords whose buildings were nationalized and who qualified for compensation. Qualifications for compensation included production of the relevant documents, such as tax clearance certificates (income, rent, personal taxes, land rent and rates, and urban house and municipal taxes), water and electricity bills (that is, documents from the Dar-es-Salaam City Council or town councils, regional water engineers' offices, and the Tanganyika Electricity Supply Company, TANESCO). The notices of assessment for compensation were issued by the treasury to the individuals concerned. Many of the former landlords whose buildings were nationalized were away from Tanzania; they had emigrated to Britain, Canada, India, and Pakistan. Thus only a few hundred people were available for submission of compensation claims. One of the major conditions for payment of compensation was that it would occur only if the building was acquired, purchased, or constructed during ten years immediately preceding the 1971 date of acquisition. A special committee was created to determine any payment of compensation whose value was estimated to be more than Tanzanian £5,000. The compensation was to be paid not promptly, but in 15 years' time. In the usual practice of the developing countries, this period is perfectly normal.

As regards the take-overs of foreign companies in Uganda, Britain formally called on Amin on December 20, 1972,[13] for an assurance that all British properties seized in Uganda would be "properly and fairly compensated." The initial capital cost of 34 British estates, firms, and properties taken over by the Ugandan government was estimated at around £10 million sterling. The British Foreign Office instructed Briand, Britain's acting high commissioner in Kampala, to advise the Ugandan government in writing that the British government reserved all rights of nationals in relation to property owned in Uganda. British Foreign Secretary Alec Douglas-Home denounced Amin's actions as "outrageous by any standards of civilized behavior, insulting and inhuman." In Kampala, Amin rejected Douglas-Home's criticisms of him and said that they did not represent the views of the British people. Amin reiterated that the take-overs of the British and other foreign-owned businesses were not directed at their owners, "but it was only intended to transfer the economy of the country from the hands of noncitizens into the hands of Ugandans."[14]

Amin stressed that the Ugandan government would pay compensation for the businesses it had taken over but he added that in doing so, the position of Uganda's economy would have to be considered. This remark was open to many interpretations—for instance, that compensation would not be prompt, effective, and sufficient. In any event, Amin acknowledged Uganda's legal obligation under international law to compensate for any nationalization or expropriation. Whether Uganda will honor her responsibility to compensate for the take-overs remains to be seen.

GOVERNMENT POLICY ON ALIEN INVESTMENTS IN EAST AFRICA

The Kenyan policy on alien investment in the country is particularly striking because of the country's special emphasis on ownership. Kenya has been described by many as a country with a "capitalist outlook." The immigrant communities, particularly the Europeans, always had private capital at their disposal. The concentration of the European population in colonized Kenya in the manufacturing and agricultural sectors of Kenya's economy prompted more substantial British investments in the country's large-scale industries than anywhere else in British Africa. That fact led to a tight British hold over Kenya's industrial life that remained in effect even after its independence. In the years 1963-64, for example, European-controlled firms in Kenya increased their capital by £1,109,670—the highest figure of private capital investment in the country.[15] Private capital investments, whether in European-, Asian-, or African-controlled companies, greatly increased over the years. A large part of major Kenyan firms are subsidiaries of London-based companies on the London Times list of the largest British firms. The firms with branches or subsidiaries in Kenya include Lonrho, Unilever, Dalgety, Mitchell Cotts, Brooks Bond, J. Lyons, Glaxo, British Leyland Motors, International Computers, Shell, Transport and Trading, British Petroleum, and Metal Box.

There are also well-known non-British companies operating in Kenya. The Kenyan government has given repeated assurances against expropriation and nationalization. The central aim of these assurances is to boost the confidence of those who either personally or on behalf of others have large sums of money to invest in the country. The incentives given for such investments have included the country's political and economic stability, wise leadership, and guarantees against nationalization or expropriation. Many foreign investors have been convinced by such promises and have consequently invested in the tourist and other industries of Kenya.

The Kenyan government has also placed minimal controls on investors and has issued Approved Status Certificates to legitimate alien firms seeking permission to repatriate profits. Such certificates normally signify that an investment is contributing to the economic growth of the country. Thus unlike Tanzania's leaders who assume that Africa must create most of its own capital from its own resources,[16] Kenyan leaders pay great attention to the needs and demands of private investors. The Kenyan leaders also set great store by alien private investment as a catalyst of economic growth. Private investment sources have usually dominated Kenya's development plans. This was, for instance, the case in Kenya's Development Plan of 1966-70 in which private investment was valued at Kenyan £180 million, from a total of Kenyan £325 million.[17] Dependence on private investment is virtually full in such fields as mining, manufacturing, and nonresidential construction.

For KANU's leaders, therefore, private capital is an essential requirement for economic welfare in Kenya. They have sought to deal with the question of unemployment via the long-term process of enlarging commercial and industrial opportunity. Private capital is thus welcome in the country provided it promotes the conomic development process. "If we have (and attract) capital," according to Kenyatta, "we shall have more business opportunities and employment in the country for our people."[18] For Kenyatta, therefore, and other KANU leaders, a meaningful self-reliance is possible, so long as close connections are maintained with the Western capitalist economy (international capitalism). These arguments are highly questionable and, not surprisingly, have been challenged by critics of KANU's capitalist policies and advocates of the doctrine of national control over the means of production.

In East Africa, as indeed in any other region of the developing world, there is an imperative need for the improvement of the material welfare of the people. This is essentially a matter of economic development, for any standard of living is closely connected with healthy commerce. The existence, therefore, of good legal investment guarantees in the region can be a significant factor in the attraction of much needed foreign capital, and this in turn could contribute immensely to the economic development of the region.

No doubt, the main fear of private foreign investors in East Africa, and for that matter in the developing world as a whole, has come from the feeling that sound, long-term investment in these new, highly nationalistic, and sensitively sovereign nations is subject to unusual risks of discrimination and nationalization without prompt, effective, and sufficient compensation. This fear has led to demands for specific assurances of protection of investment on the part of the would-be private foreign investors. They have been invariably concerned with governmental actions regarding (1) discriminatory rules and laws that either cut the private foreign investor's return considerably or eventually force him to surrender his business investment —what E. I. Nwogugu has described as "creeping expropriation";[19] (2) expropriation or nationalization of the private foreign investor's business without compensation; (3) export and import quotas that cripple his business; and (4) currency restrictions making it difficult or impossible for the investor to send money out of the country of investment.

In East Africa, the laws governing investment appear in the revised laws of the three countries.[20] In general, the significance of the legal investment guarantees of the three states lies in the requirement that the governments have a legal duty to protect every foreign investment in their countries and to compensate for any loss that may be brought about by changes in the governments' policies or measures. It is thus obvious that investment guarantees to foreign investors in East Africa are promised not only in the investment laws of the three nations but also in important verbal or written policy statements by the leaders. The guarantees are also provided in the development plans of the East African countries.

However, the East African investment laws do not possess specified provisions that put private foreign investors on a par with domestic investors. There is therefore no legal guarantee against discriminatory treatment of alien investors in East Africa. The lack of legal responsibility on the part of the East African nations to avoid discrimination against foreign investors is deplorable, since it is a

remarkable deterrent to foreign investment in the region. It shows
how irrational, hypocritical, and short-sighted the three countries
are, for they openly talk of freedom and attractive conditions and
guarantees of foreign investments, while at the same time they allow
discriminatory practices in the field of investment. The negative repercussions of the discriminatory investment laws and practices are
wide, far-reaching, and well known to the governments of East Africa.
They therefore know what to do to rectify the unfortunate situation.
But unless fair treatment for all investors, whether domestic or alien,
is rectified, it is difficult to imagine how the badly needed foreign capital will contribute to the economic development of the region, as it
ought to do.

With regard to expropriation or nationalization, there is, fortunately, a legal guarantee in each of the states. Thus illegal expropriation or nationalization is not permissible anywhere in East Africa.
However, there are cases when expropriation or nationalization are
always legal, even if done without compensation. Expropriation or
nationalization done in the public interest is a good case in point, and
international law recognizes it. Where the question of compensation
has arisen, and an East African state has agreed to pay it, the matter
has been considered to be within that state's domestic jurisdiction.
Therefore the meaning of the interchangeably used adjectives "appropriate," "adequate," "equitable," "just," and "fair," as well as
the period within which compensation has had to be paid, have in
practice been determined by the individual states themselves. What
is regarded as "fair" or "adequate" compensation may differ, and
does differ, considerably from one East African state to another.
For instance, whereas Section 22 C(1) of the Uganda Constitution
talks of adequate compensation, Section 19 (c) talks of full compensation. This means that, although the constitutional and other legal
guarantees of investment in East Africa are generally similar, variations exist that must not be ignored. Kenya's Sessional Paper no.
10 of 1965 indicates that nationalization is a good idea but that it is so
expensive, it will only be employed "(i) When the assets in private
hands threaten the security or undermine the integrity of the nation;
or (ii) When productive resources are being wasted; or (iii) When the
operation of an industry has a serious deterimental effect on public
interest; and (iv) When other less costly means of control are not
available or are not effective."

Kenya has acknowledged that legal responsibility to pay compensation for any nationalization or expropriation must be borne by the
nationalizing state, but, because of the high expenses involved, Kenya
would prefer to avoid such responsibility as far as possible.

As for legal provisions guaranteeing against import and export
quotas that would cripple the private foreign investor's business, the

East African laws of investment do not, again, give a specifically
worded guarantee. The investment laws only imply that such an investment should be given a chance to survive. This lack of clear
provision to regulate import and export restrictions also needs to be
rectified. The same can be said of currency restrictions in East Africa. Thus although customary international law recognizes the right
of control by a state over its currency, as an attribute of state sovereignty, the East African countries have a legal duty or responsibility
under the same law of nations not to abuse this right by manipulation
or discrimination directed primarily to injure aliens. The main interest of any alien investor is to make profit, which he can send out of
the investment country in hard currency. The problem with East Africa, and other developing regions, is that they suffer from a serious
shortage of foreign exchange. This situation forces them to impose
currency restrictions, especially on movement of money from the developing countries. The practice of the East African states has been
not to place any restrictions on remittance of profits and capital except the procedural requirement for exchange.

CONCLUSION

The essence of the responsibilities of the East African states
lies in the fact that the East African countries are answerable, legally
and morally, for every action or nonaction that violates the rights,
recognized by international law, of other states and, in our concern,
of aliens. As noted in Article 3 of the Hague Convention of 1907 on
the Laws and Customs of War on Land, state responsibility concerning international duties is a legal responsibility, and any breach of
it by an East African state constitutes an international delinquency on
the part of that state. As members of the international civilized community, the East African countries have thus a legal duty not to violate
the international law of aliens, or international treaty obligations concerning aliens.

On the issue of admission in East Africa, the East African
states operate under a duty to admit aliens, but only under the condition that they have the right to expel or exclude aliens, or certain
classes of aliens—in cases, for instance, of drug addiction, dangerous or infectious disease, or dangerous criminality. However, international law requires that exclusion be backed up by sound reasons—
that is, those recognized by international law. Most states, nonetheless, including the East African nations, insist on, and extensively
apply, the right to exclude all aliens at will. The reason for this
practice is that such a full and unqualified right of states is an essential attribute of state sovereignty.

Certain international situations exist that warrant the necessity to be oblivious about the East African states' highly sensitive consciousness of their sovereign right to exclude aliens and not to exercise the right to its fullest extent. Thus the right to exclude aliens at will in East Africa should be sacrificed for the duty to grant asylum to religious and political alien refugees. The countries of East Africa must also avoid discriminatory admission or exclusion, for the entire prohibition of the citizens of any particular state would diplomatically be regarded as an unfriendly act or an affront toward that state. However, the possibility of a complication arising from such situations is usually avoided by agreement. Most frequently, the case of reciprocal treatment of aliens by different nations is regulated by bilateral and even multilateral treaties of culture, commerce, navigation, and technical assistance. In East Africa, such treaties exist between, for instance, Kenya and Yugoslavia, Kenya and Brazil, and Tanzania and Sweden.

As for the responsibilities of the East African nations for the protection of aliens in the region, the states are under a duty to avoid a disproportionate punishment of an alien for a violation of a local law. This means that aliens seeking justice in the East African courts should not be denied it. Although this sounds quite obvious, there have been some cases whereby denial of justice to an alien has existed in East Africa. Denial of justice to an alien exists whenever the host state's authorities fail to give sufficient means of redress to the alien when his substantive rights have been violated or, if the alien has violated the laws of the host state, to observe due process of law in the prosecution and punishment of the alien offender. There is no doubt that, in East Africa, denial of justice has occurred, particularly in the fields of business (involving mainly alien Asians) and tourism (involving mainly alien Europeans). In these and other fields, inefficiency in the performance of police and judicial processes in East Africa has been noticeable; access to the local courts has occasionally been denied to aliens, for instance, in cases where alien property has been expropriated, Africanized or nationalized without effective, prompt, or sufficient compensation. Such cases have occasionally resulted in unfair treatment of aliens or unfair judicial decisions. The East African states have a legal duty to rectify such unfortunate situations both in law and practice. They have a duty to prevent injurious discrimination against aliens and to provide aliens with proper means of redress.

Each of the countries of East Africa is also under the responsibility to honor the so-called rule of local remedies. It is a fundamental rule of international law that the international responsibility of a state for an injury to an alien may not be invoked—in the form of an international claim—as long as local remedies, available to the injured alien under the laws of the host state and providing sufficient means of redress, have not been exhausted. Thus the injured alien must first have resort to the local remedies (that is, local courts of the host state), so it can be determined whether or not the alleged injury had in fact occurred, a denial of justice had taken place, a violation of international law was clear, and a degree of state responsibility had already been established. After these facts have been made apparent, the alien may lodge an international claim against the host state.

The East African countries are also responsible for the acts or omissions of their public or government officials and collective organs such as their legislatures and administrative bodies. The duties of the countries are to punish their offending nationals where necessary, and to free themselves, in appropriate ways, of any charges of international wrongdoing. They must exercise due diligence whenever necessary, in order to prevent injuries to aliens. They must reformulate their laws and reshape their policies in such a way that, where equity collides with other demands in the region, the former will prevail.

The policies of the East African governments cover agriculture, education, public services, and commerce and trade. In all these spheres, the interests of the African citizens are paramount. Government assistance is given to the Africans in every way possible. All these and other policies specifically aim at creating and upholding a strong central government and make strenuous efforts to adhere to a one-party state system. The governments demand absolute loyalties. They insist on uniformities and are suspicious of any kind of dissent. The leaders are sensitive to every indicated or proposed change in the present power structure. Indeed, the resulting mood is indicative of fear on the side of the African leaders. To non-African residents of East Africa, notably the Asians, this seems to be the case. In such policies, the Asian contribution can only be passive. And yet the governments of East Africa demand active Asian roles in the three countries.

On race relations, the government policies of East Africa aim—and rightly so—at the eradication of racial discrimination and tribalism. The governments hence want to see racial integration without specifically defining or showing what racial integration is or should be.

The racial problem in East Africa is still great, though its magnitude varies from one East African country to another. Thus in Tanzania, the problem is really one of ideology and socialism as against capitalism, rather than of racial segregation. And although racial discrimination is discernible, for instance in educational establishments—where non-Africans, notably Asians, are discriminated against despite their being citizens—it would be erroneous to conclude that discrimination in that country is an open practice. The results of discussions this writer conducted with some Tanzanian Asians indicated that no discriminatory practice exists in the business field, for instance. On the contrary, any Tanzanian citizen who acquires a trading license in the normal and legal way is free to conduct business anywhere in the country.

This is not the case in Kenya or Uganda, where the business laws openly discriminate against non-Africans, whether citizens or aliens; discrimination is also practiced in such other fields as education. Corruption is also a most serious problem in the two countries. In Kenya, there is racial discrimination backed by black capitalism with a citizenship orientation. The racial problem is made worse by nepotism, tribalism, and corruption at all levels and in all corners of life in the country. And in Uganda, discrimination against non-Africans is open, and has been described, especially by non-Africans of Asian origin, as "fascist."

NOTES

1. See L. Oppenheim, International Law, vol. 1, 8th ed. (London: Longmans, 1962).

2. An exhaustive discussion of this question appears in Don Nanjira, "The Legal Position of the United Nations Personnel and of Other International Organizations" (Master's thesis, Warsaw University, 1969).

3. Jomo Kenyatta, Suffering Without Bitterness (Nairobi: East African Publishing House, 1968), p. 40.

4. Quoted in High Level Manpower Requirements and Resources in Kenya, 1964-1970, Ministry of Economic Planning and Development (Nairobi, 1965), p. 15.

5. See for instance Daily Nation (Nairobi), October 11, 1972.

6. See East African Standard (Nairobi), June 2, 1973.

7. See National Assembly Debates (Kenya), vol. 16, 6th sess., September 4, 1968, col. 166.

8. Kenya Act No. 25 of 1964, p. 4.

9. See Daily Nation (Nairobi), December 18, 1972; and December 19, 1972.

10. Quoted in The Arusha Declaration, and TANU's Policy of Socialism and Self-Reliance (Dar-es-Salaam: Government Printer, 1967), p. 3.

11. See P. Temu, "Nationalization in Tanzania," East African Journal, June 1967. See also L. Cliffe, "Arusha Declaration: Challenge to Tanzanians," East African Journal, March 1967.

12. See Kenya, Sessional Paper no. 10, African Socialism, 1965; and Uganda, Work for Progress, Uganda's Second Five-Year Plan (Entebbe: Government Printer, 1967). See also Uganda, The Common Man's Charter, December 1969.

13. Daily Nation, December 21, 1972.

14. Ibid.

15. See Kenya, Registrar—General Annual Report 1964 (Nairobi: Government Printer, 1964), p. 13.

16. See Daily Nation, August 7, 1968.

17. See Kenya's Development Plan, 1966-70 (Nairobi: Government Printer, 1966), pp. 44 and 118.

18. Kenyatta, op. cit. See also East African Standard, February 19, 1968.

19. E. I. Nwogugu, Legal Problems of Foreign Investment in Developing Countries (London: Manchester University Press, 1965), p. 23.

20. Tanzania, Act to Give Protection to Certain Approved Foreign Investments Incidental Thereto, 1962; Uganda, Foreign Investment (Protection) Act, 1964, chap. 166; Uganda, Constitution, sec. 22; Kenya, Constitution, sec. 19, Foreign Investments Protection Act, 1964, and Sessional Paper no. 10 of 1965.

8

Some of the oldest and most serious problems in East Africa have resulted from the Asian presence in the region. The acceptance by Britain of a sphere of influence on the mainland of East Africa brought many opportunities. These included relaxation of the administrative burden borne by Britain in India, by providing an overseas outlet for India's growing population and settlement of British peoples in East Africa. But the British acceptance brought many problems and responsibilities as well.

African hatred of Asians in East Africa does exist. The question is, Why are Asians more hated and unwanted (by Africans) than Europeans in East Africa today, whereas in colonial times European policy always favored the European community in the region, and grouped Asians and Africans together and discriminated against them? A second question is, Why is the European minority more privileged than the Asian minority in present-day East Africa?

The answers to these questions should be given along the following lines. After independence, East Africans became aware of the fact that most Asians in East Africa were a British responsibility, and as such, Britain should necessarily be made to bear her burden. Also, the "dangerously" strong economic position of Asians in East Africa has caused envy and hatred among Africans.

RACIAL STEREOTYPES IN EAST AFRICA

Of all the African accusations against the Asians in East Africa, the following are the most widespread and persistent: "Asians monopolize the economy in East Africa." "Asians are bloodsuckers and exploiters—they overcharge, cheat, bargain, and do not cooper-

ate. They are mean, greedy, dirty, dishonest, secretive, unreliable,
isolated, clannish, discriminatory and contemptuous of Africans."
"Asians do not train Africans, and therefore retard Africanization."
"Asians are wealthy aliens." "Asians export all their capital from
East Africa." "Asians collaborated with the British colonizers, and
treated Africans as 'boys' [servants]." "Asians are fence-sitters.
They have not shown loyalty to their [East African] country of residence." "Asians are arrogant and feel superior towards Africans."
"The Asian educational system was designed to promote the economic
benefits of Asians only, and to transmit and preserve Indian exclusi-
vist culture in East Africa."

Regarding Europeans, Africans have observed: "The European
is a respectiable man; he is a powerful, tough and aggressive guy,
unwilling to share his technical know-how with Africans"; "the European is a 'little lord' in East Africa, but in his own country, he is the
lowest type of porter; he discriminates against Africans and constantly
suffers from pride and superiority complex."

On their part, Asians have accused Africans of being "lazy, in-
efficient, irresponsible, dirty, awkward, primitive, and incapable of
doing hard work or acquiring skills."

Finally, Europeans in East Africa accuse Asians of being "mean
traders and exploiters of Africans. They [Asians] send out much of
their profits to India or to relatives elsewhere abroad. They bring in
from India large numbers of children and relatives. They are generally
treacherous, spread disease, and scandalize Africans." As regards
European accusations against Africans, "the African is lazy, dull,
and stupid; but he is likeable, and spoilt by education and political development."

The above racial stereotypes had their origins in the British colonial doctrine of racial compartmentalization. Therefore, it can safely
be argued that Britain bears some responsibility for the "killing" of
Asians in East Africa whether by mistrust, hostility, or rejection.

The issue of state responsibilities both under domestic and traditional international law was discussed, in the East African context,
in Chapter 7. It was also established in that chapter that state policy,
law, and practice vary from one nation to another. Asians of East
Africa who bear passports of the United Kingdom and its colonies are
certainly entitled to British citizenship and owe allegiance to the United
Kingdom. Thus British Asians have the right to enter Britain, which
is their country of nationality, while Britain has the legal duty to accept or admit them into her territory. Britain has formally accepted,
though conditionally, her legal obligation for her East African subjects
of Asian origin. This policy has been exercised by successive British
governments, which have denied entry into Britain to or imposed controls and restrictions upon the East African Asians bearing British
citizenship.

The implication, then, of the expulsion—in more recent years—
of Asians from East Africa, and the restrictions on the immigration
or entry of the British Asian expellees into the United Kingdom, have
had, inter alia, racial, social, economic, educational, cultural, political, and legal repercussions.

Until the passing, by the British Parliament of the so-called
Commonwealth Immigrants Act of 1962,[1] no restriction was imposed
on any person bearing citizenship of the United Kingdom and its colonies. In a House of Commons debate, for instance, a private member's
bill demanding immigration control introduced by a Conservative M.P.,
Cyril Osborne, the British Conservative government categorically rejected every proposal for introducing an immigration control law.
David Renton, a junior minister at the British Home Office, ending the
discussion on the bill, declared that "Her Majesty's Government will
not contemplate legislation which might restrict the historic right of
every British subject, regardless of race or colour, freely to enter
and stay in the United Kingdom."[2] Pressure, however, continued to
be exerted upon the Conservative government for enactment immediately of a control legislation on Commonwealth immigrants coming
into Britain.

In early October 1961, an annual conference of the Conservative
Party in Brighton marked the turning point in the British traditional
policy supporting the right of entry, or open-door policy, regarding
Commonwealth immigration into the United Kingdom. The Macmillan
government capitulated to the demands caused by the increase in the
numbers of Commonwealth immigrants into the country. Other reasons for ending the open-door policy included (1) the deteriorating
economy of the country; (2) the increased losses of Conservative parliamentary seats to Labour in by-elections; and (3) the growing problems of a socioeconomic nature—for example, heavy unemployment,
problems of housing, and the lack of educational facilities for the
colored immigrants. On October 31, 1961, therefore, the Macmillan
administration announced (in the Queen's speech) that they intended to
introduce an immigration law whose central purpose would be to control Commonwealth immigrants coming to the United Kingdom from
other Commonwealth countries. The law would also empower Her Majesty's Government to expel any immigrants convicted of criminal of-
fences by British tribunals. Entry into Britain would be confined to
those Commonwealth citizens who had received labor vouchers from
the British Labour Department. Certain categories of people would,
however, be exempted from those requirements—students, visitors
(such as tourists), and dependents. British courts could recommend
the deportation of Commonwealth immigrants, and the period of qualification an immigrant had to spend in the United Kingdom for registration as a British rather than a Commonwealth citizen was raised
from one year to five years.

The second reading of the bill occurred on November 17, 1961. The discriminatory character of the bill was made manifest by the nonapplication of it to the Irish, by the labor voucher system referred to above, and by the complete disregard of consultation with the other Commonwealth nations on the issue of intra-Commonwealth immigration. Criticisms of the bill abounded both in and outside the British Parliament. Fears were expressed of the British government's neglect of Britain's international responsibilities and disturbing of the status quo of the world's greatest democracy and welfare state, via promotions of racism, ill-treatment of Her Majesty's subjects, and so forth. The British government rejected such accusations. Thus when Barbara Castle, an energetic Labour M.P., stated that the bill would certainly destroy the Commonwealth, Osborne (who had by this time been knighted for public and political services, and described in the Times (of London) of November 17, 1961, as "the spirit, if not the architect of the Bill") replied: "The Hon. Lady the Member for Blackburn said that the Bill would destroy the Commonwealth. That is irresponsible and untrue. It will not affect Australia, Canada and New Zealand."[3]

Again, the discriminatory nature of the bill is quite clear, for it would not be applicable to such typical Commonwealth nations as Australia, Canada, and New Zealand. The third reading of the bill was not obstructed, and it was finally passed in the House of Commons on February 27, 1962. Royal assent was given to the bill on June 1, 1962. The rush to Britain to evade that legislation was estimated at 86,700 Commonwealth immigrants, including British passport holders of Asian origin in East Africa.

EXODUS OF ASIANS FROM EAST AFRICA

Though the Asian problem in postindependence Tanzania has never been serious, during the 1967 Asian exodus, according to estimates by reliable Tanzanian government spokesmen, more than 300 expulsion orders were served in Tanzania to Asians holding British passports. It is certain that fears of insecurity and the existence of anti-Asianism in Tanzania were the main reasons for these Asians going to Britain on the eve of the enactment of additional immigration control legislation in Britain. Anti-Asian attitudes were far greater in neighboring Kenya, and in the mid-1960s were displayed both by Africans and Europeans. Paul Theroux has noted:

> In East Africa, nearly everyone hates the Asian.
> . . . The British have hated the Asians longest.
> This legacy they passed to the Africans who now,

in Kenya for example, hold the banner of bigotry
high. . . . Racial insult against the Asians now ap-
proaches the proportions of a fashion. [4]

Despite the major contribution of Asians not only to the economic but
also to the political development of Kenya, according to Theroux,

The reactions of most Africans and Europeans in
Kenya to the Asian presence are flagrantly racist.
Yet the racism always contains nationalist senti-
ments, as if every good Kenyan must be anti-
Asian. Occasionally innuendo is used, but the tar-
get of the innuendo is always unmistakable. A collection of clippings from the East African papers
regarding the Asians is a little chamber of horrors. [5]

In 1967, Kenyatta warned non-Africans against abusing Africans and
the Kenyan government. [6] Such warnings and accusations were common
material of political speeches in Kenya in 1967. When, however,
Theroux dared to regret racial abuse and thinly veiled menaces in the
speeches of Tom Mboya, then minister for economic planning and development, and of Davis Ogina, then secretary of the KANU Mombasa
branch, his (Theroux's) letter to the Daily Nation (January 28, 1967)
provoked accusations from Africans denouncing him and the Asians in
familiar racial tones: "There is certainly a crisis being created by
the arrogant and negative behaviour and attitude of Asians in this country. . . . [7] It is quite stupid of him to try to lecture us on what to do.
If I knew which country Mr. Theroux comes from, I would have given
him a piece of my mind. . . ." [8] "One way or the other, Asians in
Kenya must be made to modify their unscrupulous trade attitudes at
once. We cannot brag about building a harmonious multi-racial state
amidst trade turbulency. . . . Whatever the future will be, the Asian
community has nothing to grumble about; the present trend, whether
good or bad, is the harvest of seeds sown by themselves." [9]
        Earlier, Theroux had stated,

It should be clear that throughout Kenya, the feeling
against Asians is more than mistrust, more than
suspicion, more than a glance sideways. It is hatred
—blind, bold, crude, irrational and based solely on
race. It is unexamined by the political scientists
who picture Kenya a little paradise for race relations;
it is ignored by the millionaires who are wooed by
the Kenya Government; and it is sometimes exploited
and encouraged by expatriates and competing business-

men who see this as a chance to boost sales and, in
addition, prove their solidarity with African nationalism in Kenya. . . . Whatever happens, the incidents
of racial abuse in East Africa, which have increased
in the past year, cannot be erased. We can agree
that bigots are everywhere and that letters will be
written no matter what happens. But there is no excuse, and there should be no pardon, for any government to be committed to a policy of hate towards less
than two percent of the population. [10]

The 1962 census in Kenya showed that there were 176,000 Asians
in the country. An investigation conducted after the 1968 British Immigration Act indicated that there were 40,000 to 50,000 Asians who
were "automatically" Kenyan citizens, that 20,000 had opted for Kenyan citizenship, and that the majority of the remainder had decided to
retain their U.K. citizenship.

Regarding British citizens of European origin in Kenya, special
arrangements were made between Britain and the newly independent
states of East Africa that helped the British European citizens conquer
their problems following the transfer of power in East Africa. Pressure on the Asians obtained greater force as years passed by until
1967, when it burst into flames. In the summer of that year, the implementation of the Africanization/Kenyanization programs was accelerated. And the enactment of the immigration and business licensing
legislation in the country made things worse for the British Asians.
When such Asians, for example, applied for employment that could
be occupied by Africans, work permits to such Asians were issued
for only three or six months per annum. That discriminatory treatment of British Asians in Kenya, plus the deadline set by the British
government regarding entry into Britain by her subjects, compelled
the Kenyan Asians with British citizenship to leave the country.

A large exodus of such Asians occurred in the late summer and
early autumn of 1967. The Asians went either to India or to Britain.
The rate of Africanization in Kenya grew, while certain politicians in
Britain decided to exploit the situation and use it as a political weapon. In the first six months of 1967, the monthly rate of the Asian
exodus had not passed 1,000. In August 1967, the monthly rate was
1,493, and a month later, the total was 2,661.

The Kenyan Asian Debate in the
House of Commons

The right of Asians in Kenya with British citizenship to enter
Britain was the subject of debate in the House of Commons in Novem-

ber 1967. The House was discussing the so-called Expiring Laws
Continuance Bill. Roy Jenkins, then home secretary, defended the
right of the Asians to come to Britain while former Conservative Colonial Secretary Sandys and others demanded that such Asians be kept
out of Britain. The fact that East African Asians dominated the debate, which dealt with the question of immigration in general, showed
the heavy pressure to which the British government was being subjected because of Britain's responsibilities for East African Asians
with British citizenship. To the Kenyan Asians who remembered the
original (independence) conditions on which the Asian community in
Kenya would retain their U.K. citizenship, it was unbelievable that
Sandys, the very person who had made the arrangements, now turned
his back on the Asians.

    The Asian fear, hence, that an immigration law was eventually
to be enacted to control, limit, or repeal the right of entry into Britain by Commonwealth subjects led to a very rapid exodus to Britain.
The Kenyan government accelerated it, by deciding to Africanize
20,000 jobs formerly held by noncitizens (Asians). In January 1968,
the Kenyan government devised a new system to effect a rapid application of the laws against the employment of noncitizens. Thus the three-
month expiration period on work permits was replaced by visitors'
permits expiring in a further three months. After this time, the affected people were expected to have wound up their affairs and left
Kenya. Bonds were to be paid to the Kenyan government for deportation costs, if and when necessary. The last date by which applications
were to be made was March 7, 1968. The maximum period for which
work permits could be issued was to be 24 months, and this only if the
employer was ready to sign a certificate stating that the individual
was personally necessary to the advancement of his (the employer's)
business, and that it was impossible for a local citizen to occupy his
position. This condition is still observed today under the work permit system. The condition multiplied the exodus of Asians to Britain.
The racists in Britain also intensified their racism, and that doubled
the fears of British Asians in Kenya; Sandys became more racist than
ever before. On February 9, 1968, Enoch Powell, another extreme
Tory rightist, attacked the regulations governing the entry of dependents of immigrants into Britain; at a Conservative dinner in Walsall,
Powell is quoted to have said, "It is hard to describe such a policy,
or lack of a policy, as anything but crazy." According to Powell, the
problem could be solved either by preventing the dependents of immigrants from entering Britain or by stopping the granting of vouchers,
or both. The News of the World of February 11, 1968, contained an
article by Osborne that warned that unless a check was imposed upon
immigrants coming to Britain, there would be more "blacks than
whites here in seventy years time." The battle to endorse racial pre-

judice continued to be fought in and outside Parliament. James Callaghan, the finance secretary, was moved by Prime Minister Harold
Wilson from the Treasury to the Home Office, while Jenkins, the home
secretary, became chancellor of the exchequer. The liberal leader,
Jeremy Thorpe, remarked after the Cabinet reshuffle that Callaghan,
having devalued the pound, was moved to the Home Office to devalue the
passport. Callaghan toughened the unwillingness of the British government to accept its responsibility for British citizens of Asian origin
in East Africa. In the House of Lords, however, there seemed to be
a general acceptance of that responsibility. Lord Stonham, for instance, minister of state at the foreign office, when asked by Lord
Milverton about the influx of Asians into the United Kingdom, replied
that Asians "are citizens of the United Kingdom and Colonies. . . .
Numbers of them have been coming here for some years, but the rate
of arrivals has recently risen. In 1967, the total was 13,600. . . .
It should be clearly understood that there is this statutory obligation."
The Times (London) declared, "The British Government of the day
[Kenya's independence in 1963] has changed since then, but the obligation has not."[11] And on February 13, 1968, Callaghan announced in
the Commons that he would be introducing legislation "to close the
loophole in the law that allowed illegal immigrants" into the country
who had been undetected for a period of over 24 hours. That warning,
plus the acceleration of Africanization in Kenya, plunged the affected
Asians into a crisis. They feared that they might eventually become
stateless persons. The chaos in Nairobi thus doubled from day to day.
Asian leaders in Kenya desperately assessed the causes of the Asian
exodus and held Britain entirely responsible for the resulting deplorable situation. The leaders stated that only about 50,000 Asians
could go to Britain, and not the various totals of from 10,000 to 250,000
publicized in Britain. Kenya was also accused of causing problems
by accelerating her program of establishing the rights of (African)
citizens to jobs ahead of noncitizens. The British government consequently sent, on February 18, 1968, Malcolm MacDonald, the British
representative in East and Central Africa, to Nairobi to discuss the
possibility of reducing the tempo of Africanization, so that Britain
would not be obliged to take action to limit the influx. The MacDonald
mission was fruitless even though he was very much respected by Kenyatta and other Kenyan leaders.

    The British Labour Cabinet was thus compelled, under mount-
ing pressure, to introduce a law planned not only to amend the previous immigration legislations of 1961 and 1965 but also to prevent the
Asian community in Kenya from using their British citizenship as a
weapon for permission to enter the United Kingdom. The decision to
enact such legislation was taken on February 22, 1968. The announcement of this decision made things worse for U.K. citizens in Kenya.

The rush to Britain, which had hitherto been at the rate of about 750 a day, now became about 1,430 a day. Panic and confusion reigned both at the Nairobi Embakasi Airport and the British airports. The assets of the affected Asians in Kenya were sold at minimal prices. The intended legislation mainly affected the heads of Asian households. The rush, confusion, and panic of January-February 1968, plus the social human problems that ensued did not bother the British Labour government. The Commonwealth Immigrants Act of 1968 was hence passed by the British Parliament on March 1, 1968, and had immediate effect.

The British Immigration Act of 1971

Judging from the debates in the British Parliament, to which the writer listened in 1969-70, immigration into Britain is a crucial issue in British politics. The Labour party lost to the Conservatives in the British general election of 1970. One of the major issues in party policies discussed both in and outside Parliament was the question of Britain's responsibilities for Commonwealth citizens. Although it was still generally accepted that Britain was responsible for such citizens—including East African Asians with U.K. citizenship—the view was that it was essential to impose restrictions and controls on the entry of such "Commonwealth persons" into Britain. The realization of this view was through the adoption of new immigration regulations, including the Immigration Act of 1971. This extensive act was also intended to impose controls on the entry into Britain not only of British subjects but also of the nationals of non-Commonwealth countries. The central purpose of the Immigration Act of 1971 was to simplify and better the United Kingdom's immigration laws by assimilating the position of aliens and Commonwealth citizens, and replacing desperate and piecemeal legislation by a single and permanent statute. The act specified that in promulgating immigration rules, the minister responsible for immigration matters might take account of citizenship and nationality. It was expected that this power would be employed to deal with the special position of the nationals of the European Common Market countries. The act of 1971 divided prospective entrants into the United Kingdom into eight classes: (1) patrials; (2) settlers; (3) Common Market nationals; (4) nonpatrial Commonwealth citizens with U.K. grandparents or grandpatrials; (5) nonpatrial citizens of the United Kingdom and its colonies with U.K. passports; (6) nonpatrial citizens of the United Kingdom and its colonies without U.K. passports; (7) Commonwealth citizens, British-protected persons, and citizens of the Republic of Ireland (not being patrials, settlers, grandpatrials, or citizens of the United Kingdom and its colonies); and (8) aliens other than Common Market nationals.

Robert Carr, then home secretary, described as "myth" any allegations that the British government wished "to treat Commonwealth citizens as aliens."[12] However, the Immigration Act of 1971, like the other new immigration regulations introduced by Carr and approved by the Commons on February 21, and by the Lords on February 27, 1972, all reduced the right of entry into Britain of British citizens of Asian origin in East Africa. They also had the effect of evading Britain's international obligations for such Asians.

The putting of restrictions on the entry of such persons into the United Kingdom must not, however, be confused with Britain's acceptance of her obligations toward such persons. A good instance of Britain's recognition and acceptance of her international responsibilities for U.K. subjects within the British Commonwealth was clearly indicated by the British government following the expulsion, by Uganda's Amin, of Asians holding British passports in the country.

U.K. Laws Relating to Aliens

The East African laws relating to aliens have, no matter how ambiguously, indicated who is an alien in East Africa and who is not. Under the U.K. laws relating to aliens, every British subject (alias Commonwealth citizen) had the right, in common law at least, to enter the United Kingdom. This doctrine was endorsed by the British Nationality Act of 1948 (examined in Chapter 2). The doctrine was also endorsed, in the strict sense, by the Commonwealth Immigrants Act of 1962. This was clearly shown in Sections 2(1) and 3(1) and Schedule 1, paragraph 1(2) of the act, which indicated, inter alia, that if a citizen of a Commonwealth nation landed secretively in Britain, he committed no offense, for he was a British subject, and prima facie had "the same rights to be in this country as has any native Englishman." The Court of Appeal in Britain thus asserted that a Commonwealth citizen, though subject to control under the 1962 Act, might land wherever he chose, and had no obligation to search for an immigration officer and present himself for examination. This legal situation enabled citizens of the East African states, and of the United Kingdom, living in East Africa to enjoy the right to entry into the United Kingdom. The 1968 Commonwealth Immigrants Act ended the enjoyment by all British subjects of the right to enter Britain without submitting to immigration examination; this stipulation was contained in Section 3 of the Act.

The 1968 act also minimized the number of Commonwealth citizens who might remain immune from immigration restrictions. This immunity would consequently be enjoyed only by such citizens who bore a U.K. passport and had been born, adopted, naturalized, or regis-

tered in the United Kingdom. Under the Immigration Act of 1971, the
traditional right of entry into Britain was superseded by a statutory
right of abode, which was so defined that it did not encompass the
right of every person free from control to land in Britain without submitting to examination. The right of abode would be enjoyed only by
those so closely connected with Britain to qualify as patrials.

Customary international law seems to recognize a general principle of law—under the meaning of Article 38 of the Statute of the International Court of Justice—called estoppel, by which a state is prevented from denying the validity of its own actions, or from contradic-
ting the reasonable conclusions to be drawn from its own conduct.
Therefore any argument that Britain has no legal obligations toward
East African Asians, or that U.K. citizenship can be justifiably denied to such people, must be completely rejected. For in the case
of the Asians, it was Britain that had moved their ancestors to East
Africa. They and their ancestors were born and brought up in territories then under British colonial rule. It was the British government
that normally sponsored programs of moving them from one British
Empire land to another. It was Britain that recruited them to work
on the Uganda Railway. Of the treaties concluded between Britain and
other states since 1948, many have defined the expression "national
of the United Kingdom" in such a way as to include every citizen of the
United Kingdom and its colonies. Thus the United Kingdom owes to
the East African states the responsibility to admit British Asians from
East Africa.

EXPULSION OF ASIANS FROM UGANDA:
THE EXODUS OF 1972

In the summer and autumn of 1972, some 27,000 Asians arrived
in Britain from Uganda. The latter had exercised its right, announced
on August 4, 1972, to expel all Asians whom Uganda regarded as
aliens. The British government, through Carr, announced its duty
to admit the Asian expellees. Public opinion in Britain had urged the
British government to phase the influx. Carr (the home secretary),
on the other hand, clearly showed that the Conservative government
was committed to admit British Asians both on compassionate grounds
—that was why he exercised his discretionary powers to let in the
stateless husbands or heads of the British Asian families expelled from
Uganda—and as a matter of Britain's legal responsibility under customary international law.

On February 23, 1973, therefore, Carr announced to the House
of Commons his decision to admit to Britain some 300 of the Asian
men expelled from Uganda. Those who benefited from Carr's "humane

act" were not citizens of Britain and its colonies, but persons who had
considered themselves Ugandan citizens prior to the Ugandan government's project of verifying the citizenship claims of the Asian community in Uganda. However, the 300 men had an important tie with Britain: their wives were all resident there and seemingly all enjoyed
U.K. citizenship. In this regard, the 300 husbands were distinguished
from a smaller number of refugees, to whom Carr granted less specific assurances. The refugee group comprised about 100 men and
women who had entered Britain but had not yet been admitted for settlement, together with a smaller number in Europe, "whose circumstances present," as Carr put it, "strong compassionate features."
It was to this smaller group that he promised "sympathetic consideration."[13] Carr's action was commendable, for by it, family reunions
were ensured although Britain had no responsibility to admit such persons to its territory.

In a letter to the Times (London, August 19, 1972) regarding the
expulsion of Asians from Uganda Georg Schwarzenberger of London
University argued that the expulsion amounted to a breach of international law. This writer rejects that argument. It could only be justified if Amin had retained his second decree, announced on August 18,
1972, whereby all Asians—including those with Ugandan citizenship-
would be kicked out of Uganda. If Amin had in fact effected this decree
—he withdrew his announcement of August 18 on August 23—or expelled
the affected British Asians to some states other than Britain, then it
would have been right to say that his expulsion violated international
law. But as it stood, the expulsion affected British Asians only.
Moreover, Carr, along with the British lord chancellor and the attorney general, openly admitted Her Majesty's Government's duty to protect the Asian expellees and admit them, as they had "nowhere else
to live."[14]

After accepting Britain's responsibilities for the protection of
its East African nationals of Asian origin expelled by President Amin's
regime, the British government established in 1972 a Uganda Resettlement Board. The board comprised 11 members, with Charles C.
Cunningham as chairman; on the board was Praful Patel, a leading
spokesman for East African Asians in London. The purpose of the
board was to assist U.K. passport holders and their dependents who
were ordinarily resident in Uganda on August 4, 1972—the day Amin
announced his expulsion of British Asians from Uganda—and the children of any such persons born since then.

In a 1974 report, the board outlined its efforts to, inter alia,
establish centers as temporary institutions to provide emergency accommodation. The resettlement of the Ugandan Asians was distributed
throughout Britain, in 16 resettlement centers.

Those Ugandan Asian entrants who desired to reemigrate to other countries were allowed to do so. A good number reemigrated to Canada, the United States, New Zealand, and Sweden. In short, the work of the Resettlement Board was mainly administrative in character. The board helped give the Asians a first start in the U.K. community—meeting them on arrival, organizaing the resettlement centers, and providing advice and assistance. By the time the board was dissolved on January 31, 1974, it had handled 28,608 ex-Ugandan Asians. Of this total number, 6,621 decided, when they reached Britain, to make their own arrangements for settling in the British community. The remainder were accommodated, for varying periods of time, in the resettlement centers set up by the board. As for the financial implications of the resettlement work, a summary of net expenditure contained in the board's 1974 report reveals that some £6,126,700 sterling were spent during the resettlement process.

CONCLUSIONS

If East Africa had obtained independence later than it did, perhaps the Asian problem in the region might not have been as serious as it has been. It can also be argued that if the colonial power had introduced a system of black capitalism already in the colonial times and nationalized Asians in the region, as they did with the Arabs, the Asian dilemma would not, perhaps, have existed. But East African independence found the roughly 360,000 Asians still unpopular, hated, and envied not only by the African majority, but also by the tiny but beloved and most influential European community. If the British government had accepted its responsibility for the Asians right from the start of the transfer of power, and concerned itself with the protection and welfare of the Asians as it did with the white settlers and civil servants, the Asian problem might, perhaps, have been minimized. That was not the case, for during the time that the European settlers and civil servants were being secured, via projects whereby they could, for instance, either be pensioned off on excellent terms prematurely and obtain special compensations for loss of careers, or retire in the normal way, the Asians were ignored. The Asian campaigns to get treatment similar to that accorded to the Europeans were totally rejected. Further, the British government openly demonstrated its neglect of its obligations toward its East African Asians by enacting certain legislation—a practice it has retained up to today—which affirmed the government's duties only to Englishmen, white U.K. citizens. Thus no clear responsibilities were spelled out toward nonwhite Britons who, by legal definition at least, were a British responsibility just as much as the white Britons. Ironically, Britain accepted

her responsibility for such nonwhite Britons in clauses she inserted
into the Independence Constitutions of Uganda, Kenya, Zanzibar, and
Tanganyika. The new citizenship rules introduced in Tanzania, in
practice, affected the Zanzibaris only.

Although all the citizens of Tanganyika and Zanzibar became
Tanzanian citizens, there were some exceptions. Three main classes
emerged of those citizens excluded from the citizenship after the Tan-
ganyikan-Zanzibari union: (1) Zanzibari citizens by virtue of birth,
or a father's birth, in a part of the former Sultan's possessions other
than the State of Zanzibar; (2) Zanzibari citizens who had become so
only by virtue of their naturalization or registration in Zanzibar under
the British Nationality Act of 1948; and (3) Zanzibari citizens who had
been deprived of their Zanzibari citizenship by Karume's revolutionary
council, or deported or exiled from Zanzibar. Most of the Zanzibari
citizens in the last two classes became stateless persons. About
7,000 Asians belonged to this group of stateless people. Most of them
are believed to be either in Zanzibar or in Dar-es-Salaam.

The Ugandan Asians also contained categories of persons, after
Amin's expulsions, whose legal status was more of stateless persons
than of British nationals. Britain would be exempted, under traditional international law, from responsibility toward such Asians who
would be proved to be stateless. The United Nations would, via its
High Commission for Refugees, step in in such circumstances. The
possibility of solving problems caused by statelessness in Uganda was
near completion between the British government and ex-President
Obote. An agreement was being worked out between the two sides and
was about to be signed when Obote was ousted by Amin in January 1971.
The agreement was one of the subjects of discussion in Singapore,
during the 1971 Commonwealth Conference, between British government officials and Obote, when Amin staged a coup d'etat. The British-
Ugandan talks on the proposed agreement were abandoned, and thus a
golden opportunity of solving the problem of stateless Asians in Uganda
was lost.

East African Asians can be divided into four broad classes.
First, there are those Asians who are East African nationals by virtue of their possession of East African citizenship. Although it is
not easy to quote exact figures in this category, reliable governmental
sources indicate that in Tanzania, about 20,000 Asians became citizens
by registration, whereas about 60,000 others acquired Tanzanian citizenship by the automatic method outlined in the country's legislation.
In Uganda, about 13,000 Asians became citizens by registration,
while 30,000 acquired citizenship automatically. The figures for
Kenya are estimated at 20,000 and 50,000, respectively.

Second, there are those Asians who are nationals of Britain and
its colonies by virtue of their possession of British passports. This

class can be subdivided into citizens and protected persons of Britain
and its colonies. We have referred to them simply as British subjects or Commonwealth citizens. Again, it is not easy to determine
the figures in this class of Asians, owing mainly to the exoduses that
have occurred at various times since independence. However, reliable governmental sources indicate that, in Kenya, there were, at independence, about 103,000 British subjects of Asian origin, of whom
about 100,000 were British citizens and the rest were British protected
persons. After the Asian exodus of 1967-68, the figures of British
Asians in Kenya were estimated at 50,000, and now they are probably
much less. In Uganda, there were about 40,000 British Asians before
the Asian exodus of 1972. Many of them were British protected persons. No accurate figures are available at the time of this writing,
but from the events that have taken place since the first expulsion order was served to the Asians in August 1972, the number of Asians in
Uganda must now be very small indeed. In Tanzania, there are most
probably less than 25,000 British Asians, many of whom should be described as British protected persons.

A third group of East African Asians are those who are citizens
of the countries of the Indian subcontinent—Bangladesh, India, and Pakistan. Apart from those Indian-subcontinent Asians who have come
to East Africa—since the latter's independence—as "expatriates on
contract," there are roughly 15,000 alien Asians, who bear citizenship
of the subcontinent's states.

A fourth class of East African Asians are those whose legal
status is either unclear or stateless. They are all categorized into
the class of stateless persons. No exact or accurate figures are
available at the time of this writing.

The balance between hopes and fears for the future of British
Asians in East Africa, as a materially comfortable, racially visible,
and powerless small minority in the midst of black capitalism and nationalism determined their citizenship. The hopeful Asians opted for
local citizenship, while the skeptical retained their British identity.
The shrewd Asians got half the members of the family to opt for East
African citizenship and not British nationality.

The middle class, comprising an alien minority, is weak and
has no independent political power because it lacks the means of perpetuating its economic power. The Africans' eagerness to step into
Asians' shoes immediately has been prompted by the former's desire
to transfer the economy of the region into African hands. The outcome
of the desire has been the policy of expulsion of the foreign middle
class. Asianism in Uganda gripped the country's army right from the
start of the military regime. In October 1971, for instance, all
Asians in Uganda were made to line up and be counted in a special
census. They were subsequently subjected to humiliation and harass-

ment, including the calling by Amin of an Asian conference in December 1971 to respond to alleged complaints against them. Many Asians were compelled to leave the country. But not all the British Asians could go to Britain because of the voucher system introduced by the immigration rules in Britain between 1962 and 1973.

The expulsion of Asians by the East African governments has been the result of an enormous crisis and pressure on these governments. A relevant question that can be asked now is whether the expulsion of Asians from East Africa was justified in international law. The response to this question must be given in the affirmative. Alien expellees may be reconducted to their home state, or state of nationality. The responsibility of the home state toward its nationals is, in fact, the corollary of the foreign national receiving a state's right of expulsion. In the case of the expulsion of British Asians from East Africa, Britain's responsibility to admit the Asian expellees is, therefore, the corollary of the prima facie right of the East African States to expel Asians who are U.K. subjects, from their territories.

The decision to expel Asians from Uganda seems to have been made on August 3, 1972. For in Amin's speech of August 12, 1972, he declared:

> Even in this case, the decision was given by God.
> When I had travelled to South Karamoja to open
> the District Show at Iriri, I, on Thursday night,
> the 3rd August, 1972 had a dream that the Asian
> problem was becoming extremely explosive and
> that God was directing me to act immediately to
> save the situation.

The presidential decrees enacted to implement the decision to expel noncitizen Asians from Uganda have included Immigration Decree no. 17 of August 9, 1972, and the Declaration of Assets Decree no. 27 of 1972. The purpose of presidential decree no. 17 was to cancel most of the work permits and residence certificates or passes, which had been issued to U.K. and colonies' citizens of Asian origin, besides nationals of India, Pakistan, and Bangladesh, under the country's immigration and business licensing legislations of 1969. Subsequent proclamations showed that Asians from Kenya and Tanzania would also be expelled, and all bearers of canceled permits, certificates, or passes had to leave the country within 90 days from August 9, 1972. However, alien Asians would be exempted from the decree if they were in Ugandan government service, if they fell within a number of professional categories, if they were owners of industrial and agricultural enterprises, or if they were owners or managers of banks and insurance companies.

Under Decree no. 27 of 1972, no Asian leaving Uganda after being served with an expulsion order was allowed to transfer any immovable property, farm property including livestock, or business to any other person. He could not mortgage his property, issue new shares in his company, change the salaries of his staff, or in any way vary the remuneration or terms of service of his company's directors. He had to make a declaration of his assets and surrender it to the commerce and industry minister. Failure to comply with these stipulations would result in a fine of 50,000 Ugandan shillings or imprisonment of up to two years or both. This is the essence of Amin's policy of "economic war," or of transferring the economy to Africans.

The 1962 Commonwealth Immigrants Act in Britain was the country's first legislation to curtail immigration from the Commonwealth to Britain. Entry was regulated by a system of job vouchers. Vouchers were divided into three categories: A vouchers for those with specific jobs to come to; B vouchers for those with special skills or qualifications; and C vouchers for unskilled workers without definite jobs arranged before arrival into Britain. Wives and children under 16 were free to accompany voucher bearers or to join husbands and parents already in Britain.

In 1965, a White Paper was passed that set a limit of 8,500 vouchers a year, of which 1,000 were reserved for Malta. C vouchers were abolished by the 1965 White Paper, and B vouchers were given preference. The most controversial of all the British immigration laws was the Commonwealth Immigrants Act of 1968, which greatly curtailed Britain's responsibilities for her subjects within the Commonwealth. The act was aimed mainly at imposing further and tighter controls on the immigration of U.K. passport holders from East Africa who were entering Britain in increasing numbers. The legislation also provided that any unlawfully entering immigrant could be deported any time up to 28 days after his arrival.

The Immigration Act of 1971 was the most extensive of the laws dealing with immigration to Britain. The act stipulates that only "patrials" are free to live in the United Kingdom and that they can come and go as they like. The act defines a "patrial" as (1) a citizen of the United Kingdom and its colonies who has that citizenship by birth, adoption, naturalization, or registration in the United Kingdom; (2) a citizen of the United Kingdom and its colonies who has a parent or grandparent who was born in the United Kingdom or acquired citizenship there by adoption, registration, or naturalization; (3) a citizen of the United Kingdom and its colonies who has been resident there for at least five years; and (4) a Commonwealth citizen with a parent born in the United Kingdom and holding U.K. citizenship, or a Commonwealth citizen who is or has been the wife of a patrial. All other persons are considered nonpatrials requiring permission to enter the United Kingdom. Permission is normally granted for a limited period and may be given subject to conditions restricting employment.

As for work permits, control over Commonwealth citizens with such permits is exercised jointly by the Home Office and the Department of Employment. Usually, permission to remain in the United Kingdom will be for one year only. After that period, permission from the Home Office is required for an extension. If Commonwealth citizens wish to change their jobs, they will have to seek the permission of the Department of Employment. After four years in approved employment, they may apply for permanent settlement and will then be free to take any employment.

In the area of citizenship, the Immigration Act of 1971 removed the automatic right of Commonwealth citizens to register as U.K. citizens after a five-year residence in the country. However, Commonwealth citizens who are settled in the United Kingdom when the act comes into effect retain their right, as will people who are patrial and the wives of the U.K. citizens. There will be no appeal against a refusal to grant citizenship.

On deportation, the 1971 act gave the home secretary wide-ranging powers to deport the family of a nonpatrial who is being deported. There is, however, a right of appeal against his decision. A deportation order can be made against a person for staying in the United Kingdom in violation of conditions, on the recommendation of a court, or if the home secretary deems it to be conducive to the public good.

On repatriation, the 1971 act contains provision for the payment of travel expenses for households whose heads are not patrial, who wish to leave the country to settle elsewhere. Assistance is nevertheless confined to those who wish to depart of their own free choice, and in whose interests this is. Eligibility is gauged according to the means and employment record of applicants.

With regard to existing residents, the 1971 act inserted an amendment that "nothing in the Act will remove any rights from, or adversely affect the status of any Commonwealth citizen already settled in the U.K." Finally, the act regulated the question of unlawful entry. The time limit of 28 days after which removal directions may not be given in respect of a person who has entered the United Kingdom illegally is abolished. The act also introduced a new offense of helping unlawful entry, for which the penalties are an unlimited fine and imprisonment of up to seven years. The court was given power to confiscate any ship, aircraft, or vehicle used.

In May 1969, the so-called Immigration Appeals Act was enacted. The act provides for a two-tiered appeals authority, comprising an Immigration Tribunal and adjudicators. Under the 1971 Immigration Act, the tribunal and the adjudicators continue to operate. Thus a person who is refused permission to enter the United Kingdom or an extension of stay in the country or a variation of entry conditions can appeal to an adjudicator against the decision of British authorities. This also applies to a person who is refused a certificate of patriality, an entry certificate, or a visa. If the home secretary rules that entry is against the public good, then the person is not entitled to appeal.

Whatever the restrictions on entry of British Asians into the United Kingdom, Britain's obligations under international law for such Asians are unquestionable. English common law, in fact, has incorporated the general and fundamental doctrine of international law that every state has a duty to admit to its territory its own nationals.

The writer cannot discover any circumstances under which Britain may argue that the East African states have a duty, under international law, to admit British nationals to their territories or not to expel them. The enactment by the British government of the British Nationality Act (no. 2) of 1964 was indicative of the country's aim to evade its duties toward British Asians, via a discriminatory legislation. The 1964 act favored European settlers in East Africa. It had the purpose of getting around the nationality legislations in East Africa, which prohibit dual nationality. Under the British Nationality Act of 1964, those "Britishers"—white European nationals—who surrendered their British citizenship to become East African citizens can, at any time, reclaim British nationality. Such Englishmen certainly possess greater rights than the nonwhite Britons whose rights and British responsibility toward them tend to be ignored.

NOTES

1. See for instance Daily Express (London), January 16, 1962; and Britain, House of Commons Debates, February 1962.

2. Quoted in David Steel, No Entry (London: C. Hurst, 1969), p. 41.

3. See House of Common Debates, February 22, 1962.

4. Paul Theroux, "Hating the Asians," Transition, no. 33 (October/November, 1967), pp. 46-51.

5. Ibid.

6. Uganda Argus, June 2, 1967.

7. Quoted in Daily Nation (Nairobi), February 2, 1967.

8. Ibid., February 7, 1967.

9. Ibid., February 13, 1967.

10. Theroux, op. cit.

11. See Times (London), February 13, 1968; and House of Lords Debates, February 1968.

12. See <u>House of Commons Debates</u> 851, col. 591, 1971; <u>Times</u> (London), September 21, 1968; and A. Samuels, "The Immigration Act, 1971," <u>New Law Journal</u> 122, p. 1028.

13. See <u>Times</u> (London), February 24, 1973.

14. Quoted in <u>Times</u> (London), September 15, 1972.

9

ALIENS AND THE QUESTION OF HUMAN RIGHTS IN EAST AFRICA

The welfare of the individual, whether an alien or citizen, has always been a question of international concern. The fact is that international law is a discipline whose primary aim is to bring security, peace, and joy to every individual wherever he or she may be. And since the individual has always played a vital role in the process of creating legal orders, whether national or international, it is only fair that his fundamental rights and freedoms should be recognized, and fully protected by the law. International concern for the well-being of the individual is not a novel thing. For, even before the establishment of the League of Nations, the issue of human rights was the subject of regulation in many bilateral and multilateral treaties. When the League was created, it dealt with the question of national minorities and human rights, which had become an international problem following the outbreak of World War I. Many documents were prepared and conventions were concluded, under the aegis of the League. For example, conventions and valuable documentations were produced at the International Conference on the Treatment of Foreigners, [1] held in Paris in 1929, and the Codification Conference held at the Hague in 1930. When the United Nations was created, it immediately became involved in the issue of human rights and fundamental freedoms. The United Nations has continued to be deeply concerned about the protection of minorities and human rights for all peoples without distinction as to language, race, religion, sex, tribe, and so forth.

TREATMENT OF ALIENS: TWO DOCTRINES

The available historical and legal materials provide evidence that the question of treatment of aliens is as old as the history of the

law and relations among nations.[2] This history reveals that two doctrines—legal and inevitably political—exist that are not only contrast-
ing but very controversial. And their political and economic repercussions are conflicting. According to one doctrine, a sovereign has absolute authority over everything and everybody within his domicile.
Therefore, no distinction whatsoever should be made between the
treatment of a citizen and an alien in the national territory of a given
state. For an alien, by voluntarily deciding to put himself within the
territorial jurisdiction of a given sovereign or state, knowingly and
willingly accepts not only the duties of allegiance—whether temporarily
or permanently—to that sovereign or state but also any other burdens
that that sovereign's or state's laws may impose generally. An alien
must hence be treated just like a citizen of the receiving state, for
both of them fall under the same jurisdiction and are subject to the
same living conditions. This doctrine thus expounds equality of
treatment under one domestic jurisdiction. The doctrine is normally
described as the theory of national treatment. Its staunchest advocates include distinguished authors such as E. M. Borchard, Carlos
Calvo, and L. Oppenheim.

According to the other doctrine, an alien is a "visitor," and as
such, he should be made to enjoy a much more favorable status than
a citizen who is completely at the mercy of his own state, which, for
the alien who owes allegiance to another state, is a host state. An
alien should, therefore, be given a special position and treatment in
the host state. The latter cannot, according to this theory, evade in
every circumstance international responsibility by arguing that aliens
and citizens had been accorded equal treatment. Clearly, then, this
latter doctrine, known variably as the theory of international treatment, the minimum standard of civilization, the civilization standard,
the international standard of justice, the moral standard of civilized
nations, and the international standard of treatment, may be disad-
vantageous to the alien in many ways. But it is an ideal one, though
it has only a few supporters, including the Italian jurist M. Anzillotti.

The present writer supports this doctrine. For it imposes international responsibility on the receiving state to grant to aliens in
its territory a treatment according to international standards—the
minimum standards at least—laid down by international law. This
means that more than equality of treatment (with its own citizens)
should be accorded to aliens by a state. This is all the more necessary if and where national standards fall below international ones.
Thus execution of an alien without trial, wanton killings of aliens by
local authorities, arbitrary or illegal arrests, detentions or imprisonments, deportations, denial of justice to aliens, unduly cruel, oppressive, or unjust treatment of aliens, and so on are all examples of
national treatment below the international standard. In these instances,

the state cannot escape international responsibility. The doctrine of
the international standard of treatment thus promotes respect for
the rights of individuals and other sovereigns. It purports to advance
the fundamental principle of international comity whereby states agree
to observe rules of convenience, politeness, and goodwill in their mutual relationships, even though they are not bound to do so by law. It
was on the basis of international comity that the Vienna Convention on
Diplomatic Relations of 1961 exempted, in Article 36, diplomats from
customs duties, taxes, and related charges.

The doctrine of equality of treatment, on the contrary, favors the
principle of equity through which the policies of justice, the open door,
reciprocity, most-favored-nation treatment, compromise, and the
like are pronounced and may be arranged by treaty. Fair enough, but
in reality, this doctrine tends to support the evasion of international
responsibility toward aliens by the host state. The denial to aliens of
political and civic rights by most states, including those in East Africa, is a good instance in point. According to the national treatment
theory, aliens might quite as well serve not only in the police force
but also in the armed forces as well of a host country. Is this not
ridiculous? The national treatment doctrine also enables many states,
including the East African states, to require aliens to obey the law as
they find it. This is perfectly normal. But the repercussions of this
requirement have a discriminatory character, since by it, aliens can
be quite easily—and are in most states—restricted, if not excluded,
from performing certain functions, be they in the legal, economic,
business, or other spheres. Thus aliens may, for example, be denied
access to legal assistance in cases before national tribunals. They
may be required to deposit enormous amounts of money, or security
in kind, for costs. East Africa applies the national treatment doctrine,
imposes restrictions on aliens, and prevents them from carrying on
certain functions. Aliens may, under national treatment, also be deported, as the East African practice has shown, without justified reasons being given by the deporting states. All these and other theories
and realities clearly show that the doctrine of national treatment is
not perfect. For, in it, there is plenty of room for the occurrence of
all sorts of discrimination and violation of human rights and fundamental freedoms.

The wide support and application of the equality doctrine, plus
the tolerance by international law of discrimination in many areas—
such as those of taxation, business, and exchange control—all clearly
reveal the existence of many loopholes in the world's legal systems,
and the imperfection of international law itself. It remains to be
seen what those international organs charged with the responsibility
of developing the law will do to remove the worldwide menace of discrimination and other violations of the basic freedoms and rights of
mankind.

EAST AFRICAN APPLICATION OF
INTERNATIONAL RULES

In practice, East Africa greatly deviates from the international rules governing the issue of treatment of aliens and human rights in general. In part, however, the East African practice conforms to these rules. We have also seen that, in law, East Africa considerably deviates from the requirements of international law regarding the issue, but it generally conforms to the international-law principles on the question. The deviation is partly due to the loopholes in international law itself and to the deliberate shortcomings of the legislations regulating the legal status of aliens in East Africa. In the Ugandan (Independence) Constitution, for example, racial citizenship provisions were deliberately enshrined. No clause was included to guarantee freedom of religious community, for instance, or denomination to provide religious instruction in the course of educating its own members. Furthermore, there was a deliberate allowance for racially discriminatory laws to be made for the employment of a proportion of African citizens of Uganda in any trade, business, profession, or occupation. The same can certainly be said of the provisions in the Kenyan legislation. Most conspicuous and least justifiable of these extraneous issues was the proposed change in the citizenship regulations by which the child of Ugandan citizens, born after a date to be specified—most probably the date the Kenyan Constitution would come into effect—would have to apply for registration as a Ugandan citizen, unless one of the child's parents or grandparents was, or had been, an African born in Uganda. Thus the existing Ugandan citizenship could be denied in the cases of certain children or other minors, before independence, who had been children of non-African citizens of Uganda. And the alterations in the citizenship law were in effect a deliberate deviation from the internationally accepted principles of nationality law, under which the child of a citizen, whenever born, and whatever his racial origin or pigmentation, succeeds to his father's citizenship. That the new Ugandan form of racial discrimination was inscribed in the same law that was supposed to guarantee against racial discrimination was a striking instance of tolerance of racialism in legislation. The outcome of such tolerance of racialism in law would inevitably be a new class of stateless persons in Uganda. Article 4 of Uganda's Independence Constitution, therefore, like the corresponding articles in the Independence Constitutions of Kenya and Tanzania, needed to be reviewed.

Not many cases of a serious nature involving aliens have been brought before East African tribunals. But because these tribunals have variably interpreted the concept of the rule of law, it is necessary to look into the meaning of this concept here. The core of the concept is the understanding that nobody is above the law and that all people should be tried in the same courts, under the same laws, irrespective of position or origin. However, the notion of the rule of law does not mean that the government, its officials, and agents—the source of the laws—are vulnerable. In England, for example, the doctrine of the rule of law went hand in hand with the expression "the sovereign can do no wrong." This inconsistency in theory is only apparent. Thus, the belief that "the sovereign can do no wrong" does not mean that "anything the sovereign does is always right." All, then, that the doctrine originally meant, and still means, is that the sovereign is incapable of wrongdoing. The modern trends in the interpretation of democracy, however, especially in the civilized world, show that this traditional notion of the rule of law is being challenged.

That aliens have rights—granted and guaranteed by international law—before municipal courts is an established and widely accepted fact. The East African states recognize this fact, fortunately. The states also recognize the existence of, and apply the internationally significant principle of, the local remedies rule (as discussed previously).

The East African nations generally permit aliens access to their courts on a basis of equality with citizens. However, the practice in the region of requiring excessive security bonds and the frequent inability of aliens to sue in forma pauperis both deserve an analysis here.

First, the East African practice does not acknowledge the historical and traditional doctrine of extraterritoriality, by which aliens are governed by their own laws, even though abroad, and may be sued only in special courts in the host state that apply that law. However, this doctrine is no longer applicable anywhere in the world today. The doctrine was once very frequently applied in the Middle and Far East.

Second, the East African practice acknowledges and applies the doctrine of reciprocity, by which the rights of aliens in East Africa depend upon the corresponding rights being accorded to citizens of the East African states in the country of aliens. This reciprocity may be either (1) de facto, when the alien will enjoy those rights that are granted by law, by the courts, or by administrative practice in his own country, to citizens of his host state; (2) legislative, when the alien will enjoy or enjoys only those rights that are granted by legislation to citizens of his host state; or (3) diplomatic, when the alien has only those rights granted by treaty or even practice (custom). Kenya extensively applies this doctrine, for instance, toward the diplomats of the socialist states except for those of Yugoslavia. This Konyan practice is questionable. The Soviet Union imposes restrictions on their movements upon Kenyan and other nonsocialist diplomats on Soviet soil. For example, a Kenyan diplomat in Moscow may not move out of a certain radius within Moscow without prior consent of the Soviet authorities. The other socialist states—Poland, for instance—affirm that they do not restrict foreign diplomats within their territories.

According to Kenyan diplomatic practice, no diplomats from East European states, except Yugoslav diplomats, are allowed to leave the Nairobi area without prior consent of Kenyan authorities. Thus socialist diplomats from Eastern Europe must apply for permission at least ten days before their intended visit up country. The applications are subject to approval or rejection. A question that could be raised about the Kenyan practice is whether Kenya imposes restrictions on the movements of socialist diplomats within its territory merely because of the restrictions imposed on Kenyan diplomats in the Soviet Union by Soviet authorities. It seems that the argument expounded by Kenya is that the socialist states are Soviet satellites, because they belong to the Soviet bloc, and, therefore, all their diplomats in Kenya must be treated in the same way (that is, on a reciprocal basis) that the Soviet Union treats Kenyan diplomats within her territory. It is difficult to justify the rationale behind Kenya's insistence that she adheres to the internationally recognized principle of reciprocity, on the treatment of diplomats, just because her ambassador to Russia, Poland, Czechoslovakia, Hungary, Bulgaria, or Romania happens to have his residence in the Soviet Union, where he is restricted, and therefore, all the diplomats of these countries should also be restricted in Kenya. Any argument, therefore, that Kenya displays preferential treatment to certain diplomats—Yugoslav diplomats and those of Western Europe (British diplomats, for instance)—and not to others, has the support of this writer. It may be argued, and rightly so, that Yugoslavia has always fought with Kenya and other developing nations in the nonaligned movement. But it has been a matter of custom and practice that Yugoslav diplomats are not discriminated against in Kenya. There is no reason why a similar custom cannot be adopted toward those East European states that do not discriminate against or restrict Kenyan diplomats in their territories. Certainly, it would be best for Kenya to revise the question of treatment of foreign diplomats in the country and to abide by the principle of reciprocity. This, as regards the East European states, means that the Soviet restrictions on Kenyan diplomats should not make the diplomats of the other socialist countries in Kenya suffer discriminatory treatment. Such behavior would also be best for Uganda and Tanzania.

The East African practice also acknowledges and applies the doctrine of restrictive systems, by which the rights of aliens are determined. According to this doctrine, equality between citizens and aliens is proclaimed in theory, but in practice, that equality is subject to so many important exceptions, combined with official and unofficial hostility, arbitrariness, discrimination, and suspicion, that any safeguards or guarantees to aliens are virtually meaningless.

Finally, the East African practice acknowledges, as we have already explained, the doctrine of equal treatment or assimilation, by which aliens are accorded the same rights as citizens in the host state, with minor exceptions, restricting commercial and political activity, and concerning expulsion from the host country. Since the 1960s, however, the commercial restrictions in, and expulsions from East Africa have certainly not been minor exceptions. Aliens have also experienced unreasonable and unjustified discrimination in the region.

INTERNATIONAL LEGAL PREVENTION
OF DISCRIMINATION

Discrimination between human beings on the grounds of race, color, or ethnic origin is a direct offense to human dignity, a denial of UN Charter principles and those of other international conventions on human rights and fundamental freedoms, and an impediment to friendly and peaceful relations among nations. All states, including the East African nations, are dutybound to promote human rights without discrimination. Prevention of discrimination is the prevention of any action that denies to individuals, or groups of individuals, equality of treatment that they may wish. Similarly, the East African states are under a duty to protect their minorities, the nondominant groups that, while wishing in general for equality of treatment with the majority, wish for a measure of preferential treatment—the international minimum standard—in order to protect them in their highly vulnerable situation before the majority of the population.

Among the international conventions adopted to regulate the observance of, and respect for, human rights and fundamental freedoms and to prevent violations of human rights everywhere in the world, the following are noteworthy: (1) the Universal Declaration of Human Rights adopted by the UN General Assembly on December 10, 1948; (2) the International Covenant on Economic, Social, and Cultural Rights adopted by the UN General Assembly on December 16, 1966; (3) the International Covenant on Civil and Political Rights adopted by the UN General Assembly on December 16, 1966; (4) the United Nations Declaration on the Elimination of All Forms of Racial Discrimination, proclaimed by the General Assembly on November 20, 1963; (5) the International Convention on the Elimination of All Forms of Racial Discrimination, adopted by the UN General Assembly on December 21, 1965; (6) the Discrimination (Employment and Occupation) Convention, adopted by the International Labour Conference on June 25, 1958; and (7) the Convention Against Discrimination in Education, adopted by the General Conference of UNESCO on December 14, 1960.

The Universal Declaration of Human Rights does not impose any treaty or contractual responsibilities upon any state. But, as an international charter of human rights, the declaration should not be ignored, because it is an important general guide concerning the basic freedoms and rights of mankind. One of its provisions is that everybody, irrespective of nationality, is entitled to freedom from torture or cruel, inhuman, or degrading treatment or punishment and to freedom from arbitrary arrest or detention. Fortunately, the Universal Declaration is frequently referred to in national legislations, such as constitutions, in judicial decisions, and even in international instruments. The East African states have based their constitutional sections relating to human rights partly upon the Universal Declaration. This practice of voluntarily including the declaration's provisions in national legislations is very important, for the 1948 Declaration on Human Rights, with no binding force, was merely a declaration without any means of enforcement.

The International Covenants adopted in 1966 concern the right of all peoples to self-determination—for example, they prohibit torture or discrimination of any kind. They call for the protection, for example, of children and ethnic, religious, and linguistic minorities. These covenants provide for means of their enforcement, although the measures of their implementation are different. They impose obligations on their signatories to promote, respect, and preserve human rights.

The other international instruments mentioned above have, as their main purpose, to prevent or eliminate discrimination in all its forms. Elimination of racial discrimination is certainly a significant aspect of the protection of human rights. The above instruments, which provide an international legal prevention of discrimination, contain practical measures for the elimination of racial discrimination and the prevention or prohibition of all practices of apartheid and other forms of racial segregation. [3]

LEGAL PREVENTION OF DISCRIMINATION IN EAST AFRICA: A SHORT COMPARISON

The question of legal prevention of discrimination in East Africa is important because verbal promises by political leaders or government spokesmen do not offer any reliable or static guarantees or safeguards. The Constitutions of Tanzania, Uganda, and Kenya are the basic laws of these countries. Constitutional guarantees or safeguards in the East African countries simply mean those constitutional provisions and devices that were designed to prevent abuse of power. A short constitutional comparison, in the areas of citizenship, human

rights, and fundamental freedoms among the East African countries,
reveals that in Tanganyika, the Citizenship Act (no. 15) of 1961 was
made part of the Constitution. In Uganda, as in Kenya, the law of
citizenship was made part of the country's constitution. The Constitutions of Uganda and Kenya only contain a Bill of Rights. The Independence Constitution of Tanganyika did not contain a Bill of Rights.
But the Preamble to the Republican Constitution of Tanzania (1965)
contains important provisions on human rights or rights of the individual, which is in the same terms substantially as the opening declara-
tory section of both the Ugandan and Kenyan Bill of Rights. The Preamble to the Tanzanian Constitution is entitled "An Act to Declare the
Interim Constitution of Tanzania (July 10, 1965," and is as follows.

> Whereas freedom, justice, fraternity and concord
> are founded upon the recognition of the equality of all
> men and their inherent dignity, and upon the recogni-
> tion of the rights of men to protection of life, liberty
> and property, to freedom of conscience, freedom of
> expression and freedom of association, to participate
> in their own Government, and to receive a just return
> for their labours:
> And when men are united together in a community
> it is their duty to respect the rights and dignity of
> their fellow men, to uphold the laws of the State, and
> to conduct the affairs of the State so that its resources
> are preserved, developed and enjoyed for the benefit
> of its citizens as a whole and so as to prevent the ex-
> ploitation of one man by another:
> And whereas such rights are best maintained and
> protected, and such duties are most equitably disposed
> in a democratic society where the Government is re-
> sponsible to a freely elected Parliament representative
> of the People and where the courts of law are free and
> impartial:
> Now therefore this Constitution, which makes pro-
> vision for the Government of Tanzania as such a demo-
> cratic society is hereby enacted by the Parliament of
> the United Republic of Tanzania.

The view is expressed, in a government paper entitled "Proposals
of the Tanganyika Government for a Republic," published on May 31,
1962, that "the rule of law is best preserved, not by formal guarantees
in a Bill of Rights which invite conflict between the executive and the
judiciary, but by independent judges administering justice free from
political pressure."

Constitutional provisions in the legislations of Uganda and Kenya regarding the protection of individual rights and freedoms, and the prevention of every kind of discrimination, can be outlined as follows. Chapter 5, Section 70, of the Kenyan Constitution corresponds to Section 3 of Chapter 3 of the Ugandan Constitution. Under Section 70 of the Kenyan legislation, every person in the country has the right to enjoy fundamental rights and freedoms, including the right to life, liberty, security of the person, and equal protection of the law. Also, any deprivation of personal property must be followed by compensation. Section 72 of the Kenyan Constitution talks of exclusion, admission, deportation, extradition, restriction, and control of aliens. These provisions are in line with international law rules. The corresponding provisions in the Ugandan Constitution appear in Section 10 of Chapter 3. Emphasis in the Ugandan provisions is placed upon the protection of the right to personal liberty. Kenya's Section 74, Chapter 5, of the Constitution corresponds to Uganda's Section 12, Chapter 3, of the Constitution; the talk is about protection from inhuman treatment of every person in the country. In all these provisions, there is a general conformity to international law rules relating to the prevention of discrimination and the respect for, and observance of, human rights. Kenya's Section 75(1) provides protection from deprivation of property. Thus, no illegal expropriation or nationalization of any personal property may be effected without prompt payment of adequate compensation. Similarly, nationalization or expropriation of such property without compensation may be lawful only if it is done for public purposes, such as defense, public safety, public order, public morality, health, town and country planning, or the development or utilization of any property in such manner as to promote the public benefit. The corresponding section in the Ugandan Constitution is Section 13. Of importance is the provision in these sections that a person whose property is compulsorily expropriated has a right of direct access to courts, including the High Court, for determination of his interest, legality of expropriation, compensation, and the like. The question of slavery and forced labor does not, really, arise in East Africa, for it is simply nonexistent. But Sections 73 and 11 of the Kenyan and Ugandan Constitutions respectively provide that individuals must be protected from slavery and forced labor. Sections 76 to 84 of the Kenyan Constitution and 14 to 22 of the Ugandan Constitution, respectively, deal with protection against arbitrary search or entry; provisions to secure protection of law; protection of the freedom of conscience; protection of the freedom of expression; protection of the freedom of assembly and association; protection of the freedom of movement; protection from discrimination on grounds of race, color, sex, language, religion, and the like; derogation from fundamental rights and freedoms; and enforcement of the protective provisions.

PREVENTION OF DISCRIMINATION
IN KENYAN LAW

Only a few cases have taken place in which the prevention of
(racial) discrimination in law has appeared in practice. A good example was the fascinating case of Wadhwa v. City Council of Nairobi in
1968. In that case, the extent to which racial discrimination is prohibited by the Kenyan Constitution was displayed. The events of the
case were as follows: Six Asians, citizens of the United Kingdom and
its colonies, were given notices to leave their stands in the Nairobi
City Market, following a resolution by the Nairobi City Council that
non-Africans be given such notice, and that applications for the tenan-
cies of the stands thereby rendered vacant be invited from suitable
Africans. Subsequently, in correspondence with the plaintiffs' advocates, the Nairobi City Council affirmed its aim as being to allocate
the stands to "Kenya citizens of African origin." Four of the Asian
plaintiffs had been born in Kenya, but because their parents had not
been born in that country, they did not automatically become Kenyan
citizens under Section 1(1) of the Kenyan Constitution. It was noted
previously that this subsection guaranteed automatic Kenyan citizenship only to citizens of the United Kingdom and its colonies or to British protected persons who had been born in Kenya and were, on December 11, 1963, such citizens and protected persons. All other persons
would acquire Kenyan citizenship only by registration, if their applications to register as Kenyan citizens would be submitted before a specified date, and approved by the Kenyan government. Four of the
Asian plaintiffs had so applied, although at the time of the court hearing their applications had not been processed, and certificates of citizenship had not been issued. The right to become a Kenyan citizen
is not dependent on the exercise of any discretion by any government
official, but it is an absolute right on the showing of proof that the
applicant falls within the appropriate category. However, the legal
status of such a citizen is less than that of a person who automatically
became a Kenya citizen, because a citizen by registration may be deprived of his citizenship—and this has already been done, as noted
previously—on the grounds, inter alia, that he has shown himself to
be disloyal or disaffected toward Kenya. This is, in fact, the mes-
sage in subsection 1 of Section 8 of the Kenyan Constitution.

The ruling in Wadhwa v. City Council of Nairobi was interesting.
The learned judge held that all six Asian plaintiffs had to be treated
alike as being citizens of the United Kingdom and its colonies and that
the four who had applied to be registered as citizens of Kenya could
not be treated as Kenyan citizens, since they had not yet obtained
their certificates of registration.[4]

It seems that the right thing for the plaintiffs to have done would
have been to apply to the court for a declaration that the four were en-

titled to be treated as citizens, and that the Immigration Department
had, therefore, the duty to issue at once the required certificates to
them. The court held, however, that the Nairobi City Council had
acted in a discriminatory manner, contrary to the Kenyan Constitution,
by treating Asians who were not Kenyan citizens less favorably than
Kenyan citizens of African origin. Thus even though the Asians were
aliens in East Africa, the Nairobi City Council discriminated against
them. It was hence "immaterial for the purpose of this suit whether
or not they [were] citizens of Kenya."[5]

Section 26 of the Kenyan Constitution prohibits every kind of
discrimination, which was defined as follows:

> affording different treatment to different persons at-
> tributable wholly or mainly to their respective de-
> scriptions by race, tribe, place of origin or resi-
> dence or other local connection, political opinions,
> colour or creed whereby persons of one such descrip-
> tion are subjected to disabilities or restrictions to
> which persons of another such description are not
> made subject or are accorded privileges or advan-
> tages which are not accorded to persons of another
> such description.

This exhaustive definition of "discrimination" was inserted by
the colonial draftsmen into every independence constitution of a would-
be ex-British state. Noteworthy in the above definition is the deliberate omission of "the grounds of nationality or citizenship." The purpose of the omission was to make room for the making of laws, and
thereby also make room for loopholes in the legislations, which would
in whole or in part permit discrimination on the grounds of citizenship
or nationality. Room was also made for discrimination in governmental policies and practices and by private individuals.

That the legislations of the East African states both prevent and
permit racial discrimination is illustrated by Section 26 of the Kenyan
Constitution. For, whereas some of its subsections, notably subsection (3), prohibit every kind of discrimination, subsection (4) tolerates
discrimination both on the grounds of race and citizenship. Subsection (4) provides that a discriminatory legislation shall not be uncon-
stitutional "so far as that law makes provision: (a) with respect to
persons who are not citizens of Kenya." Hence, preferential treatment is possible in Kenya for African citizens and noncitizens as
against Asians or Europeans who are or are not African citizens.
This complex legislative situation exposes lots of contradictions. The
aforementioned Asian plaintiffs were free to appeal to the High Court
for redress. But the rights granted to individuals under Section 26

are enjoyed by Kenyan citizens only. Hence, aliens who are discriminated against on nationality grounds in Kenya have little or no chance
of obtaining redress even if they appeal to the Kenyan High Court.
However, Commonwealth citizens enjoy, under Section 10(1) of the
Constitution, a better (preferential) treatment than any other nationals
who are ordinary aliens in Kenya. But this section is contradicted
by Kenya's Land Control or Trade Licensing Acts, which heavily favor
Kenyan citizens of African descent. Section 10, then, is concerned
with the granting of recriprocal rights and privileges and not with the
restriction of rights accorded by the Kenyan Constitution.

Subsections (1) and (2) of Section 26 of the Kenyan Constitution
deal with discriminatory laws or actions by public officers or authorities. However, subsection (7) of that section makes discrimination by
private individuals illegal: "no person shall be treated in a discriminatory manner in respect of access to shops, hotels, lodging houses,
public restaurants, eating houses, beer halls or places of public enter-
tainment, or in respect of access to places of public resort maintained
wholly or partly out of public funds or dedicated to the use of the general public." The lack, however, of a provision whereby an injured
party can obtain damages for (illegal) discrimination has by itself encouraged discrimination by individuals in their private capacity.

This state of affairs exists in the other countries of East Africa
as well. Unless the contradictions in the laws are removed and the
loopholes in them corrected, it is difficult to imagine how the situation
of aliens in East Africa will rise distinctly above the average of the
international standard of treatment.

So long as the situation remains as it is, accusations of discrimination and violation of basic human rights will prevail. And so long
as the East African practice is allowed to go against East African law,
negative reactions to the practice will not be confined to East Africa
but will have international repercussions, as when Amin expelled the
Asians in 1972. Kenya's violation of her constitutional provisions in
the 1960s was also internationally condemned.

BRITISH NATIONALITY AND STATUS
OF ALIENS ACTS

The British Nationality and Status of Aliens Acts (1914-43) divided, in the eyes of English common law, the world's population into
two sections: aliens and British subjects. British subjects in British
colonial possessions were divided into two groups: Natives of a colony—
born in His Majesty's dominions such as Kenya Colony—were normally
called British subjects; and natives of a protectorate, trust, or mandated territory such as Tanganyika, Uganda, or the Kenya Protectorate
were normally called British protected persons.

The enactment of the 1948 British Nationality Act terribly complicated the whole situation. British nationality was replaced by British subjecthood/Commonwealth citizenship. National groups were thenceforth divided into the following: British subjects or Commonwealth citizens including citizens of the United Kingdom itself; British protected persons; citizens of the Republic of Ireland who are not British subjects by virtue of their being outside the British Commonwealth of Nations; and aliens, anyone who is not a British subject, a British protected person, or a citizen of the Republic of Ireland.

The legal problems of Asians in East Africa have stemmed from the British Nationality Act of 1948. The Asians expelled from East Africa were British subjects and protected persons, a British responsibility. They were given an option at independence in East Africa to retain British subjecthood or to acquire East African citizenship. About 400,000 Asians opted to remain British citizens. [6]

We noted in Chapter 2 that jus soli and jus sanguinis are the two primary doctrines of international law that govern the question of acquisition of nationality. Of these two doctrines, the jus soli is the usual and fundamental doctrine governing the question. But there is no legal obligation on the part of states to confer their nationalities on persons. However, although a person may not obtain a right of residence or business on a state's territory, even if he was born there, it is possible that he may obtain an acquired right of business. He could hence also acquire a right of residence. It might, therefore, be argued that aliens in East Africa of Asian origin possess, by virtue of their long residence and conduct of trade in East Africa, or could acquire, a right of permanent residence and trade in the region.

Acquired rights can be defined as "any rights, corporeal or incorporeal, properly vested in a natural or juristic person, and of an assessable monetary value." The doctrine of acquired rights thus empowers international law to protect the acquired or vested interests of individuals not protected by jus soli. The commercial privileges of Asians in East Africa who are not African citizens are acquired rights, and the affected alien persons, whether physical or juristic, should have the right to bring cases before tribunals. A license lawfully granted to exercise a business is an acquired right. Its bearer should not, therefore, be deprived of it without sound reason. It is a freedom granted lawfully to an individual to conduct business. This is an acquired right that none of the East African states takes into consideration before issuing notices to surrender businesses or expulsion orders to alien Asians in East Africa. In such circumstances, the expellees should be accorded a right to indemnity, if and when such expulsion orders are served to them.

One of the serious problems facing expelled Asians from East Africa is to find another home to settle in. We have seen that many of

the Asian expellees who failed to acquire East African citizenship had
hoped eventually to settle in their country of citizenship—Britain. But
not all of them settled in Britain. For example, according to a survey
undertaken in Kenya in 1968, of the Asians intending to emigrate from
the country, only about 18 percent preferred to settle in the United
Kingdom, about 67 percent preferred India, and about 6 percent preferred Canada. Not many wanted to go to the United Kingdom because
they feared being subjected to the racism there that had prompted the
enactment of the 1968 Immigration Act. Thus, of the roughly 67,000
British passport-holding Asians in East Africa, only about 12,000
wanted to go to the United Kingdom. The Indian government also introduced legislation restricting the entry of East African Asians into
India. But there was not much enthusiasm among the Asians for emigration to India or Pakistan, even though these two countries offered
the Asians the best places from the cultural and religious viewpoints.
Britain offered better educational and living standards.

Apart from Britain and the Indian subcontinent, Canada also offered prospects for settlement, and some of the Asians expelled from
East Africa in the mid-1960s decided to emigrate to Canada. In 1968
alone, it was estimated that 5,000 Asians went to Canada. But, again,
the immigration controls in Canada were also strict, and it seemed
that only those Asians with definite professions and skills would be allowed to settle in that country. On the African continent itself, Zambia agreed to absorb some East African Asian expellees for work on
the Tanzania-Zambia (Tan-Zam) Railway. Ethiopia also recruited a
few of them. The refusal by these and other countries to absorb the
Asian expellees from Kenya and Tanzania was prompted by the British
Immigration Act of 1968. The countries believed that by absorbing
British Asians, they would be bearing Britain's burdens; and that they
were unwilling to do. Pakistan introduced strict immigration controls.
Thus the "slamming of doors" in the world to Asians in East Africa
created a most serious situation of statelessness among the Asians.
That unfortunate situation led to the conclusion of an agreement between
India and Britain in July 1968.

The purpose of the Anglo-Indian Agreement was to arrange for
the resettlement of persons of Indian origin holding U.K. passports
and resident in Kenya, who were compelled to leave and wished to go
to India. Where such persons were denied permits for residence or
for the practice of their trade or profession or where their livelihood
was curtailed by restriction of their right of trade, the British High
Commission would place an appropriate endorsement in their passports giving the holders the right of entry to the United Kingdom. The
Indian government agreed to provide, via the appropriate Indian authorities and representatives in Kenya, any such persons, if they were
not disqualified from admission into India, with visas for entry into In-

dia, with a view to possible eventual settlement. The necessary administrative procedures were instituted in the British and Indian High Commissions in Nairobi. The results of the Indo-British arrangements were long queues of Indians at the High Commissions of the two countries in Nairobi. Many of the Asians had lost their jobs and were thus desperately eager to go to India or Britain. The 1,500 vouchers annually available to them to enter the United Kingdom were too few. Thus be 1968, a good 40,000 had emigrated to India and settled there permanently.

Another serious problem caused by the expulsion of Asians from East Africa has been the splitting up of families and capital. This has weakened the economic and industrial capacities of the Asians, and it is, in itself, a very sad experience and a serious violation of the Asians' fundamental family rights. The financial losses, physical separations, inconveniences, sufferings, and other evils are all instances of violations of basic human rights.

The British Commonwealth Immigrants Act, passed by the British Parliament on March 1, 1968, produced perhaps the most serious and negative repercussions for the Asians expelled from East Africa. For the first time, citizens of the United Kingdom and its colonies were deprived of their inalienable right to enter any part of the territories of which they were citizens. Until the enactment of the (British) Commonwealth Immigrants Act in February 1962, it was a matter of principle that all citizens of Commonwealth countries, including citizens of the British colonies, had the free and unrestricted right of entry into the United Kingdom. But the situation was changing, with the belief in Britain that that country was a welfare state, with the growing rate of immigration in that state, with the emergence of former British dependencies—including those in East Africa—to full statehood, with the resulting burdens imposed upon Britain, and with the strains imposed upon her social and welfare services. The 1962 Immigration Act introduced many restrictions that curtailed the number of Commonwealth immigrants into the United Kingdom. The expelled East African Asians were affected very badly, for the discriminatory legislation was aimed only at Commonwealth citizens and those of the United Kingdom and its colonies whose place of origin and home was in a colony. Those Commonwealth citizens resident elsewhere—for example, in Canada, Australia, or New Zealand—continued to enjoy the right of entry into the United Kingdom. The excuse, a lame one, given by Britain for the control of the influx of certain Commonwealth citizens into the United Kingdom, whether for employment or as a result of expulsion, was the necessity to avoid racial friction in the United Kingdom caused by such forces as lack of employment, housing, and schools for immigrants.

Britain's decision to join the Common Market had, as its aim, to secure her economic survival. In order for her to have a chance, it was felt that entry into the United Kingdom of Commonwealth immigrants had to be limited. These were some of the crucial problems that caused restrictions on the right of entry into the United Kingdom of some Commonwealth subjects and that led to the imposition between 1962 and 1971 of immigration controls upon Commonwealth citizens.

In short, Britain's rejection of Commonwealth immigration was motivated by the fear of "diluting" English culture and traditions; the determination to preserve the welfare state, by, for instance, avoiding strains on Britain's social services; complaints against the behavior of immigrants, which tended to be "uncivilized" or below English standards; the fear that racial events in the United States might be repeated in the United Kingdom; and fears of overpopulation.

One of the staunchest advocates of exclusion or strict control of (Commonwealth) immigration into Britain was Enoch Powell, the Conservative M.P. for Wolverhampton in the British Midlands. Although a very strong scholar, Powell has always been extreme in his racist attitudes. He began advocating a racist doctrine after the expulsion of British Asians from Kenya in 1967 and their admission into Britain in February 1968. In a speech to the Annual Meeting of the West Midlands Area Conservative Association, an area with a huge colored population, Powell announced his famous three-point doctrine for the solution of the (racial) immigration problem in the United Kingdom: Legislation against racial discrimination should be enacted at once; further immigration into the United Kingdom should be suspended indefinitely; and voluntary repatriation of colored immigrants should be encouraged officially.

EXPULSION OF ASIANS FROM UGANDA IN
1972: INTERNATIONAL IMPLICATIONS

The expulsion of Asians from Uganda in 1972 sparked a series of international implications. It could be argued that, in the strict sense of municipal law, a citizen of the United Kingdom and its colonies, or of Bangladesh, Kenya, Tanzania, or India is not an alien in Uganda; but that the citizen of Pakistan is, because the latter is no longer a Commonwealth country. Since Uganda continues to subscribe to the Commonwealth Code of Nationality, the expression "alien" refers only to those people who are citizens of independent states outside the Commonwealth and Ireland, and to stateless persons. However, because the common legal status of British subjects now has relatively little, or no, effect on the legislation governing transactions between Commonwealth governments, the right under traditional international law to expel aliens embraces the right of a Commonwealth country to expel those people who are exclusively citizens of other Commonwealth nations. It has been estimated that 14,451 Asians

acquired Ugandan citizenship by the automatic process. According
to reliable Ugandan sources, 8,791 Asians acquired Ugandan citizenship by registration. About 70,000 Asians became aliens in Uganda,
or citizens of the United Kingdom and its colonies, by association
with India, Pakistan, Bangladesh, Kenya, or Tanzania by birth or
descent. The exodus of Asians from Uganda after the expulsion orders
of 1972 was accelerated as the November 8, 1972, deadline approached.
By that time, the British High Commission in Kampala had issued entry permits into Britain to about 15,000 Asians. Processing continued
at the rate of about 1,200 a day. The number of Asians expected to
enter Britain was estimated at 30,000. The fighting on the Ugandan-
Tanzanian border in the previous week had slowed down the process,
for some Asians were kept at home, while others in up-country areas
were physically unable to reach Kampala.

Thus the Ugandan government issued new regulations to ensure
that the Asians did not delay their departure after receiving final
clearance. By that time, no word had been uttered regarding the sale
of, or compensation for, Asian properties in Uganda. Instead, all
outgoing Asians had to buy their air, rail, or sea tickets at the same
time as they obtained their exit papers. The airlift of Asians to Britain ran at 500 to 600 people a day. Several countries—including Canada, the United States, and Sweden—volunteered to absorb the expelled
Asians. The Canadian airlift was under way, and about 1,500 Asians
who had received entry visas to Canada were flown to that country.
Most of the Asians who left Uganda for Canada were either stateless
or Ugandan citizens. The Canadian Immigration Office was, at the
time of the dealine, also still processing another 6,000 applications
for entry visas to Canada. By the same time also, about 1,000 of the
4,500 Indian citizens had already left, and 1,000 British Asians had
been granted Indian visas. Other expelled Asians were expected to
go to countries other than Britain, India, and Canada. These other
countries included Australia, Malawi, New Zealand, Mauritius, Pakistan, and Bangladesh. Britain exercised her responsibilities for those
Asians by holding consultations for accommodation with some 50
states.

Under normal circumstances, one would expect India, Pakistan,
and Bangladesh to accommodate, next to the United Kingdom, the
largest numbers of the Asian expellees. But that was not the case,
for, as we have seen, these countries enacted legislation restricting
the entry of East African Asians. India's Constitution bestows the
right of entry and free movement, residence, and settlement in its
territory only upon its own citizens. Moreover, the Kenyan Asian
crisis led to the enactment on March 6, 1968, of a regulation applicable to the citizens of the United Kingdom and its colonies whose passports showed Kenya as the country of residence.[7] The regulation pro-

vided that citizens of that category should no longer be allowed to enter India freely but should be required to request permission to settle in the country. The effect of that regulation was followed by the signing of the Indo-British agreement explained above.

Citizens of the United Kingdom and its colonies resident in Uganda continued to enjoy the right to enter India freely until 1972. Hence, a restriction was imposed upon the British citizens of Asian origin in Uganda in implementation of the Indian home secretary's announcement that, should a similar exodus of Asians take place anywhere else in the Commonwealth, "we shall not hesitate to extend [the restriction] to other countries also."[8] In line with that announcement, the Indian government later amended its immigration laws in order to impose controls on the admission of citizens of the United Kingdon and its colonies holding passports specifying Uganda as the bearer's country of residence.[9] In September 1972, an Anglo-Indian agreement was concluded whereby thousands of those affected by the alteration in the Indian legislation would now be admitted to India for settlement. The administrative arrangements for the implementation of the 1972 agreement are similar to those made in connection with the Kenyan Asians in 1968.

STATELESSNESS

The expulsion of Asians from East Africa and the refusals to accept them in Britain and the Indian subcontinent have caused serious problems for refugees and stateless persons. As we have explained, it is a general principle of international law that no state is dutybound to accommodate stateless persons or refugees. However, the international community has promulgated some rules that demarcate a state's right to expel stateless persons. It now seems that the expulsion of stateless persons is permissible only if undertaken in the interests of "public order or national security."[10] The unlawfulness is obvious where statelessness is the outcome of a denaturalization decree by the expelling state. Similarly, a state that deprives individuals of that state's citizenship in order to render them stateless violates international law.

Thus to those Asians who obtained Ugandan citizenship but were later deprived of it by any action, the principle applicable is that third states have no duty to recognize the deprivation of Ugandan citizenship, if the deprivation was motivated by racial considerations. A third state may thus continue to regard such Asians as Ugandan citizens, and may return them—if expelled—to Uganda, or if Uganda refused to readmit them, a third state may hold Uganda entirely responsible to make reparation for any expenses that may result from the need to

accommodate the expellees. The case is not the same, however, with
those persons who have never possessed Ugandan citizenship. For
such persons are, and have always been, citizens of the United Kingdom and its colonies, if, of course, they fall within Section 2 of the
Uganda Independence Act. Such persons are unquestionably a British
responsibility and must, therefore, be admitted to Britain.

     The class of stateless Asians created following President Amin's
expulsion orders remained the most intractable of the many problems
the orders produced. No official figures were released on the number
of stateless Asians, but the estimate was put at 16,000 people who had
been divested of Ugandan citizenship in the government's "verification"
campaign. Asians exempted from expulsion by virtue of their Ugandan
citizenship or professional skills were then being required to buy
identity cards to facilitate their continued stay and movement in Uganda. The stateless Asians, however, had no national identity, and no
easily identifiable future, unfortunately.

                    Gross Violation of Human Rights

     The wholesale expulsion of Asians from Uganda, with expropria-
tion of their property, has profoundly offended world opinion. The expulsion of Asians, whether from Uganda, Kenya, or Tanzania, is
bound to do substantial and lasting damage to the East African economy.
Vigorous denunciations of Amin's racism by African leaders in Uganda
itself, and in Tanzania, Zambia, Kenya, and elsewhere, were no
doubt in part an expression of the leaders' concern for its effects upon
the future of the area as a whole. Evil as these expulsions are, they
have certainly served to distract attention from the lawlessness and
brutality with which the Ugandan government and armed forces have
been acting toward their fellow Africans. The arrest by soldiers of
Uganda's Chief Justice Kiwanuka in the High Court building in Kampala
was an outrage against the rule of law. There are persistent reports
that Kiwanuka was beheaded within a few hours of his illegal arrest.
No reasons have been given for his arrest. It may be that, as a former prime minister and as a person of stature and recognized integrity, he was thought to be a possible alternative head of state. It
may be that his independent judgment in a habeas corpus application,
shortly before he was seized, incurred the wrath of the authorities.
Prominent African Ugandans, and other Africans from other countries, have also mysteriously disappeared. A "disappearance" in
Uganda has come to be tantamount to clandestine murder by the Ugandan Army. Whether the murders have been effected as a result of
fear on the part of the mostly undereducated Ugandan Army that the
Ugandan African elite might take over power or as a result of revenge

is not clear. The truth is that the actions of the Ugandan Army have been in direct and gross violation of human rights and fundamental freedoms. Unless an end is put to the disappearance and possible murder of prominent personalities in Uganda, accusations will continue to be leveled against the Ugandan government. President Amin's hypocritical condemnations of the disappearances, his promises of severe punishment to those army personnel found guilty of such murderous and barbaric acts, his dissociation of himself and his government from such acts, and his explanations that such disappearances have been caused by flights or escapes to other countries will not help end the outcries against Uganda's violations of human rights. For in addition to prominent personalities, hundreds of less-well-known suspected opponents of Amin's regime have disappeared and are believed to have been murdered in all parts of the country, particularly in the northern districts of Acholi and Lango. The latter is, notably, ex-President Obote's district. Disappearances have also occurred in Buganda.

Defiance of the rule of law in Uganda extends to the treatment of suspected petty criminals. For example, on July 28, 1972, three suspected thieves were publicly executed in a field at Lugazi, a tiny town near Kampala. The executions were performed by members of the so-called Public Safety Unit, composed of selected public officers. There was no trial, no conviction, and no sentence. This is but one instance of a practice that has been continuing indiscriminately elsewhere in Uganda, including the police barracks at Naguru—another tiny town near Kampala—Mbale, and other places. It seems that the senior superintendent of the Public Safety Unit has been given unlimited power of execution.

On the international scene, Amin has stressed that Uganda is not a lawless state. In defending his policy of "economic war," for example, Amin has made it clear that he is not at all a racist. In a note to UN Secretary General Kurt Waldheim, Amin declared that the Asian expellees "are being allowed to take their personal belongings as well as reasonable amounts of cash with them. . . . There has not been any single instance of confiscation of property. [Allegations of] harassment and maltreatment which might have reached you have been entirely unfounded, or at any rate grossly exaggerated."[11]

However, in spite of earlier reports, the expulsion policy was not extended to the refugees living in Uganda under the auspices of the UN High Commission for Refugees (UNHCR). These groups comprise Sudanese and Rwandese, 33,600 of whom live in settlements organized by the UNHCR. Some Sudanese had, by the adoption of the expulsion policy in Uganda, already been repatriated following the Sudanese Peace Agreement. Others were expected to follow them.

The Ugandan Asian Problem at
the United Nations

At the United Nations itself, the probem of the Ugandan Asians
was brought before the General Assembly in September 1972, when the
then British foreign and Commonwealth secretary, Alec Douglas-Home,
requested the assembly to discuss the problem without delay, owing
to its serious nature. That British request was later withdrawn, but
the East African states had already adopted their stands on the question. Kenya's stand, in the formulation of which this writer was
greatly involved, was important. Kenya's total opposition to all forms
of racial discrimination and denial of fundamental human rights and
freedoms was reaffirmed. Her strict adherence to the international
instruments preventing all sorts of discrimination, particularly the
Universal Declaration of Human Rights of 1948 and the two United
Nations Covenants of 1966, to which she is a party, was declared.
Her firm support of these and other antidiscrimination instruments,
particularly the UN Declaration on the Elimination of All Forms of
Racial Discrimination proclaimed in 1963 and the convention on the
same subject adopted in 1965, was stated with precision. Kenya's
stand further revealed the country's commitment to uphold, at all
times, all these instruments, to take all necessary measures for their
universal implementation, and to cooperate with the United Nations
to champion the cause of human rights.

Elimination of the myriad violations of human rights in the
world, whether at the centralized or decentralized level, requires,
in Kenya's view, closer cooperation of all states to suppress these
violations and eliminate inhuman acts of terrorism. While, therefore, commending the work of the United Nations and other international
bodies charged with the duty of enforcing measures taken to prevent
violations of human rights and freedoms, Kenya expressed the view
that it was still imperative for those bodies to respond with prompt-
ness and skill to the requests made in the UN resolutions, despite
the difficulties of the task and their heavy programs of work. The
language used in Kenya's stand was dogmatic, without any element of
condemnation of Uganda's attitudes toward her Asians. Tanzania was
direct in her condemnation of Amin's policy, which she described as
racist. President Nyerere himself once remarked that, while it was
normal to expel aliens from a country, Amin's decision to expel Ugandan citizens who were Asians could not be less than racial. Criticisms similar to the Nyerere remark compelled Amin to cancel his
expulsion decree requiring all Asians to leave the country and to retain the one directed against alien Asians in August 1972. In short,
then, Kenya—like Tanzania—expressed the view in its public statements that national judicial safeguards for the protection of human

rights, as well as the international legal prevention of discrimination provided for in the international instruments referred to above, should be upheld.

Although the UN General Assembly did not discuss the Ugandan Asian problem, Uganda's permanent representative to the United Nations, G. S. Imbingire, made a policy statement on the issue in the assembly on October 6, 1972; Uganda affirmed that of the nearly 60,000 Asians affected by Amin's expulsion decree, about 55,000 were British nationals. Therefore they were entirely a British responsibility. It was the United Kingdom that had organized an exodus of its subjects from the Indian subcontinent to Uganda at the close of the 19th century. Ambassador Imbingire also blamed many of the affected Asians, who had "deliberately and voluntarily rejected Uganda's offer" to them of its citizenship. The damage done by those people to the Ugandan economy, of which they controlled about 90 percent, said the ambassador, was enormous; the resulting outflow of capital greatly handicapped the country's economic advancement. Imbingire noted that "there was [therefore] no alternative but to ask those aliens to depart for their countries of nationality," for Uganda had the right to ask them to go. Imbingire, however, acknowledged that many of the Asian expellees would become stateless persons, but he continued to blame them because they had deliberately refused to renounce their British nationality and take up the Ugandan one within the period of three months that they had been given. Imbingire then assured the assembly that the expelled Asians still in his country would not be subjected to inhuman treatment after the November 8, 1972 deadline. They would certainly not be thrown into concentration camps. These specific assurances had already been communicated by President Amin to the UN secretary general, in a letter. Transit out of the country of those Asian expellees was protected by police escorts. Imbingire then informed the assembly that President Amin had noted that many Asians entering the United Kingdom from Uganda were being accommodated in camps similar to concentration camps.[12]

The matter of the Ugandan Asians was also taken up by the UN Subcommittee on Human Rights—a branch of the UN Commission on Human Rights. A proposal that the subcommittee should send a telegram to Amin, expressing serious concern at his proposed action, was defeated by 14 votes to one, with six abstentions. A proposal to add the words "and expulsion" to a motion condemning racial discrimination in immigration policies of states was also defeated with only three votes in favor. However, a draft resolution referring to the Human Rights Commission the issue of international legal protection of human rights of noncitizens was carried by a small majority: 12 to one with ten abstentions.

The most active aspect of the UN involvement in the matter has, however, been the work undertaken by the UNHCR. This organization has not only communicated regularly with the Ugandan government in order to secure the welfare of the refugees under UN mandate, but it has also taken measures to ease the condition of the expellees. On October 19, 1972, for instance, the commission communicated with 16 states with a view to securing the temporary or permanent settlement in those states of Asian expellees who appeared to be stateless. From the start, the UNHCR has closely cooperated with the Intergovernmental Committee on European Migration with a view to facilitating the travel of Asians expelled from Uganda. It is hoped that the UNHCR will establish closer working relationships with the UN Commission on Human Rights, now that the latter's Subcommission on Prevention of Discrimination and Protection of Minorities has devised a new procedure for dealing with communications to the UN secretary general alleging violations of human rights and fundamental freedoms throughout the world.

The new procedure was, in fact, laid down by the UN Economic and Social Council (ECOSOC) in its Resolution 1503, adopted at ECOSOC's 48th Session in 1970. Under the new procedure, three stages are now operative.

First, the subcommission—which is a government-appointed but independent body of legal experts—is authorized to appoint a working party.[13] The purpose of the latter is "to consider all communications, including replies of Governments thereon . . . with a view to bringing to the attention of the Sub-Commission those communications, together with the replies of Governments, if any, which appear to reveal a consistent pattern of gross and reliably attested violations of human rights and fundamental freedoms."

Second, the subcommission is requested to consider the communications brought before it by the working party, and any replies of governments and any other relevant information "with a view to determining whether to refer to the Commission on Human Rights particular situations which appear to reveal a consistent pattern of gross and reliably attested violations of human rights requiring consideration by the Commission."

Third, the Commission on Human Rights, after examining any situation referred to it, is asked to determine "whether it requires a thorough study by the Commission and a report and recommendations thereon to the Council," and "whether it may be a subject of an investigation by an ad hoc committee to be appointed by the Commission, which shall be undertaken only with the express consent of the State concerned and shall be conducted in constant co-operation with the State and under conditions determined by agreement with it."

On August 4, 1971, the subcommission adopted a resolution
setting out the procedures for dealing with the question of the admis-
sibility of communications and laying down the standards and criteria
for judging this, as well as rulings relating to the sources of communications, the existence of other remedies, and their timeliness. Ad-
missible communications may originate from individuals or groups
who are victims of violations, persons having direct knowledge of violations, or nongovernmental organizations acting bona fide and not
politically motivated and having direct and reliable knowledge of such
violations.

This new system of suppressing violations of human rights in
the world is a most useful one. The East African states should strictly
observe the new international rules for preventing discrimination.
The new procedure is significant, because for the first time within
the framework of the United Nations, there is a procedure under which
private individuals, nongovernmental institutions, and governments
alike can raise complaints about violations of human rights within a
given state and have those complaints investigated and reported on by
an impartial international body. The new procedure came into operation for the first time in 1972. The working group met in New York
in August 1972. It considered questions of human rights in Greece,
Iran, and Portugal. Other areas where human rights have been reported to have been violated include Bangladesh, Northern Ireland,
Portuguese Africa, Turkey, South Africa, Rhodesia, and Uganda.

Tribalism's Impact on Human Rights

Tribalism has a great impact on human rights and race relations in East Africa. To eliminate racial discrimination and thus
ensure respect for human rights in the region, it is necessary to get
rid of nepotism and tribalism.

The racial and tribal distribution patterns of wealth in the East
African states originated from discriminatory colonial policies and
practices, and from non-African control over private investment capital, which both protected and maintained the privileged positions of
the immigrant communities—and their favored African tribes. The
racial and tribal inequalities and separatisms made integration impossible. They have continued to endanger tribal and racial harmony and
equality in the region.

SOME PRACTICAL PROPOSALS FOR BETTER
TREATMENT OF ALIENS IN EAST AFRICA

The East African states are under a moral duty and a legal responsibility, imposed upon them by international law, to treat aliens

according to international standards dictated by the civilized states.
What does this mean? It means, briefly, that by the time they acquired independence and joined the international community, the East
African people and their countries were supposed to be mature enough
to differentiate between what is and what is not acceptable in international behavior, and to accord an egalitarian and just treatment to all
people irrespective of origin, color, language, and the like.

The doctrine of sovereign equality for all states was strengthened
in 1646 by the distinguished Dutch jurist Huig de Groot, who, in his
De Jure Belli ac Pacis Tres Libri (Three Books on the Law of War
and Peace), strongly condemned savage wars and chaos. De Groot
appealed to all states to honor the existing universal standard of justice applicable to all states and individuals and to regard themselves
as equals, irrespective of their size, population, wealth, or power.

International standards require that the dignity, freedom, life,
property, and safety of aliens be protected sufficiently. Because the
standards are sanctioned by international law, they are acceptable to
the international community, to which the East African states belong.
Therefore, these states are under an international obligation to shun
every practice that is contrary to the above universal standard of
justice. They are also dutybound to honor or fulfill their international obligations resulting from international practice and custom,
for example, honoring or exchanging diplomatic representation, settling international disputes by peaceful means only, and granting aliens
a minimum standard of treatment.

The idea that rules of international law can be applied directly
to individuals without the intervention of their own state is as old as
the entire history of modern international law.[14] There has been no
epoch comparable in significance to the glorious years marking the
end of the 15th century and beginning of the 16th century. It was in
this most significant era that the discovery of the New World occurred,
and that there lived many great persons, including one of the fathers
of international law: Francisci de Vittoria.

Vittoria was a professor of theology at the Spanish University
of Salamanca. His fame rests on his lectures, which his enthusiastic
students compiled and published after his death. In brief, Vittoria's
lectures asserted the rights of the native Indians in the New World,
and the responsibilities Spain owed them, even though they were considered barbarians. Vittoria argued that the individual is the ultimate unit of all law, national and international alike, in the double
sense that the obligations of international law are ultimately addressed
to the individual, and the development, the welfare, and the dignity of
the individual are a matter of direct concern to international law.[15]
Vittoria recognized that both the new system of states and the new law
among states that were springing up were not confined to Europe or
Christendom but that they belonged to the whole world.

Another founder of international law was the Swiss lawyer Emmeric de Vattel, who in 1758 published the famous <u>Le Droit de Gens, ou Principes de la Loi Naturelle, Appliques a la Conduite et aux Affaires des Nations et des Souverains</u> (The Law of Nations or the Principles of Natural Law). Vattel and Vittoria founded the two doctrines of treatment of aliens in international law. Vittoria was the father of the national treatment doctrine. Today the three states of East Africa are among the staunchest advocates of the doctrine, and apply it unreservedly. Vattel was, on the other hand, the founder and father of the international treatment. In Chapter 8 of his abovementioned book, he outlined principles of international law, whose main objective was to secure the rights of aliens and foreign states, and to prevent the "peace of nations from being disturbed by the disputes of individuals." According to Vattel, an alien is accorded access only on the understanding that he will be subject to the general laws created for the maintenance of good order. Further, an alien must always be regarded as a citizen of his own state and treated as such, without being obligated to bear public burdens directly concerned with the citizenship of the host state.

It has been argued by several writers on international law that no one standard should be taken as dogma. This writer, however, supports the international standard of treatment, without, however, condemning the national treatment standard. In this way, the writer acknowledges the view that the legal status and treatment of aliens are a matter for national legislation alone to determine. But international law cannot remain indifferent if the host or receiving state behaves toward aliens in a manner inconsistent with, or contrary to, the fundamental principles of international law. Aliens must be treated according to standards laid down by international law.

The East African nations cannot thus evade the burdens of strict observance of this fundamental rule of international law. Although the East African governments have a right (that is, are permitted by international law) to expel aliens generally, the law of nations imposes upon the governments certain conditions, culminating in international legal, and even moral, responsibility, under which they may expel or deport aliens. Justified reasons for expulsion of aliens include prostitution and other similar corrupt social vices and evils; vagabondage; disease; conviction for a crime against public order and security; espionage, conspiracy, piracy, and other forms of political intrigue; abuse of the flag (of an East African state); resistance to, or complete disregard of, the law; and violation of a human right or fundamental freedom established by law.

Although the East African states have absolute powers regarding the treatment of persons, and their rights and duties within the states' territories, international law exerts a protective influence, which lim-

its state absolutism and exclusive jurisdiction over aliens. This reduction of state absolutism in the treatment of aliens within state
boundaries is the central purpose of international instruments on human rights and fundamental freedoms. The East African states should
accept the restrictive influence that international law claims to exercise upon the East African laws relating to aliens. Existing laws of
East Africa should comply with the requirements of international law.
Those laws that do not should be repealed and replaced by others that
will comply with the demands of international law. Similarly, those
laws that are missing but are essential to regulate certain crucial
situations of aliens must be enacted at once. The legal position of
aliens in East Africa is a matter of international law, which sanctions
their rights in that region. The countries of East Africa should remember that aliens, once admitted into their territories, are, in a way,
legal subjects and should be accorded certain minimum of rights. In
international practice, apart from being subjected to the territorial
burdens of the receiving state, aliens also bear the burdens of their
own (protecting) state. Therefore, aliens owe two kinds of allegiance,
to their host state and to their home state, and, as such, deserve a
right to privileged treatment in the former state, and diplomatic protection from their own country. This right presupposes the legal institution of citizenship. Is it not ironical that international law grants
protection to people when they reside abroad, which it denies to them
in their own country? It is because of these two jurisdictions to which
aliens are subjected that international law intervenes and regulates
the question in order to avoid difficulty by demarcating the rights and
duties of states in the treatment of individuals.

International law does not recognize the theory of national treatment. The standard established by international law is that of international civilization, and it is this standard that the East African nations should apply, if they truly want to belong to the civilized society
of nations and avoid international delinquencies. The international
standard gives aliens all the rights essential for their existence,
without restricting the sovereignty of the host state.

NOTES

1. See League of Nations, Preparatory Documents, C.I.T.E. 1,
1929, and Proceedings, C.I.T.E. 62, 1930, pp. 419-21.
2. See for instance Charles de Fisscher, Theory and Reality
in Public International Law, trans. P. E. Corbett (Princeton, N.J.:
Princeton University Press, 1957); E. M. Borchard, The Diplomatic
Protection of Citizens Abroad or the Law of International Claims
(New York: Banks Law Publication, 1927); F. de Vittoria, De Indis

et de Jure Relectiones, trans. John Pawley Bate (New York: Oceana
Publications, 1964); E. de Vattel, Le Droit des Gens, Ou Principes
de la Loi Naturelle, Appliques a la Conduite et aux Affaires des Nations et des Souverains, trans. George D. Gregory (New York:
Oceana Publications, 1964); Marek S. Korowicz, Introduction to International Law (The Hague: Martinus Nijhoff, 1959); S. Krylov, Les
Notions Principales du Droit des Gens (la Doctrine Sovietique du Droit
International) -70 HR,411 (The Hague: Academie de Droit International,
1947).

3. See Human Rights: A Compilation of International Instruments of the United Nations (New York: United Nations, 1967).

4. See Wadhwa v. City Council of Nairobi (1968), p. 409.

5. Ibid.

6. See for instance Bulletin of the International Commission of
Jurists, no. 34, p. 36.

7. See House of Commons Debates 769, col. 185; and House of
Lords Debates 296, cols. 391-92.

8. Quoted in Times of India, March 7, 1968.

9. See Times (London) August 7, 1972.

10. See for instance United Nations, Doc. E/Conf.17/5, The
U.N. Convention Relating to the Status of Stateless Persons, 1954.

11. See United Nations, Office of Public Information, NV/318,
October 10, 1972.

12. See U.N. Monthly Chronicle, October/November, 1972.

13. See Review of International Commission of Jurists, no. 11
(December 1973), pp. 27 ff.

14. See for instance Peter P. Remec, The Position of the Individual in International Law According to Grotius and Vattel (The Hague:
Martinus Nijhoff, 1960).

15. See "The Grotian Tradition in International Law," British
Yearbook of International Law 23 (1946), pp. 27 et seq.

10

CONDITIONS
FOR THE ELIMINATION
OF RACIAL DISCRIMINATION
IN EAST AFRICA

The survival of aliens in East Africa depends, and will, no doubt, continue to depend upon the fulfillment of many conditions, not only by the countries of East Africa and their (private) nationals but also by the aliens themselves. Effective and lasting solutions will thus have to be found to the numerous existing racial and other problems resulting from such forces as (1) tribalism, whose impact on racial and communal relations and the general position of aliens in East Africa is enormous, (2) racism, (3) Africanization, and (4) the more difficult and complex legal questions of aliens in that region.

ELIMINATION OF TRIBALISM IN SOCIETY

The wide misuse of the expression "tribalism" requires one to be cautious when dealing with it, and to avoid it altogether if one can. However, because tribalism greatly affects some aliens economically, socially, and even politically, in East Africa, mention of it cannot be avoided here. For our purpose, it is here used to mean ethnicity or "ethnic particularism." Tribalism is a form, by definition, of group identity. That is, it is a strong ingroup loyalty and sentimental attachment to one's own group and its traits. The impact of tribalism on race relations in East Africa is not a novel thing. There are, however, certain ethnic groups in the region who have maintained, following the colonial policy of divide and rule, a feeling of superiority vis-a-vis the other ethnic groups. The most widely quoted are the Wachagga of Tanzania, the Baganda of Uganda, and the Kikuyu of Kenya. The Luos and certain other ethnic groups were also used by the colonizers in the advancement of tribalism.

208 ALIENS IN EAST AFRICA

The main advantage of tribalism is that it serves, however indirectly, the cause of regional unity by blurring national boundaries. Its greatest disadvantage is its advancement of exploitation. The colonizers failed to eradicate tribalism because they failed to introduce a system of direct rule at all levels of government. Instead, they introduced a system of indirect rule. They refused to train local Africans for governmental posts. Instead, the colonizers employed traditional and tribal authorities who could not help clinging to their own tribal principles. Another disadvantage of tribalism is that since there are many tribes (more than 120 in Tanzania, 31 in Uganda, and 27 in Kenya), it is an isolating force that limits a person to the often tiny world of the tribe.

The results of tribalism include many factors that have a negative bearing on the position of aliens in a country afflicted with animosity, hostility, resentment, envy, corruption, social and political instability, and insecurity. Whereas aliens may regard tribalism as the main source of economic, educational, racial, sharp cultural, tribal, social, political, and all other forms of developmental compartmentalization and social injustice, the envious and less favored underprivileged individual African citizens and tribes have voiced a twofold resentment: against tribalism, and against uncooperativeness and unwillingness by non-Africans—whether citizens or aliens—to share their knowledge with Africans by teaching or training them in skilled jobs. This common charge has united native Africans against aliens in East Africa.

Adjustment, then, of racial and tribal imbalances in all spheres of life in East Africa requires the development of equal educational opportunities and the recruitment into public service of people with education and experience. The stress on individual merit means that some of the more educationally advanced tribes and aliens should continue to be favored in the East African civil service recruitment, until such time as the rest of the population acquires the same educational standards and accepts the same values as do the better-educated citizens and aliens. It also means that development of the East African countries must be done in such a way as to eradicate the existing tribal imbalances and develop the less developed regions. Education, then, is the basis of social justice and progress, legal dignity, and racial and tribal harmony. Education plays a significant role both as an agent of social change and as an investment in training and skills.

EMPHASIS ON INDIVIDUAL MERIT

There are many reasons why many aliens in East Africa will be retained in good positions for a long time to come. The present shortage of sufficiently skilled African architects, dentists, doctors,

and engineers is a serious problem that cannot be solved overnight.
It is the greatest impediment to the economic and political development
and stability of the region. A premature departure of alien workers
from East Africa would certainly slow down development and create
increased unemployment. The East African governments are aware of
this fact and continue offering good working conditions to expatriates
who intend to take, or already hold, jobs in the region.

However, for those resident aliens, especially Asians, who leave
school before the fourth form, there is simply no future, except for
girls who can be expected to marry and become housewives. The refusal in Kenya to renew the work permits of all noncitizen typists, except in a very few cases, is a good example; the Employment Department in Kenya directed that such secretaries not have their work permits renewed after June 30, 1974[1] in order to create vacancies for
Kenyan citizens. East African government projects to educate Africans, whether locally or overseas, have increasingly been intensified.
Scholarships from abroad are granted to African citizens mainly.
Aliens in East Africa must make their own arrangements for the education of their children and training of their people to become teach-
ers, doctors, lawyers, and the like, if they expect to survive and
prosper in the region.

What aliens in East Africa should do, it appears, is create associations for raising funds, scholarships, and so on, for sending
their children to schools and universities. It also appears imperative
that, in this great venture, the aliens of East Africa be assisted by the
governments of East Africa, India, Bangladesh, Britain, and Pakistan.
Alien communities in East Africa should also assist in the important
task, whether individually or collectively. Thus the advantages of obtaining higher education and skills, open to aliens in East Africa—
mostly those of Asian origin—include their ability to perform useful
services on their own behalf and on behalf of the Africans and to obtain access because of their skills to nearly any country in the world
if they must leave East Africa in due course.

The emphasis on individual merit means that Africanization,
which should be "citizenization" (making opportunities equal for all
citizens) whether rapid or gradual, can only be justified if no fall is
experienced in the standards of efficiency. Otherwise, the economies
of the East African states are bound to suffer seriously from the
(negative) repercussions of Africanization. It is essential that Africanization should remain compatible all the time with developmental
goals. Also, Africanization should not be carried out at the expense
of justice. Therefore, corrective justice of bringing about equity or
reallocating resources by offering Africans more opportunities than
the other races—citizens or noncitizens—is a discriminatory practice
that should be abolished. Racial discrimination in employment must

also be eliminated. This is one of the crucial conditions for alien survival in East African society. The East African governments should differentiate between Africanization and Kenyanization/Ugandanization/Tanzanization. The evils of the unmade distinction have been many and varied. They have hit the alien very hard. If Africanization means transferring the country's assets, resources, and entire economy to Africans on an equitable basis, then Ugandanization, for instance, means transferring such assets, resources, and the economy to Ugandan citizens, irrespective of color. The interchangeable employment of these two expressions has led to a lot of confusion, corruption, and victimization of the innocent. So long as, however, Africanization remains as expensive as it is today in East Africa, foreign investments will continue to pour into that region. And so long as investment agreements continue to be signed between the East African and other governments, the practice of exchanging specialists will prevail.

This is all the more so since the young graduate entrants are arrogant and like changing jobs frequently in order to meet better conditions of work to suit their better qualifications. This situation in turn retards the tempo of Africanization and is, therefore, also a condition for the retention, by aliens, of their good positions in East Africa. Most of the local staff, however, hate the idea of continued recruitment and maintenance of foreign personnel who cost the East African governments huge sums of money. The argument of the local personnel must be rejected, because developmental needs cannot be sacrificed for any equity or superiority demands by the locals. If the local staff are not capable or are scarce and the governments decide to retain expatriates, that is perfectly justified as a step toward achieving the equity that is so badly needed for the development of East Africa. If the expatriate staffs stay and do not deter, but rather assist, in the Africanization of jobs—and this is the aim of most expatriate staffs—then they should not be accused of frustrating the local staffs.

On their part, however, aliens—especially those of Asian origin—must show their willingness and ability to comply with the developmental requirements of the region, where, after all, the aliens do not have full rights. But if aliens in East Africa are expected to train Africans more efficiently, then it is certainly desirable that they be integrated and fully accepted into the East African society. This requirement calls for full respect of the acquired rights and vested interests of aliens in the region.

Ghana's Kwame Nkrumah said, about racialism:

> The foulest intellectual rubbish ever invented by man
> is that of racial superiority and inferiority. The fact
> is that the powerful forces which seek to block the ad-

vance of the 280 million Africans to a place of full
equality in the world community, and which strive
to maintain neocolonialism, or even overt colonial
domination and white supremacy rule in Africa, find
it their interest to perpetuate the mythology of racial inferiority. Thus it is not simple ignorance of
Africa, but deliberate disparagement of the continent and its peoples, that . . . Africans must con-
tend with. [2]

East Africa is a mixed society. What does this mean? Many
things. For instance, it is a society in which its members, whether
nationals or not, want to make a home, on a permanent or temporary
basis. East Africa is also a multicultural society—that is, it is a
society in which there is ethnic diversity. It is also a multiracial society. If aliens are to survive in such a society, there must be absolute equality in the areas of knowledge and culture; equal opportunities
for all; equal legal administration for all; and equality in spiritual matters.

JUSTICE AND EQUAL DISTRIBUTION OF
WEALTH IN SOCIETY

The present setup of the East African society does not, unfortunately, make it a perfect multiracial society. Human relations in
East Africa are full of racial and other tensions, whose causes include cultural, religious, social, economic, traditional, tribal, lin-
gual, and educational differences. The core of the racial threat (that
is, feelings of racial antagonism and suspicion) in present-day East
Africa is still the economic and social imbalances separating Asians
from Africans. The struggle for uhuru (independence) in East Africa
was promoted by the feeling of humiliation of being ruled by aliens.
Politically, the Asians identified themselves with this humiliation.
There was also the humiliation of disease, ignorance, and poverty,
which became clearer after the attainment of independence. The challenge, then, to the non-African communities, particularly Asians,
was whether they would continue showing that they were willing to
share that humiliation with the Africans. What the Asians could do in
the circumstances was contribute generously to the economic progress
of East Africa. In this way, the attitudes and spirit of the body politic
would be immensely bettered.

If harmonious race relations are to be achieved in East Africa,
aliens (especially Asians) and East Africans must alter their attitudes
toward one another, and remove the traditional barriers existing be-

tween themselves. Asians, whether nationals or not, must disregard
their racial prejudices and attitudes of cultural arrogance. They must
also change their patterns of economic activity and be willing to assist
Africans in business, trade, and other undertakings. Africans, on
their part, should show their readiness to end revengeful practices
and guarantee the security of Asians in the region. Citizen Asians,
Europeans, and any other national (citizen) minorities in East Africa
should not be regarded as second-class citizens.

Another way of easing the communal and racial tensions in East
Africa is to establish genuine cooperation among the various ethnic
and racial groups in the region. What are needed are national, or
even regional, voluntary organizations of both Africans and other racial groups devoted to the creation and continuance of sound race relations, such as the Community Relations Committee (CRC) established
in January 1970 by the National Christian Council of Kenya (NCCK) and
composed of nations and aliens from all walks of life, with different
religious, racial, and ethnic backgrounds. It has already done useful
research on some of the complex problems resulting from the mixture
of tribes, cultures, and races in Kenya—problems of employment,
youth, students, Africanization, and racial minorities.

The CRC is one of the very few organizations in Africa that
work for the ideals of harmonious mixed societies. The CRC is the
only organization of its kind in East Africa. The creation of similar
committees in Tanzania and Uganda is desirable. It would also be
useful to create a similar organization on an East African regional
basis, whose primary function would be to coordinate the activities of
national committees. In fact, each East African city, town, or province requires an active organization, first, to direct its attention to
immediate problems of racial difficulties and, second, to plan long-
range efforts to eliminate racial discrimination. The inflammatory
statements—some with racist tones—made over the years by East African politicians regarding the racial problem in the region can only
alert East Africans to this great social problem, which, if unchecked,
could explode into open violence.

Since the governments of East Africa and the Indian subcontinent
(India, Bangladesh, and Pakistan) reject the notion of dual nationality,
alien Asians who want to reside in East Africa should be offered and
should seize the opportunity of acquiring East African citizenship.
Those large numbers of Asians who wanted to stay in East Africa but
did not opt for such citizenship during the two-year period of grace
starting with the date of independence in East Africa did themselves
enormous harm. Those Asians who are now permanently resident in
the region should fully participate in the building of a successful and
prosperous East African multicultural society. For example, East
African Asians should intensify their efforts to assist Africans in all

the key fields of development. This type of action will demonstrate to Africans that Asians in East Africa are committed to it and to its prosperous future.

EFFECTIVE INTEGRATION IN SOCIETY

No doubt, one of the important conditions for the elimination of racial discrimination in East Africa is strict observance of the constitutional provisions guaranteeing equality of rights and treatment of all people, irrespective of tribe or race. However, constitutional guarantees and safeguards, together with a mere setting side by side of races in East African schools and universities, and in places of residence and employment, will not, by themselves, solve racial and communal tensions in East Africa. What is needed is some form of effective integration: a relationship in which the hatred toward national minorities diminishes, or disappears altogether. Integration can be of two types: pluralism, also known as accommodation, and assimilation. Pluralism advocates the continuation of the minority as a distinct group or unit within the larger society, while retaining community awareness.

Assimilation rules out every diversity between groups as such, for example, in family life, culture, religion, club associations, and other sociocultural institutions. Assimilation further implies the complete disappearance of minorities.

Resident aliens in East Africa have these two types of integration open to them. However, the continued existence in the region of racial tensions despite the prevalence of pluralism in East Africa is a clear indication that pluralism has not been an effective type of integration. It therefore appears that assimilation would be the better form of integration in the region. But the strong tendency toward pluralism makes the realization of assimilation remote. In the circumstances, it seems that pluralism will prevail in the region.

If East African society is to be a pluralistic society in which racial harmony is ensured, the conditions that must be fulfilled can be summed up as follows:

1. The racial, ethnic minorities must be accepted as full members of the society (or their country of residence), in which they can thus play a role on an equal footing with the majorities.

2. The minorities must accept, and be loyal to, the country of residence; they must also respect the fundemantal aspirations of the majorities, who, in turn, are obligated to be tolerant and understanding.

3. The existing intraracial institutions must be reconstructed in such a way as to promote trust and goodwill among the various racial groups in East Africa.

4. All forms of legal disrcimination must be removed at once, in law and in practice.

Some Asians refused to become citizens of East Africa, partly because of much confusion and misunderstanding about the implications of East African nationality. Primarily, their refusal to opt for this nationality and instead retain that of Britain, Pakistan, or India was inspired by the fear that to release their foreign nationality would be to surrender the right to any kind of protection in the event of persecution or property confiscation.

INTERNATIONAL PROTECTION OF HUMAN RIGHTS IN EAST AFRICA

International implications of the problems of aliens—and for that matter any other racial minorities—in East Africa will continue to occur as long as the African (ruling) majorities fail to understand, and find the right solutions, to the problems, and the racial or ethnic minorities—citizens and aliens alike—remain persistently arrogant. In this case, the immigrant minorities will, or should, have the right to seek assistance from outside countries—whether of their origin, like India, Pakistan, or Bangladesh, or of their nationality, like the United Kingdom. International law recognizes the right of a state to intervene in order to protect the lives of its citizens abroad. Forms of intervention by the protecting state against the host state include, first, bringing the problem before an international community such as the United Nations, the Organization of African Unity, the British Commonwealth Conference, the East African Community, or the Afro-Asian Consultative Organization. Any of the organizations may either discuss the problem and recommend solutions to the countries concerned or set up commissions of inquiry to investigate and report on the problem. This procedure has been very widely used by the United Nations. Other forms of intervention are diplomatic protests against the state alleged to be persecuting, or to have persecuted, a citizen of another (home) state, in reality a form of minimum interference; severance of diplomatic relations with the state in which the citizens of the protecting state are, or have been, persecuted; direct military intervention to protect the home state's nationals abroad (as applied by the Belgian government in July 1960, against the Congo); and risking war (as Turkey has repeatedly done against Cyrpus, where Turkey feels committed toward its minority nationals).

To what extent the governments of the United Kingdom and the Indian subcontinent would feel themselves morally obliged to interfere in East Africa, if ever there was a case of the persecution of alien minorities in East Africa, is in doubt. The reactions of these governments to the expulsion of Asians from East Africa in 1967, 1968, and 1972 indicated that government intervention in East Africa would be a last resort. This leaves diplomatic protests, bringing the problem before the international community, and "wars of nerves and words" as the forms of intervention most likely to be used, should such expulsions and other kinds of mistreatment of alien Asians occur again in East Africa. One thing that seems certain is that the abovenamed home countries (governments) will not intervene in East Africa just because of the economic imbalance between alien Asians and the Africans in East Africa. Even if a strong position were to be justified by persecutions of such alien Asians in East Africa, it is very difficult to imagine a military intervention in the region by Britain, Bangladesh, India, or Pakistan. The most serious repercussions of the alien problem in East Africa might appear on domestic lines—on the politico-economic fronts. This has already happened.

A very curious phenomenon regarding the position of the Asian minority and the issue of human rights in Uganda has been the report of the Geneva-based UN International Commission of Jurists (ICJ).[3] The ICJ report bitterly accused President Amin's government of creating a reign of terror in Uganda, through massive violations of human rights, arbitrary arrests, torture, and murder. The comprehensive 63-page report declares that "by a series of decrees overriding all constitutional safeguards, and by a system of arbitrary repression operating outside any legal framework, there has been a total breakdown in the rule of law." The ICJ report further states, "The effect of these massive and continuing violations of human rights has been to create a reign of terror from which thousands of people from all walks of life, Africans as well as Asians, have sought refuge in voluntary exile. Those remaining are in a constant state of insecurity." The report, based on statements from Africans, Asians, and Europeans who were in Uganda after Amin's coming to power in January 1971, condemns Uganda's failure to uphold even the minimum judicial safeguards for the protection of human rights. Amin was accused of overriding the Ugandan Constitution by arbitrary decrees. The expulsions of Asians from Uganda in 1972 involved serious violations of human rights because, the commission argued, the expulsions were based on an explicit policy of racial discrimination. Similarly, "the banishment of all Asians recognized as Uganda citizens to a remote and unfamiliarly rural life was an act of racial discrimination which had the (no doubt intended) effect of driving almost all of them out of the country."

The report sparked off a host of negative reactions on the part of Amin's regime. The British Broadcasting Corporation's (BBC) commentaries on the report prompted General Amin to threaten taking drastic steps against Britain—by closing down the British High Commission in Kampala and expelling all British nationals in Uganda—if the BBC did not stop broadcasting "malicious propaganda against Uganda."[4] The BBC alleged that over 200,000 people had been killed in Uganda during the Ugandan "crisis." Amin was about to carry out his threatened "drastic steps" when President Kenyatta phoned to advise him not to do so. However, Amin soon greatly regretted having gone along with Kenyatta's request, when an editorial in the Kenya-government-backed Daily Nation of June 8, 1974 condemned Amin's threats against Britain. The editorial affirmed that "the ICJ is an independent organization whose members are professional lawyers of the highest standing and integrity . . . drawn from all over the world." Amin's immediate reaction to the above commentary was to ban "'all imperialist' newspapers for their perpetual stand against the Uganda government, where they distort the true picture of the country and, at times, fabricate stories on issues which have never taken place."[5] The papers banned included (London papers) the Observer, the Daily Telegraph, the Times, the Sunday Express, News of the World, and the People, and (Kenya-based papers) the Daily Nation, the Sunday Nation, the Sunday Post, and the East African Standard.[6] The ban was still effective as of June 20, 1974.

Uganda bitterly condemned "our brothers in neighbouring Kenya who are supporting imperialists" and seriously warned these "brothers" of their "provocative propaganda which Uganda hates because of the strain or interference with such [a] good relationship."[7] That accusation against "our brothers in Kenya" was promptly responded to in another editorial in the Daily Nation of June 10, 1974:

> It is not necessary for us to whine because of insults hurled at us by a spokesman of General Amin. If the Uganda Military spokesman calls us imperialists, or imperialist propagandists, or fabricators of issues, none of these things objectively represent what we are doing. They are simply . . . in the mind of the speaker. . . . In our editorial of Saturday, June 8, we stated, among other things . . . that the nature of the document is such that it is imperative for the Uganda government to give a satisfactory counterexplanation. We reiterate this position to-day. The present regime stands accused at the bar by world public opinion. And just what is General Amin trying to deny? . . . We are committed to the prin-

ciples of good neighbourliness and peaceful coexistence. But we are not committed to lavishing praise
on our neighbours whether they are right or wrong.[8]

Later in the same week, Amin paid an unannounced visit to Kenyatta
at State House in Nairobi. Although the real purpose of that visit
was not revealed, it was presumed that the two heads of state discussed
the ICJ report.

The above example reveals one significant thing. The survival
of aliens in East Africa will depend upon international interest in the
position of aliens in that region. The work of international bodies
concerned with the promotion of human rights, such as the UN High
Commission for Refugees and the UN Commission on Human Rights,
will have to be intensified. Individual states will have to offer their
good services and show interest in the maintenance of respect for human dignity. They will have to observe the principle of humanitarianism. Canada did this, for instance, when she announced her readiness
to accept up to 6,000 of the Asians expelled from Uganda in 1972.[9]
Other governments, notably those of the United Kingdom, India, Bangladesh, and Pakistan, will have to be willing to accept their moral and
legal responsibilities (imposed upon them by international law) for
people of Asian origin in East Africa.

One of the things these governments could do to ensure alien
Asian survival in East Africa is introduce a system of agreements
similar to the one signed between the British and Indian governments
in July 1968. These two governments made arrangements for the resettlement of British Asians resident in Kenya at the time of their expulsion from that country in 1967-68. The right of entry into either
India or the United Kingdom was endorsed by the U.K. passport
holders. Where there is no mother country to appeal to, appeal can
be made either to humanitarianism or to standards of justice and morals.

The economic position of the African is rapidly improving. This
development might help ease racial tensions in East Africa and lead
to a complete integration of the pluralistic type. If the Indians and
Goans in East Africa were to be integrated completely with the Africans, the Indian and Goan mentality—of culture consciousness, for
instance—would be destroyed. But the continued existence in postindependence East Africa of purely Asian associations such as the Patel
Club and the Goan Institute in Nairobi is a clear indication of the determination of the Asian community to maintain their cultures and isolation. So long as this mentality prevails, the problems of Asians will
survive, despite the existence of such integrating associations as the
Lions Club.

ASIAN TENDENCY FOR PLURALISM
OR ACCOMMODATION

The Asian tendency is still for pluralism or accommodation.
Asians have accepted African political victory and the new civic and
political institutions. Beyond this, Asians would prefer to uphold their
old mentality. But they should realize that acceptance of, and respect
for, the new leadership, complete allegiance to the host state—which
requires aliens (Asians) to invest locally rather than export their capital outside that state—and economic assistance to Africans, particularly in the creation of an African business class, are all prerequi-
sites to any integration.

In the political sphere, integration is possible, but it is hindered
by the inclination in the East African states toward a one-party system
—in practice, at least, although in law, two-party or multiparty systems are permissible. Political leaders in a one-party system have
the advantage of imposing policies, without opposition, that may obviously be risky and even dangerous to racial harmony and nation-
building. The concept of the government-opposition party system
should be applied in East Africa. For aliens, however, the one-party
system is ideal, for no menace exists from any other party that loses
that the aliens do not support. Asian participation in politics was
most active in Tanganyika, where the African leadership practiced
the most liberal racial policies of all the three states. That was possible to a large extent because Tanganyika had—and still has—a one-
party system. In Tanzania, Uganda, and Kenya, fewer efforts have in
general been made to involve the minority groups in political parties
and activities.

In the economic field, which is the key field that will determine
Asian survival in East Africa, African hostility toward Asians can be
ended through Asian support to Africans via training and advice, guid-
ance, leadership, credits and loans, and economic partnership.
Asians should also be encouraged to participate in trade unions, which
are a good area of racial integration. Trade unions in East Africa
have been very race-minded. This must be stopped if integration is
to be achieved. Unfortunately, a part of the hatred meted out to Asians
in the region is a function of their being distinctive, and possessing
more wealth than the East Africans.

The policies of the East African states toward Asians differ
from one state to another. There is a lot of rhetoric in these policies,
and what is laid down in law is quite often disregarded in practice.
However, the established official East African government policies
toward Asians are as follows:

1. The official policy of the three states is equal treatment and justice (of rights and duties) for the Asian citizens.

2. The expression "Africanization" is used in different senses. It is sometimes interchangeable with "localization," meaning "citizenization." But it often implies replacement of white by black, "blackenization." The work of aliens and minority Asian citizens is appreciated, but the two categories of Asian minorities (aliens and citizens alike) are indiscriminately blamed for retarding the process of Africanization because of their reputation for devious business practices. Harsh punishment is threatened for those who frustrate or undermine the policies of Africanization.

3. Promises are made regarding security and full government protection of minorities.

4. Asians are persistently accused of racial arrogance, exploitation, isolation, and exporting large sums of money from East Africa. Amin has accused them of "milking the cow without feeding it." Hence Asian and other racial minorities are called upon to identify themselves with the commitments and aspirations of the African majority populations. Asian isolation must be ended at once for the sake of national unity and progress.

5. Discrimination against Asians, especially in business and schools, is practiced most frankly in Uganda and Kenya. Tanzania claims, with considerable justification, to have abolished discrimination in law and in practice. But in certain areas of employment, Asians simply do not qualify even if they are citizens. Thus, in the Foreign Office, Tanzania has offered the post of ambassador to one Asian only (at the Hague). In the Kenyan and Ugandan diplomatic corps, there are no Asian ambassadors.

6. Priority is given to African demands for human rights, dignity, and socioeconomic and educational equality. Hence equity in East Africa usually means raising the sociomaterial standards of Africans above those of the Asians and Europeans.

7. The central aim of the East African states' general economic policies toward Asians is to eradicate Asian dominance in the economic and commercial fields. In Tanzania, this is reflected in her socialization of the economy as outlined in the Arusha Declaration of 1967. In Kenya, the economic policy is that of Africanization of commerce and industry. In Uganda, the economic policy is a combination of Africanization and socialism (as in Tanzania). This is reflected in the so-called Common Man's Charter, adopted by Obote's Uganda People's Congress at its conference on December 18, 1969,[10] and in the country's Development Plans of the 1960s. In the spirit of the Arusha Declaration, the government of Uganda proclaimed, in May 1970, partial or complete nationalization of the major sections of the Ugandan economy: import and export trade, the oil companies, banks, mining

companies, public transport companies, and all manufacturing and plantation industries.

8. Integration is called for on a basis of complete multiracialism, which is strongly believed to offer an excellent opportunity for harmonious race relations. Both types of integration (explained above) are favored. However, some African leaders have shown preference for total assimilation, especially via intermarriages. The Zanzibari government required this, particularly under Karume's leadership. Karume decreed in 1970 that Arabs and Asiatics encourage the marriage of their daughters to Africans. He himself took one Asian girl as a wife under his own decree. His ministers widely made use of his ruling. Mainland Tanzania also showed a predilection for assimilation, but not by the Karume method.

Compromise and natural inclination offer a better chance of promoting racial harmony and integration than force or coercion. There is at present no standard well-defined homogeneous culture in East Africa. The radicalism of the African cultures, the conservatism of the Asian cultures, and the self-conscious aggressive outlook of Western culture meet in East Africa but do not make integration by the assimilation method practicable. If dominance of any of these three cultures is to emerge, it will be the Western one.

Some government leaders in East Africa have not shown a marked preference for either of the two methods of integration. This has been the case among the Kenyan and Ugandan leaders, who have done very little to clarify their integration policies, despite their continued references to racial integration. However, Uganda's Amin has shown that he prefers assimilation to accommodation. His schemes of settling Asians in the rural areas are a good case in point. In Kenya, the tendency has been a preference for accommodation. This attitude has been reflected in political speeches of Kenyan government leaders. President Kenyatta has reiterated his love of and determination to maintain African cultures, traditions, and customs, which he believes must never be diluted. He has also reiterated the Kenyan government's policy of fully protecting minorities and their denominational beliefs, plus cultural and other rights.[11]

To survive in East Africa, Asians must also divorce themselves from corrupt practices and people. The East African governments have a duty to eliminate corruption, in all its forms, in practice, and not just superficially. The duty of the governments is, therefore, to establish impartial bodies to inquire into the possibilities of ending corruption in society. The presidents of East Africa have occasionally expressed their serious concern about corruption, and allegations of corruption, in their respective countries. But Amin has been unique in his style of condemning corruption. He has on a good number of

occasions promised to establish an independent organ to probe into
charges of corruption in Uganda.[12] Amin's idea is definitely commendable. It should be realized and spread throughout East Africa.
President Kenyatta has particularly condemned, in various speeches,
"those disgruntled elements and economic prostitutes" who, by their
corrupt practices have frustrated his government's policy of Africanization. Obviously, he was referring to both Africans and Asians.
Alien survival in East Africa will depend on the acceptance of responsibilities by the East African states toward aliens. Discrimination
against brown and white citizens must be stopped. The concept of the
integrity of citizenship must be upheld.

LEGAL CONDITIONS FOR SURVIVAL OF
ALIENS IN EAST AFRICA

On the legal front, there are five areas where the legal conditions for the survival of aliens in the region are crucial: equality in
the administration of justice; the legal problems of minorities in East
Africa; the need to review East African legislation affecting aliens
in the region; the question of statelessness in East Africa; and what
the legal status of aliens in East Africa should be.

In the legal sphere, the expression "arbitrary arrest" is used
to mean arrest or detention either on grounds or in accordance with
procedures other than those established by law or under the provisions
of a law, the basic purpose of which is incompatible with respect for
the right to liberty and security of person. The term "arrest" is
used to mean the act of taking a person into custody under the authority
of the law, or by compulsion of another kind, and includes the period
from the moment he is placed under restraint up to the time he is
brought before an authority competent to order his continued custody
or to release him. The expression "detention" means the act of con-
fining a person to a certain place, whether or not in continuation of
arrest, and under restraints that prevent him from living with his
family or carrying out his normal occupational or social activities.
The expression "exile" is used to mean the expulsion or exclusion of
a person from the country of which he is a national and the banishment of a person within the country by way of forcible removal from
the place of his habitual residence.

The legal and procedural rights of aliens in East Africa, which
international law imposes upon the East African states as duties toward aliens in their territories, include the right of habeas corpus;
access to East African courts; a fair, nondiscriminatory, and un-
biased hearing in the determination of criminal charges; the right to
be heard by an independent and impartial court; the right to be heard

by their (aliens') lawful judges; the right to be informed of the offense of which they may be accused and of their procedural rights; and the rights to defend themselves in person, to counsel, to a prompt and speedy hearing, to a public hearing, to a just decision rendered in full compliance with the state's laws, and to appeal to a higher court.

A prima facie reaction to the above legal rights of aliens in East Africa may be that they are too obvious to need any mention here. But violations of these rights abound. Discriminatory procedural legislation against aliens based upon nationalistic and ideological considerations has been enacted in East Africa. Cases brought before East African courts regarding, for example, nationalizations, compensations, and the like have on occasion been discredited in court decisions. Survival of aliens in East Africa requires that constitutional and statutory safeguards of fundamental human rights be implemented. No doubt, the best protection for aliens—and citizens alike—against excesses committed in the name of national emergency is via the courts. To function properly and impartially, these courts must be independent. They are an institutional machinery for enforcing guarantees of basic freedoms and rights of mankind. Therefore, courts comprising judges subject to political influence and pressure are not courts at all. Aliens require, for their protection in exacting their procedural safeguards and guarantees in courts, fair treatment based upon the integrity, impartiality, and independence of the courts.

The East African countries have a heavy responsibility to enhance their judicial systems, because any neglect of these will certainly lead to a breakdown in fundamental human rights and freedoms. Luckily, the courts of East Africa, including the East African Court of Appeal, are independent. And so long as their independence prevails, alien survival in the legal field can be anticipated. The local remedies rule, for East Africa, essentially means that cases involving aliens must be given exhaustive treatment at the local-court level before letting them mushroom into international disputes. The East African governments should execute their moral and legal responsibilities toward aliens. For example, their actions infringing on the property rights of aliens should be corrected by compensation. The East African courts must maintain the international legal order. They must continue settling disputes between citizens and aliens impartially. They should intensify their fair application of the local remedies rule.

A clear distinction should be drawn between expropriation and nationalization. Expropriation is mainly of individual or personal assets. It involves the compulsory purchase of particular pieces of property. Nationalization involves, on the other hand, mainly purchase of private-corporation assets. It has usually different motivations and is of great economic and political significance. Further, expropriation is normally done by a permanent machinery for enabling

individual acts of expropriation to be carried out when necessary.
Nationalization is, on the other hand, normally done by the government
of the nationalizing state. That government needs powers to carry
through nationalization. These powers are normally granted through
special legislation.

Private investment is essential for the economic development of
East Africa. If increased foreign capital is to be invested in the region, the East African nations should ensure that no such capital is
discriminated against and that fair treatment and distribution of it
are assured. Similarly, expropriation, nationalization, or other similar dispossession of private property must be accompanied by a fair,
adequate, effective, and prompt compensation. Furthermore, the East
African states should carry out their international obligations arising
from bilateral and multilateral treaties. The states must honor their
international obligations regarding foreign investments. They should
set up impartial tribunals, where these do not exist, for settlement
of disputes, and make maximum use of the services of such tribunals.
The existing divergences in the East African laws governing private
alien investments in the region necessitate conclusion of an East African multilateral convention to regulate such investments. This would
be a good way of maintaining the confidence of private alien investments, on which the economies of East Africa heavily depend. Enactment of new laws, and review of the existing legislation relating to
aliens in East Africa, the proper interpretation of these laws, the
strict observance of them by their makers and by citizens and aliens
in East Africa are all necessary for the survival of aliens in East Africa. There is an imperative need to codify or establish an East African law of aliens that will clearly lay down rules to govern the general position and treatment of aliens in East Africa.

The techniques for achieving minimum standards of procedural
justice in the courts of East Africa include (1) avoidance of incompe-
tence in court administrations by enacting impartial and nondiscriminatory legislations; (2) according aliens access to international legal
assistance where possible and necessary; (3) removing, by legislation,
all existing loopholes in formal legal mechanisms, including the
existing legal provisions for discrimination; (4) removing inadequacies
of the economic, social, and political environment within which legal
mechanisms must function, by encouraging foreign investment; (5) establishing local bar associations where they do not exist and encouraging them to revitalize or alter judicial procedures; and (6) establishing political and economic stability. All these measures are essential
and have a direct bearing on the position of aliens in East Africa. The
granting to aliens of procedural rights in the region means that the
East African states are under an international duty to open their courts
to aliens. Such granting is a most important protection against the

violation of the substantive rights of aliens. These include the (human) right to freedom of movement within and outside a state's border, and the right of exit (to leave the country) from his country of sojourn, which should not be subject to any arbitrary restrictions.

The above human rights are legal rights that were recognized by the 1948 Universal Declaration of Human Rights. In exclusively criminal proceedings, of particular significance are the right to have enough time to prepare a defense; the right to cross-examine witnesses for the prosecution; the right to have an interpreter, without charge, if the accused cannot speak or understand the language employed in the court; freedom from what is known as self-incrimination, that is, freedom either to give evidence on oath at the trial of the accused, if he so wishes to testify, or to make an unsworn declaration at the end of the trial but before judgment is passed; the right to compensation for wrongful conviction; and the right not to be placed in double or multiple jeopardy.

In assessing the procedural rights of aliens before East African courts, the latter should seriously consider the possibility of applying the international standard rather than the national one. Extralegal problems affecting aliens should be avoided. The national standard of treatment was not, it seems, calculated to protect aliens but to protect the state from aliens. However, to be complete, treatment of aliens should be subject both to the national and international treatment concepts. One of the reasons why the writer insists on the introduction and wider application of the minimum standard of treatment in East Africa is that it offers a much better opportunity of showing a country's pride and hospitality. In the alien, man discovered the concept of humanity. The alien was protected in the ancient world— as numerous passages in the Old Testament reveal—because he was a fellow human being.

Aliens in East Africa are a minority who, when rejected by East African states and refused entry to any other states, become stateless persons. Statelessness is one of the greatest challenges facing international law. The problem was regulated by Article 15 of the 1948 Universal Declaration of Human Rights, to which the East African states are signatories: "Everyone has the right to nationality." The lack of uniformity in the East African citizenship laws, and the rule, in the more recent years, by presidential decree—particularly in Uganda and Kenya—have inevitably given rise to complex problems of statelessness in the region. The presidential decrees have, in most cases, bypassed the existing constitutional and other legal (statutory) safeguards and guarantees assured to aliens. International law principles have also, on occasion, been disregarded. While rule by decree in East Africa cannot be said to have entirely ignored the crucial dogma of rule of law, where aliens have been concerned, presidential decrees have deprived aliens of their legal rights. Good cases in point have been decrees enacted, particularly in Uganda and Kenya, to denationalize some citizens, to arrest, detain, imprison, or expel them arbitrarily, and so on. A wider employment of the doctrine of presidential rule by decree in East Africa will certainly imperil the position of aliens in the region. To avoid this possible danger to the status of aliens in East Africa, the East African states should ratify and strictly observe all international conventions whose central aim is to reduce or eliminate causes of conflicts of nationality laws that prompt statelessness. A good example of such conventions is the Convention on the Reduction of Statelessness adopted, within the UN framework, in 1961.[13] Article 1 of the Convention imposes on the contracting states compulsory application of the doctrine of jus soli in certain cases in order to reduce or eradicate the possibilities of statelessness. Thus the parties to the convention agreed to grant their citizenship to people born in their territory who would otherwise be stateless and to people not born in the territory of a contracting state who would otherwise be stateless if the nationality of one of their parents at the time of their birth was that of the state.

For aliens not to become stateless persons in East Africa, the states of that region will have to stop denationalization of their citizens, and grant, on moral and humanitarian grounds at least, their citizenships to persons who would otherwise be stateless; and to (continue to) allow refugees and stateless persons to enjoy minimum rights and essentials of life. For example, stateless persons and refugees should be allowed the use of identity or travel documents, and to enjoy privileges of admission into East Africa, with rights of residence, of practicing professions, of carrying on businesses, and so on and so forth. When expelling, deporting, or returning aliens to the frontier under police escort, the East African countries should remember that expulsion or reconduction must be effected without unnecessary injury; detention prior to expulsion must be avoided, unless the alien refuses to leave, or is most likely to evade the East African (state) authorities; deportation of aliens should not be to a country or territory where the person or freedom of the alien would be menaced, owing to the alien's race, religion, nationality, or political opinions; and the deportee or expellee should not be exposed to unnecessary indignity.

If the legal position of aliens—whether stateless persons, refugees, residents, or sojourners—in East Africa is to measure up to the international minimum standard of civilization, aliens may not be obliged to perform military service in East Africa. However, those aliens who are resident in the region, unless they prefer to leave their country of residence, may be compelled—but under the same conditions as citizens—to perform such essential functions as fire protection and police or militia duties for the protection of their domicile

against natural dangers or disasters not resulting from war. The
East African countries should extend to aliens, whether resident or in
transit through their territories, all individual guarantees extended to
East African citizens, and the enjoyment of basic civil rights without
detriment, as regards aliens, to legal provisions governing the scope
of, and usages for, the exercise of the aforementioned rights and
guarantees.

Aliens, on their part, must avoid involvement in the political activities of their host state in East Africa. In cases of such involvement, aliens must be made liable to the penalties established by the
laws of the East African host state.

SUMMARY

One of the conditions for the survival of aliens in East Africa is
to find lasting solutions to the racial tensions in the region. These
solutions necessarily include (1) adjustments and adaptations, by the
racial minorities, to the changed circumstances in which they now find
themselves. They should, for example, consider the necessity of
learning the languages, customs, and traditions of the other races.
Revisions of attitudes are also required on the side of the African majorities. Behaviors and feelings of prejudice should be stopped. Distinctions should be made between minorities who are aliens and those
who are citizens. This is necessary particularly where the Asian
community is concerned. Tribalism is a backward and barbaric doctrine. The attainment of independence in East Africa was premature.
As such, it has created and even intensified intratribal tensions and
conflicts. The Zanzibari revolution, the army uprising in Tanganyika,
the Obote-Kiwanuka clashes in Uganda, and the Oginga schism in Kenya
in the 1960s were all symptoms of the unpreparedness of the leaders
of East Africa when they acquired independence. In such conditions,
no lasting guarantees can be assured to aliens. The economic rivalries and inequalities and the imbalanced distribution of educational,
social, and other facilities also justify the above assertion of unpreparedness for independence.

Integration and cooperation are required at the national and regional levels. Swahili is used as an administrative lingua franca in
Uganda, Tanzania, and Kenya; it is the language of popular communication. English is the official language of East Africa. The best way
for aliens to communicate in the region is to learn these two languages.
Apart from these common working languages in East Africa, other
factors supporting East African unity include the existing common
economic, social, and political interests; a common ex-British colonial rule; similarities in the economic potential and development; the

existing common problems—for example, border disputes—whose solution requires East African unity at federal level; and the possession of common properties such as boundaries, customs, traditions, railways, and roads that were separated by the colonizers.

A prima facie reflection on the above factors excludes alien interests in the necessity for East African unity. But a closer examination of the factors reveals that, if legal unity, for instance, were to be achieved in East Africa, the position of aliens in the region would perhaps be improved. As things stand, that position is blurred. Alien employees, for example, working for the East African community have complained of mistreatment in their employment conditions. They have on occasion been refused compensation for injuries done to them. In recent years, Kenyan and Tanzanian citizens have been loath to work in the East African Community Offices in Uganda, owing mainly to the "disappearances" and other alleged violations of human rights in Amin's Uganda. If the East African states could conclude conventions among themselves on such crucial questions as dual nationality and diplomatic or consular relations, the position of aliens in the region could be made much clearer.

Opportunities for effecting complete legal unity exist in East Africa. The legislations of the East African states are essentially based on English common law. This is revealed by the following considerations. Kenya, Uganda, and Tanzania have, really, a common visa and passport area. As regards Kenya, for instance, the following countries do not require visas to enter Kenya: all Commonwealth countries, including Tanzania and Uganda; Denmark, Ethiopia, Italy, Norway, San Marino, Sweden, Spain, Turkey, Uruguay, and West Germany. All that the nationals of these countries need are valid return tickets to their own countries, and the right travel documents, including passports. Once admitted, aliens from the above states are granted passes and certificates according to the types of visit of the aliens. All other countries require visas to Kenya. Visas are of two types: referred visas, which are granted after obtaining permission from the Kenya Immigration Department; and ordinary visas, which can be obtained from any Kenyan embassy abroad, or other embassies authorized to do so by the Kenyan government.

The position is similar in Uganda and Tanzania, although minor differences exist. In Tanzania, for instance, a circular was issued in 1972 by the Tanzanian Tourist Office to the effect that from June 1, 1973 all Kenyans and Ugandans of African origin should be required to hold valid passports if they desired to enter Tanzania. Thus by that circular, the existing immigration rules requiring all immigrants into Tanzania to possess valid passports but exempting indigenous Africans from Kenya and Uganda were amended. The period within which people from the Commonwealth states and the Nordic nations

could stay in Tanzania was unaltered—three months. Exempted also
from visas are members of African tribes indigenous to Mozambique,
Rhodesia, Burundi, Rwanda, and Zaire. Tanzania has many refugees
from these countries. It was also provided in the circular that pas-
sengers entering Tanzania in the course of a continuous and unbroken
journey leaving by the same ship or aircraft need not have visas,
but they cannot leave the aircraft or ship.

Similarly, resident aliens in any of the East African territories
holding valid immigration interstate passes issued by any of the three
governments do not need visas. The circular further provided that an
ordinary single-journey visa might be granted without reference to
the principal immigration officer, except to citizens of Albania, Bulgaria, Czechoslovakia, East Germany, Hungary, North Korea, South
Africa, North Vietnam, Poland, Saudi Arabia, South West Africa,
Syria, and Portugal. Citizens of Argentina, Colombia, Ethiopia,
Israel, Mexico, Peru, Salvador, and Uruguay might be accorded continuous visas for all journeys within a 12-month period except when
more restrictive visas are specifically authorized.

The current situation in East Africa with regard to visas is
that all visitors to any of the three states require passes except for
members of tribes indigenous to Tanzania, Uganda, and Kenya. Also,
the general policy of these states is that all travelers, by any means,
wishing to visit any of the three states are divided as follows: African
citizens of an East African country do not need a passport or pass to
enter another East African state; however, it is advisable for them to
have identity cards or other useful documents. All other people,
whether Africans, citizens, or not, must bear passports or any other
valid travel documents. The above considerations indicate there is
a need for uniformity in the laws of aliens in East Africa. This legal
uniformity can be achieved by reframing the existing laws and adopt-
ing the required laws, in such a way as to avoid every possible diver-
gency. For example, the rules for the expulsion of aliens should be
made uniform. A possible consideration here would be enacting a
rule that would limit the right of an East African state to expel aliens
from its territory.

As the UN Covenant on Civil and Political Rights declared, an
alien who is legally in the territory of a state that is party to the covenant "may be expelled therefrom only in pursuance of a decision
reached in accordance with law." Hence, before expelling an alien, a
state is required, by international law, not to do so capriciously or
arbitrarily and to be prepared to give sound reasons for an expulsion
at any time, if called upon to do so by a recognized international court.
Also the expelling state has a duty to have an alien's case reviewed
by—and be represented for the purpose before—the competent authority.
If the expelling state fails to do this, it may be accused of violating

the minimum standard of substantive justice, and its action may constitute an international delinquency. Therefore, expulsion of aliens should be effected without injury to them or their interests or rights, whether acquired or vested. Arbitrary arrest, detention, exile, denationalization, or expropriation of property are not allowed by the 1948 Universal Declaration of Human Rights.

What aliens in East Africa should hope for is a steady growth of a civilization in East Africa not entirely like their own but comparable to it in certain respects. They should work for a true democracy with a liberal economy whose main aim is to provide for an increased standard of living for every inhabitant of East Africa. Aliens who come to East Africa as expatriates—to serve the East African governments on contract—must make sure that they get accurate and relevant instructions about the East African way of life. Once in East Africa, expatriates should be encouraged to contribute commensurably to the process of nation-building via, for instance, guest membership in voluntary or philanthropic organizations such as Maendeleo Ya Wanawake (Women's Organization), the Kenya National Christian Council, and the Kenya Freedom from Hunger Campaign Council. Aliens in East Africa should also hope for freedom for all people from fear and discrimination of every kind. They should further wish for the promotion of social harmony and mutual respect; the promotion of African art and culture; the promotion of peaceful multiracialism; and a mutual study, understanding, and sincere appreciation by all the ethnic and racial groups of one another's character, history, and potentialities in the modern world. Aliens should also understand that the whole of Africa is now living in a transitional period, worsened by pressures of alien civilizations. The entire East African region is still in the first postindependence phase.

The grounds for racial harmony and coexistence now exist in East Africa. Isolationism can now be broken down without much trouble. Wealth and jobs can now be distributed with justice, security, and stability. The roles and position of aliens in East Africa can now be properly assessed, appreciated, and corrected where and when necessary. But much still needs to be done if Tanzania, Uganda, and Kenya are to be an East Africa in which multiculturalism and multiracialism can thrive, whether independently of each other or by integrating—an East Africa in which citizens and aliens alike can enjoy the civilized treatment of substantive justice.

The topic of aliens in East Africa is too broad to be exhausted in this, its first overall assessment. One therefore hopes that other writers on East Africa will give this important subject further consideration and thereby further clarify and illuminate the position of aliens in the region.

NOTES

1. See Daily Nation (Nairobi), March 9, 1974 and March 23, 1974.

2. See ibid., November 26, 1964.

3. See for example ibid., June 5, 1974, June 8, 1974, and June 10, 1974.

4. Ibid, June 8, 1974.

5. Ibid., June 10, 1974.

6. Ibid.

7. Ibid.

8. Ibid.

9. See for example ibid., August 26, 1972.

10. See Uganda, The Common Man's Charter: First Steps for Uganda to Move to the Left (Entebbe: Government Printer, 1969).

11. See for example Daily Nation (Nairobi), June 2, 1973.

12. See for instance ibid., July 24, 1973.

13. See United Nations, Document A/CONF. 9/15.

DANIEL D. C. DON NANJIRA is a diplomat in the Kenyan embassy in Washington, D.C. Before being posted to the embassy, he worked in the United Nations and in the Americas Division of the Kenya Ministry of Foreign Affairs. He reactivated the Kenya National Coordinating Committee on United Nations Day and as chairman renamed it "The Kenya U.N. Day Celebrations Committee" in 1972. He also served as chairman of the Kenya Human Rights Day Committee and as legal adviser of the Kenya Delegation to the Second UNCTAD Session on the Economic Rights and Duties of States, held in Geneva in 1973. He successfully completed a UN training course on the control of narcotic drugs and psychotropic substances.

Dr. Don Nanjira received his early education at St. Peter's Catholic Seminary, Kakamega (Kenya) and gained a magna cum laude Master-in-Laws Degree from the University of Warsaw, Poland, specializing in public international law, organization (the United Nations), and diplomacy. He traveled widely as a student, both in Eastern and Western Europe. He was admitted to the M.Sc. Course in International Relations at the London University College and obtained his magna cum laude Ph.D. from the University of Nairobi, Kenya.

MULTILATERAL SANCTIONS IN INTERNATIONAL
LAW: A Comparative Analysis
C. Lloyd Brown-John

THE ORGANIZATION OF AFRICAN UNITY AFTER
TEN YEARS: Comparative Perspectives
edited by Yassin El-Ayouty

PATTERNS OF POVERTY IN THE THIRD WORLD: A
Study of Social and Economic Stratification*
Charles Elliott,
assisted by Francoise de Morsier

A SOCIOECONOMIC PROFILE OF SOUTH AFRICA
William Redman Duggan

CRIMES AGAINST INTERNATIONALLY PROTECTED
PERSONS: PREVENTION AND PUNISHMENT: An
Analysis of the UN Convention
Louis M. Bloomfield
Gerald F. FitzGerald

*Also available as a Praeger Special Studies Student Edition.